Every Day a HOLIDAY

Celebrations *for the* Whole Year

Silvana Clark

Revell
Grand Rapids, Michigan

Published by Fleming H. Revell
a division of Baker Publishing Group
P.O. Box 6287, Grand Rapids, MI 49516-6287
www.revellbooks.com

Printed in the United States of America

Library of Congress Cataloging-in-Publication Data
Clark, Silvana.
    Every day a holiday : celebrations for the whole year / Silvana Clark.
       p.   cm.
    ISBN 0-8007-5877-3 (pbk.)
    1. Holidays. 2. Games. 3. Creative activities and seat work. I. Title.
    GT3930.C58   2004
    394.26—dc22   2004005161

To my husband,
Allan,
who for the past twenty-seven years
has made every day a special holiday
simply by being my best friend.

Preface

Think back to last February 14. You probably had red hearts decorating your windows and lots of glittery valentines on the kitchen table. What about last Thanksgiving? Did you make Thanksgiving place mats and fill a cornucopia with nuts and fruit? Now think back to January 19. Did you celebrate National Popcorn Day? No? Did you celebrate *Wizard of Oz* Day on August 15?

Don't worry. You'll never miss out on celebrating another holiday again! *Every Day a Holiday* is filled with over three hundred untraditional and slightly wacky holidays. You'll find great ideas, recipes, and craft projects to celebrate Dr. Seuss's birthday. Make your pastor feel extra special as you honor him or her during Clergy Appreciation Month. Don't forget to have fun with Grandma and Grandpa as you celebrate Grandparents Day.

In our fast-paced society, parents often wistfully say, "I wish our family spent more time together." Here's your chance to make every day a special day by celebrating some of the holidays described in this book. Don't worry. There's no need to look all over town to find matching tablecloths and party hats that say "Today Is National Pig Day." All the ideas are simple to do without hours of advance preparation.

Think about the memories you are creating when you wake up your children on the first Sunday in August (National Family Day) with a lively polka. Celebrate National Self-Esteem Day on May 15 by giving a cheer for each child at the dinner table. Try this:

2, 4, 6, 8
Who do we appreciate?
Yeah-h-h-h Allison!!
(Wearing a cheerleader's uniform is optional.)

Yes, your children may think you are slightly crazy as you start celebrating these unusual holidays. More than likely, though, they'll think you are a fun-loving parent. It's all too easy to get stuck in the day-to-day routine of school, work, church, ballet, etc. Sometimes a family just needs to celebrate!

Think back to your own childhood. What memories stand out? Can you even remember what you got for Christmas when you were eight years old? You probably do remember moments like the time your family had a flat tire and waited in a tiny roadside café, drinking hot chocolate together. Maybe you remember how good it felt to see your dad come home from work and know you'd soon have a high-spirited wrestling match in the living room. It's those small, "insignificant" moments that remain with us as positive memories of growing up. *Every Day a Holiday* is designed to help you quickly find some way to celebrate every day. It might just be sticking a Twinkie in your daughter's lunch with a note saying, "Happy Twinkie Day!" Maybe you'll get more involved and invite the neighbors over to help celebrate Jellybean Day.

If you are a teacher or youth group leader, this book also helps add an extra bit of pizzazz to ordinary days. Encourage students to think how the class can celebrate Read a New Book Month in December. Perhaps your youth group could collect puzzles to donate to a homeless shelter in honor of National Puzzle Day on January 29.

So the next time you feel life could use a little creativity and fun, pull out this book and *celebrate*!

JANUARY

National Hot Tea Month
National Oatmeal Month

Weeks to Celebrate

1st Full Week • National Letter Writing Week
2nd Full Week • National Pizza Week
2nd Full Week • National Printing Week

Days to Celebrate

1st Monday • Organize Your House Day
2nd Monday • Clean Off Your Desk Day
3rd Friday • National Hat Day
Usually 4th Sunday • Super Bowl Sunday
4th Tuesday • Speak Up and Succeed Day
4th Thursday • National Clashing Clothes Day

1 New Year's Day
3 Drinking Straw Patented
4 National Trivia Day
8 Rock and Roll Day
   (Elvis's Birthday)
8 Joy Germ Day
11 Use More of Your Mind Day
11 National Thank You Day
13 National Snow Day
13 National Frisbee Day
14 National Volunteer Day
14 Take a Missionary to Lunch Day
15 Martin Luther King Jr.'s Birthday
16 National Nothing Day

17 Shari Lewis's Birthday
18 Winnie the Pooh Day
19 Tin Can Day
19 National Popcorn Day
21 Chinese New Year
22 Polka Dot Day
23 National Pie Day
24 TV Game Show Day
25 A Room of One's Own Day
27 National Bubble Wrap
   Appreciation Day
27 National Activity Professionals Day
29 National Puzzle Day
31 Inspire Your Heart with Art Day

National Hot Tea Month

Winter is a perfect time to enjoy a cup of tea. Children might enjoy a mild tea flavored with milk and sugar. Incorporate a silly tea party into your celebration.

Celebrate with Fun

- Invite your family to a tea party based on the Mad Hatter's tea party in *Alice in Wonderland*. Send out invitations saying "Don't be late for a very important date!" State the location and time for your tea party, even if only family members are invited.

- Play a game of "Queen of Hearts." Toss a deck of cards into a bowl. Mix well! Make sure cards are facedown. Take turns quickly reaching into the bowl to select a card. First person to pick the Queen of Hearts wins a prize. Repeat several times.

- Pick 2 people in your family to stuff pillows under their shirts and pretend to be Tweedledee and Tweedledum. Call them by those names throughout the party.

- Be sure to sing "I'm a little teapot, short and stout; here is my handle, here is my spout. When I get all steamed up, hear me shout, 'Tip me over and pour me out!'" Act out the motions to really celebrate National Hot Tea Month. Make up other verses to go with the song like, "I'm a little teapot, straight and tall. If you let me go, then down I'll fall . . ."

Celebrate with Crafts

Ask for help making decorations for your party. Pass out white paper and black and red markers. Ask people to draw enlarged versions of playing cards. Hint: Unless you're superartistic, don't bother trying to draw a Jack, Queen, or King.

One lump or two? Some children have never seen sugar cubes. Buy a box and make some cubed sculptures. Give everyone a handful of cubes and a small bowl of frosting. Use wooden craft sticks to spread the frosting on the cubes as "cement." Try building an igloo or other structure with the sugar cubes.

Celebrate with Food

Purchase an assortment of teas. Try a few new flavors. Offer a "Tea Smorgasbord" so people can sample a variety of flavors.

The British enjoy cream tea. Add a "spot" of cream (or milk) to your tea for a European flavor.

Bake cupcakes in your favorite flavor. Frost as normal. Use gel frosting to write "Eat Me" on top, just like the cupcakes Alice in Wonderland ate.

For more ideas, see www.teausa.com.

National Oatmeal Month

Start off a cold winter day with a bowl of steaming hot oatmeal. Enjoy the nutritious good taste throughout the month.

Celebrate with Fun

- Go ahead! Have everyone improve their complexion with this oatmeal mask. Mix 1 cup oatmeal with ½ cup warm water. Spread a small handful of the mushy oatmeal mixture on your face. Let dry for 5–10 minutes. This is the time to take pictures of your family with their oatmeal face masks! Wash the mixture off and marvel at your smooth skin.

- Collect a number of small household items like paper clips, plastic spoons, coins, and buttons. Drop them into a bowl of uncooked oatmeal. Reach in and try to identify objects using only your fingers—no peeking! Are you brave enough to try the same experiment using cooked oatmeal?

- Younger children enjoy playing with a water or sand table. Be different and set out an oatmeal table. Fill a dishpan with 2–3 cups uncooked oatmeal. Add a few action figures and other small toys and let children enjoy!

- Write the word *oatmeal* on a piece of paper. How many words can you make using the letters o-a-t-m-e-a-l?

Celebrate with Crafts

Mix up a batch of oatmeal clay. Stir together 1 cup oatmeal and ½ cup flour. Add ½ cup water. Mix well. If dough is too sticky, add a small amount of flour. Knead on a floured surface. Use oatmeal clay to make natural-looking pottery.

Celebrate with Food

Want to quickly cool your oatmeal? Fill an ice cube tray with milk and freeze. Put the frozen milk cubes in a bowl of hot oatmeal. They will quickly cool the oatmeal without diluting the taste.

Try these 3-minute no-bake cookies. In a saucepan, heat 2 cups sugar, ½ cup milk, 1 stick margarine, and ⅓ cup cocoa. Boil for 3 minutes. Remove from heat and stir in 3 cups oats. Drop mixture by teaspoonfuls on wax paper. Let cool before eating. (Make sure an adult is present when boiling the cookie mixture.)

For more ideas, see www.quakeroatmeal.com

National Letter Writing Week

We all know it's easy to dash off an e-mail message to Aunt Martha and Cousin Howard. Bring back the forgotten art of writing letters this week.

Celebrate with Fun

- Brainstorm with family members about relatives and friends who should receive letters. Track down their actual snail mail addresses.

- Write a round-robin letter. One family member begins writing about the weather, then stops mid-sentence and passes on the letter. The next person continues, writing about the new puppy's antics. Continue until everyone has added a few lines. Younger children can draw pictures or decorate the envelope.

- Write a short greeting with the plastic magnetic letters on your fridge. Stand your child in front of the message. Take a picture to send to a friend.

- Write a letter in secret code. Use a cotton swab dipped in lemon juice to write a short message on paper. Mail to the recipient with instructions to hold the letter over a hot lightbulb. The heat causes the lemon juice to turn brown and legible. (Write the instructions in visible ink or the person will wonder why you sent a blank piece of paper.)

- Select family members' names. Write your designated person a short letter and place it on his/her pillow.

- Make a family time capsule in a 5-lb. coffee can. Each family member brings 2–3 small items of importance to store in the can. Add report cards, photos, and a daily newspaper. Write a letter to yourselves describing daily routines and what each family member enjoys doing. Seal the can, then store in a safe place until you open the can in 15 years.

Celebrate with Crafts

Make some extra-special writing paper. Set out a variety of solid-colored paper. Pour a thin layer of different-colored paint on several paper plates. Dip assorted household items in the paint and stamp on the paper. Try pencil erasers, fork tines, buttons, or pasta wheels. Let paint dry and use your designer paper for prolific letter writing.

Celebrate with Food

Eat some paper. Call a few Asian food stores and ask if they carry edible rice paper. Purchase some and enjoy eating what looks like actual paper but is totally edible.

National Pizza Week

Pizza is the universal favorite food for kids of all ages. Have fun eating pizza and playing pizza-related games this week.

Celebrate with Fun

- Have a pizza-pan relay race. Stand 3–4 empty soda bottles on a pizza pan. Use a stopwatch to time people running from one location to another as they hold the pizza pan. If bottles fall, they need to start over.

- Set up an easy Frisbee golf course outside. Number 9 paper plates 1–9. Use a thumbtack or duct tape to attach paper plates to a "safe" target like a tree, the mailbox, or the garage door. Take turns throwing Frisbees (flying pizzas—see the "Celebrate with Crafts" section) at the targets.

- Many families enjoy eating pizza while watching a movie. To ensure quality film choices, try this technique. In a notebook, collect movie reviews from newspapers and magazines. When a movie is released on video and DVD, check the review in the notebook to see if the movie is appropriate for your family. If it is, then you can all eat your pizza while enjoying a suitable and fun movie.

Celebrate with Crafts

Purchase inexpensive solid-colored Frisbees for each family member. (Or look in the back of the garage for Frisbees you used last summer.) Bring out permanent markers and decorate Frisbees to look like pizzas. Don't forget to draw anchovies!

Celebrate with Food

Naturally you'll want to eat pizza during this special week. Order pizza to be delivered one day and try your own variations on homemade pizza another day.

Make pita pizza: Place several pieces of pita bread on a cookie sheet and bake at 250 degrees for 10–15 minutes until crisp. Let everyone spread pizza sauce on their pita and top it off with olives, pepperoni, and cheese. Put back in the oven until cheese is melted.

Make a pizza "sandwich": Lightly butter a frying pan and add a flour tortilla over low heat. Spread with pizza sauce and the usual assortment of meat, vegetables, and cheeses. Place another flour tortilla on top and cook like a grilled cheese sandwich.

Make homemade white bread dough in your bread machine. Remove dough before the baking cycle. Roll dough into individual pizzas and top with favorite toppings.

National Printing Week

Newspapers, billboards, and computers all use various methods of printing. Imagine what a colorless world it would be without printed signs or clothes.

Celebrate with Fun

- Look for various forms of printing around the house. Research these questions with your children: How do prints get on shirts? What technique is used to print money?
- Visit a museum with an early printing press. Computer-savvy children will be amazed at how each letter had to be individually placed by hand.

Celebrate with Food

Use your thumb to "print" thumbprint cookies. Make your favorite sugar cookie dough. Roll ¼-inch thick and cut into circles. After washing hands, have children press thumbs into the center of the cookies to make thumbprints. After cookies bake, spoon 1 tsp. jelly into the thumbprint indentations.

Celebrate with Crafts

Do some printing during National Printing Week. Begin by making a "Balloon Blob" print. Set out construction paper and shallow containers of paint. Blow up small balloons and tie shut. Dip the bottom of a balloon in paint and "bounce" the paint-covered balloon on the paper. Repeat with different colors, overlapping prints.

Use yarn and an ordinary tin can for another type of print. Remove can's label and make "squiggle" designs on the can with glue. Cover all the glue with thick yarn. Let dry overnight. Pour paint in a paper plate. Roll yarn-covered can in the paint, then onto paper. Roll the can back and forth and around to create a pattern from the raised yarn.

Save ahead some Styrofoam meat trays. (For safety, wash trays in soapy water and mild bleach solution.) Use a chopstick or blunt item to "carve" designs in meat trays. Draw simple pictures or abstract patterns. Brush over designs with thin layer of paint. Cut paper the size of the meat trays. Place on top of paint. Press down and rub gently. Lift to reveal a reverse print of the design in meat tray.

You've probably printed using apples or potatoes. Make some "moon" designs by cutting a piece of celery in half. Dip in paint. Press on paper to form tiny *C* shapes or moons.

Organize Your House Day

Feeling overwhelmed with the clutter in your house or in your children's messy rooms? Start the New Year with a plan to reduce clutter and get your house organized.

Celebrate with Fun

- Yes, it can be fun to get organized. Make a schedule. Maybe you can't get the whole house organized today, but you can do 30 minutes every day this week. Set a timer, and when the timer goes off, stop for the day.

- Do your children have small toys or craft items scattered around their rooms? Purchase plastic tackle boxes with small storage compartments ideal for organizing tiny items. Let the kids take "before" and "after" pictures of their rooms. They'll feel better living with less clutter.

- Go through the magazines you've been saving. Quickly tear out those recipe or craft ideas you wanted and toss the rest of the magazine.

- Try the "King Is Coming" approach for a quick house cleanup. Tell everyone, in a very proper British accent, "The King is coming! We must clean the house because the King is coming." Everyone then runs around picking up so the house is clean when the King arrives.

- Give each family member a colored laundry basket for their clean clothes from the dryer. They put their own clothes away in the proper drawers. Give them matching colored boxes by the front door labeled "Launch Pad." That's where they store backpacks, ballet shoes, permission slips, and other items needed to "launch" them off for the day.

Celebrate with Crafts

Get crafty with decoupage to help young children know where to put their things. Glue pictures of socks, shirts, and pants on your child's dresser drawers. Cover with a layer of decoupage. Now your nonreader has no excuse for leaving clothes on the floor.

Divide a family chore chart into sections listing each person's daily and weekly chores. Everyone's first "chore" is to decorate their section to reflect their personality.

Celebrate with Food

As a family, sit down and plan out a week's worth of menus for dinner. Make an organized list of what ingredients you need and what ingredients you'll need to buy. Dinner preparation will be much easier with this advanced preparation.

More ideas: www.organizedtimes.com

15

Clean Off Your Desk Day

Look at both adult's and children's desks and you'll usually find a cluttered assortment of papers and a few snack food wrappers. Start off the New Year by cleaning off your desk.

Celebrate with Fun

- If younger children don't have desks, help them clean out their toy box. Sort out all the toys and discard ones with broken parts. Donate toys in good condition that your child no longer wants.

- Be ruthless when it comes to cleaning your desk. Do you really need those expired coupons for turkey stuffing?

- At the office, announce in advance that today is a special day to clean off your desk. Set aside 15 minutes for everyone to do what they can to reduce the clutter.

- At home, plan a "Trade-It" night. Give everyone 20–30 minutes to clean up their desk (or toy box). Ask them to bring any unwanted scissors, staplers, pens, or rolls of tape to a central location. Trade unwanted items for something you need. Your extra roll of Scotch tape could be traded to your son for 2 fine-tipped permanent markers.

- Give everyone a set of new markers, pens, or pencils to proudly display on their clean desk.

- Take "before" and "after" pictures of your desk. Hopefully the "after" picture shows some improvement!

Celebrate with Crafts

Purchase a plastic stacking tray for each family member. Let everyone decorate their own tray with stencils, paint, and markers. Place the stacking trays in an easily accessible location. Each person is responsible for putting their important paperwork in their tray. This includes bills to pay, field trip permission slips, and overdue library notices. Hopefully this reduces desk clutter.

Celebrate with Food

Enjoy a snack on your clean desk. Eat some foods that are "neat" to eat. Try apple slices, tomato soup in a thermos, carrot sticks, Jell-O, and water from your water bottle. No crumbs allowed on your clean desk!

Cut off the tops of several oranges. Scoop out the orange from inside, as if you were cleaning out a pumpkin. Mix the orange pulp with vanilla yogurt, and put back in the hollowed-out orange shell. Eat directly from your organic bowl! You won't have any food-encrusted bowls on your spotless desk.

National Hat Day

Baby boomer moms probably remember going to church as little girls and wearing adorable white hats with pink ribbons. Here's a chance to update your style in hats.

Celebrate with Fun

- Play an adapted game of musical chairs. Place hats in a circle on the floor. Have equal amounts of hats and children. When music starts, have children walk around hat circle. As music stops, they put on the hat closest to them. No need to eliminate children. They'll all enjoy participating by putting different hats on their heads.
- Hat Toss: Set several sturdy hats on the floor and make a tape or string line 2–3 feet away from the hats. Have children stand behind the line and try to throw small balls or sponges into the hats.
- Young children will enjoy this simple sing-a-long game: Give each child a hat to wear as you sing these words to the tune of "The Farmer in the Dell": *My hat is big for me, My hat is big for me, It's so big I cannot see, I'll put it on my knee.* Change last word to *neck, elbow, toe,* etc. as kids take turns putting hats on different parts of the body.
- Find old hats from the dress-up box and model them as you sing, "Put on your Easter bonnet, with all the frills upon it . . ."

Celebrate with Crafts

Place 2–3 sheets of newspaper on top of child's head. Wrap several strands of masking tape around the crown of child's head, forming a bowl with the newsprint. Roll the edges of the paper tightly up toward the tape. Each child has a custom-fitting hat they can decorate with paint, markers, and glitter. Wear the hats at dinner.

Give each child several empty Styrofoam cups. Have them decorate the outside of the cups with permanent markers or brightly colored crayons. Place cups on a cookie sheet in a preheated, 325-degree oven for 45–60 seconds. The cups will shrink in size while intensifying in color. Remove from oven and cool before handing to children. Hats fit on Little People or other small dolls.

Celebrate with Food

Give each child a pineapple ring and half a canned peach on a plate. Place the peach cut side down on the pineapple ring for a tasty hat-shaped snack. Decorate the rim of the "hat" with raisins or sunflower seeds.

Super Bowl Sunday

Put on your football shirt and bring out the snacks. It's time to root for your favorite team. Even if you are not a football fan, get in the spirit by simply enjoying the festivities.

Celebrate with Fun

- Purchase some inexpensive indoor/outdoor "grass" carpet at the hardware store. Place it in front of the TV to create the feeling of Astroturf. (It's cheaper than buying Super Bowl tickets!)
- Speaking of tickets, invite friends over with invitations that look like Super Bowl tickets. Use a computer or just hand print the tickets to look like high-priced, highly coveted tickets to the big game.
- In every crowd there's a non–football fan. Ask one to give a 5-minute "unfootball" presentation during halftime. This can be an entertaining lecture on how to grow radishes or the best way to select a new washing machine. The contrast between their presentation and the rowdiness of the football game always draws big laughs.
- Younger children usually get restless during the game. Send them off to another room to come up with a cheerleading routine to perform during halftime. Naturally, adults will respond with a standing ovation and loud football cheers. Children who don't want to be cheerleaders can form their own marching band by finding instruments around the house or simply hitting 2 empty paper towel tubes together. They can practice a marching band routine before performing for the adults.
- Tape a paper goalpost to a wall. Use a balloon to try to make a field goal.
- Advertisers pay millions of dollars to air their commercials during the Super Bowl. Give people score sheets to vote for their favorite commercial.

Celebrate with Crafts

Paint white lines on a green tablecloth to look like a football field. Ask everyone to draw their favorite football player on the "field."

Cut a football shape out of a sponge. Dip in paint and decorate paper plates with football designs.

Celebrate with Food

Ask the appliance store to save you a large refrigerator box. Let children decorate it to look like a concession stand at a football game. Cut out a "window" so children can stand inside and serve popcorn and chips. Charging $4.00 for a bag of popcorn is optional.

More ideas: www.superbowl.com

18

Speak Up and Succeed Day

Studies show public speaking is the number one fear of adults. Yet we all know the importance of being able to effectively communicate in front of a large group. Use today to improve your family's public speaking skills.

Celebrate with Fun

- Make sure your family never runs out of conversation starters. Use strips of paper to write down topics for discussion. Each night at dinner, select 1 strip of paper. Take turns so everyone has a chance to share their opinions. Topics can include: What exotic pet would you like to own? Share a time you helped someone. What would you do if you won the lottery? What is one thing you'd like to change at church? Describe your idea of a perfect vacation.

- Set up a friendly "debate" among family members. One person speaks up for the need to get a raise in her allowance. She presents clear ideas on why her allowance is too low. Another family member presents the opposing view that all family allowances are adequate. Debate is a great way to practice public speaking!

- When watching TV, turn off the sound during commercials. Take turns providing the dialogue for the actors. This gives everyone experience in quick thinking.

- In the morning, ask everyone to prepare a short 2–3 minute speech on any topic. In the evening, listen to everyone's after-dinner speech. Applaud for everyone!

Celebrate with Crafts

Make a "Table Topics" box for the kitchen table. Find a box about the size of a tissue box. Cut an opening in the top and paint the box a solid color. Cut out a variety of pictures from old magazines. Glue on pictures of animals, people, or food items until the box is covered. Fill the box with the "conversation starters" mentioned under "Celebrate with Fun" above.

Celebrate with Food

If you're going to be a professional speaker, you'll need to use a microphone. Start out by making an edible microphone. Have each family member stick a pretzel rod into a large marshmallow. Sing into it, and then eat it for a snack.

National Clashing Clothes Day

Preschoolers who dress themselves look like they celebrate National Clashing Clothes Day on a regular basis. The rest of us, however, might need some ideas.

Celebrate with Fun

- Talk to your child's teacher or principal about organizing a large-scale celebration of Clashing Clothes Day. Encourage children and teachers to wear mismatched socks, clothes, and hair ribbons. Offer lighthearted awards for "Best Use of Mismatched Shoes," "Best Mismatched Shirt and Pants," and "Best Mismatched Hair Accessories."

- If you have a major business presentation to make today, it's probably best not to arrive wearing a polka-dotted blouse with a plaid skirt. Instead, designate dinnertime at home as "Clashing Clothes Time." In order to be served a meal, everyone must appear wearing their most clashing outfits. This means flowered shorts, striped tops, clashing socks, and different shoes. Be sure to take a picture of your well-dressed family and send it to Grandma.

- Make sure to wear mismatched pajamas when everyone gets ready for bed.

- Bring out all the dolls and stuffed animals in your house. Make a group effort to dress them in an assorted collection of mismatched clothes. Watch out, Barbie!

- Instead of simply wearing clothes that have clashing patterns, dress in clothes from other family members. Have Mom wear her daughter's cheerleading sweater while the kindergartner wears Dad's necktie.

- Designate the youngest member of your family to bang 2 pot lids together to make a clashing noise. (Okay, it's actually a crashing noise.)

Celebrate with Crafts

Give everyone a piece of construction paper and assorted family photographs. Cut out your face from the pictures and glue it on the paper. Use an assortment of scrap wrapping paper or fabric to design clothes to go with your self-portrait. Make sure the clothes clash.

Celebrate with Food

Mismatch your evening meal; Combine traditional foods from breakfast, lunch, and dinner. Your family might enjoy pancakes, peanut butter sandwiches, and pork chops as their culinary tribute to Clashing Clothes Day.

New Year's Day

Instead of just celebrating on New Year's Eve, start the year with a full day of party activities. Get everyone involved in planning and participating.

Celebrate with Fun

- Any Italian relatives in your family? Do you like pasta? That makes you semi-Italian. In that case, celebrate with a southern Italian tradition that's sure to be a hit with your kids. (It also will give your neighbors second thoughts about your sanity.) Toss pots and pans and other household items out the windows to celebrate the New Year.

- Cut leftover Christmas wrapping paper into 6″ x 1″ strips. Loop together and make into long chains to decorate the house.

- Assign every family member to plan 15 minutes of entertainment. Even a 4-year-old can lead everyone in a rousing game of Duck, Duck, Goose. Teenagers can play their favorite CD and ask parents to dance to the beat. You'll end up with party fun you never thought was possible!

Celebrate with Crafts

Make supershakers for all-day noise. Track down empty wrapping paper tubes and cut into 6-inch sections. Staple one end shut. Fill rest of tube with 1 Tbs. dried rice or popcorn. Here's the tricky part: "Twist" the unstapled end in the opposite direction and staple shut. This forms a strong shaker that will last for many noise-filled hours. Decorate with markers and stickers.

Here's another great tradition you can start on New Year's Day: Gently poke a hole in both ends of a raw egg. Blow in 1 end to remove the egg white and yolk. (Use those for scrambled eggs tomorrow.) Very carefully break away the shell from around 1 hole until it is the size of a dime. Rinse the egg. When dry, partially fill with tiny scraps of confetti. You can use a hole punch to punch out tiny confetti circles. Tape the opening shut. Make sure everyone has a confetti-filled egg. Gather as a group, count to 3, and proceed to crack your egg over someone's head!

Celebrate with Food

Set out all the holiday leftovers on a large table. Ask your children to create fancy names and label the food. Leftover mashed potatoes become "Fluffy Clouds," Grandma's fruitcake can be labeled "Edible Brick," and sweet potatoes take on a new flavor when called "Orange Soufflé."

21

Drinking Straw Patented

In 1888 Marvin Stone of Washington, D.C., made a drinking straw out of paraffin-covered paper. Before that, straws were made from rye. Today, straws are used for much more than drinking.

Celebrate with Fun

• Organize "Straw Olympics." Challenge each other to amazing feats of skill using straws. Here are some Olympic-caliber events:

1. Straw toss: Stand on a designated line. Toss a straw as far as you can. Measure each toss to determine the winner.
2. Participants kneel on the floor with a straw and Ping-Pong ball. On "Go!" each person blows through the straw, trying to blow their Ping-Pong ball over a finish line 8 feet away.
3. Balance a straw on your fingertip. Time each other to see who can keep it balanced the longest.
4. Give participants small glasses of water (equal amounts in each glass). Set empty glasses 5 feet away. On "Go!" each person uses their straw as a suction device. Push the straw into the water. Place a finger on top of the straw to form suction. Race with the water-filled straw to your empty cup. Lift your finger to let the water flow out. Repeat the process until 1 person has emptied their glass.

• Cut tissue paper into stamp-sized pieces. Use the straw to "inhale" and pick up a piece of tissue paper. Now try picking up 2 pieces of paper. Who has the lung power to pick up 8 or 10 pieces of tissue paper?

Celebrate with Crafts

Make some prehistoric necklaces by cutting about 1 inch on each side of the flexible part of 20 straws. These are your dinosaur bones. Thread floss through the centers and bend the straw sections in different directions to look like bones. Tie the floss and wear your Flintstone style necklace.

Make unique bubble prints. Fill a shallow bowl with ¼ cup water, ¼ cup liquid dishwashing detergent, and 2 Tbs. liquid tempera paint. Use a straw to blow bubbles in the liquid solution. As soon as the bubbles come over the top of the container, gently put a piece of white paper on the bubbles. Remove the paper to reveal your round bubble prints.

Celebrate with Food

Purchase some red licorice twists. (Twizzlers work well.) They are edible straws. Cut ½ inch off each end. Put the licorice twist in water or milk and use as a straw.

National Trivia Day

You probably know someone who immediately can name the main export crop of Bolivia, tell how many teeth a piranha has, and locate where the deepest lake in America is found. Now it's your turn to learn some obscure facts for National Trivia Day.

Celebrate with Fun

- Here's a great game that changes as family members add new trivia questions. Give everyone a few index cards. (To get a wider variety of questions, e-mail or call relatives and ask for their suggestions.) Write down a trivia question related to a family member on each card. This could be "What did Jamie hit the first day she got her driver's license?" or "Where did Michael leave his stuffed rabbit on vacation?" After collecting trivia questions, pass them out and try to answer the questions. The next time you gather for a family get-together, hand out more blank cards so you can collect additional questions.

- Amaze family and friends by casually inserting these bits of trivia into everyday conversation: There are 1,200 different varieties of watermelons. There are more than 1,750 O's in a 15 oz. can of Spaghetti O's. July contains the most birthdays. The average child watches 40,000 commercials a year.

- When you get tired of verbal trivia, show your family how to turn a penny green. Pour several tsp. vinegar in a cup. Drop in a few pennies. The next morning, you'll have green pennies.

Celebrate with Crafts

Make a "Footprint Trivia Chart." Trace around each family member's foot on a piece of construction paper. Then measure how many of Dad's footsteps there are from the refrigerator to the TV and the number of Jenny's footsteps from the front door to the mailbox. Record the numbers on a chart. When friends come over, ask, "Did you know it takes Emily 53 steps to get from the bathroom to the kitchen?" Now that's trivia!

Celebrate with Food

Come up with your own trivia relating to food. Set out a variety of foods such as candy bars, chips, or boxes of Jell-O. Ask family members to come up with "Food Trivia Tidbits." You'll discover facts such as: the average bag of chips has 242 chips, a box of Jell-O contains fumaric acid, the circumference of a can of corn is 6 inches. Eat as you discover trivia.

Rock and Roll Day
(Elvis's Birthday)

In 1935 Elvis was born in Tupelo, Mississippi. Rumors insist he's still alive today. Have you seen Elvis lately?

Celebrate with Fun

- It wouldn't be Rock and Roll Day without an Elvis impersonation contest. Invite friends over to dress up in their white jumpsuits, blue suede shoes, and slicked back hair. See who can do the best imitation of Elvis crooning.

- Show your children how you danced when rock and roll was "real" dancing. Demonstrate your skill at doing the Freddy, the Swim, and the Pony. Threaten your children with extra chores if they don't join you in this trip down memory lane.

- Practice your manners today. Every time you say, "Thank you," be sure to say, "Thank you—thank you very much," with an Elvis twang.

- Play a round of "Song Charades." Write song titles on paper. Take turns selecting a title and acting it out. Or try "Name That Tune." Get a tape or CD of well-known songs. Play the first 2–3 bars and see who can guess the song first.

More ideas: www.elvis.com

Celebrate with Crafts

Still have a record player? First use it to show your children how you used to play rock and roll records. Then use it for spin art. Cut out circles from lightweight cardboard and punch holes in the middles. Place 1 circle on the record player. Turn to 78 speed and drop a few drops of paint on the revolving cardboard. Instant spin art!

Elvis was known for his shaggy hair. Make your own Elvis heads using pantyhose. Cut a section of pantyhose 8–10 inches from the toe. Fill with 2 cups sawdust. Top with ½ cup potting soil on which you sprinkle ¼ cup grass seed. Shape sawdust and soil into a round "head." Set Elvis head in a shallow container of water so sawdust and dirt absorb water. Use puff paints to draw eyes, ears, and mouth on Elvis. Place in a sunny location. It won't be long until Elvis has a full head of luscious green hair!

Celebrate with Food

Elvis is known for enjoying fatty, greasy, high-calorie foods. Go ahead and eat a meal that ranks low on nutrition. How about fried chicken, potatoes with extra butter, and biscuits with honey? Be sure to have Elvis singing in the background as you eat.

Joy Germ Day

This day is designed for you to share your joy with others. The theme for the day is "For Doom and Gloom—There's No Room."

Celebrate with Fun

- Find a roll of adding machine paper so you can make a l-o-o-o-n-n-g list of things that make your family happy. Lay the paper on the floor. Write (horizontally) all the people and activities that give you joy. See how long you can make your list describing the joyful and positive aspects of your family experiences. Tape the list around the perimeter of a room so everyone can review it.

- Make some paper "germs." Write down a compliment for someone like "You made a great dinner tonight, Mom." Give the "germ" to another person. Be contagious—spread positive germs to as many people as possible!

- Do you know what JOY stands for? The letters can help you prioritize what is important in your life. Every time you hear the word *joy*, think: J = Jesus, O = Others, and Y = You. If we put Jesus first in our lives, then think of others, and then think of ourselves, we'll have a joyful life.

- As a family, think of the most positive person you know. List adjectives to describe him or her. Let this person be a role model to your family on the importance of thinking optimistically.

- Use a concordance to find references to joy in the Bible. As you discuss the fruit of the Spirit from Galatians 5:22, notice that joy is a very distinct characteristic of a Christian.

Celebrate with Crafts

Use 3 paper plates to make a J-O-Y wall hanging. Give each person 3 paper plates. Write a large *J* on 1 plate, *O* on another, and *Y* on the last. Decorate the plates with lace around the edges or other trims. Outline the letters with glue and then sprinkle with glitter. Staple the plates together so they spell out JOY vertically to stand for Jesus—Others—You.

Celebrate with Food

Purchase several oranges and cut into eighths. Leave on the peelings. Have everyone in the family put an orange slice in their mouth, with the peeling facing out. Smile! Look at each other with bright orange, joyful grins!

More ideas: Contact Joy Germ Unlimited 315-472-2779

25

Use More of Your Mind Day

Here's a day to turn off the TV, bring out the dictionary, and get your brain working at full speed.

Celebrate with Fun

- Know anyone who belongs to Mensa? This organization is open to the top 1 percent of the population, those with extremely high IQs. See if any of your family members qualify by taking a Mensa sample test available on www.mensa.org. Try taking the test as a group. Maybe they'll let you join based on your combined IQs!

- Get a copy of a *Reader's Digest* magazine. As a group, try to come up with the correct answers for the monthly "Word Power" feature. Try to use the words in everyday conversation during the week. It isn't every day you'll hear your second grader say, "Look, Mom! The light from the candle is beginning to wane."

- Take a well-known song and change the words to fit your family. How about "Dad's dreaming of a new lawnmower, just like the one that used to work . . ." Try to include everyone's name in the song at least once.

- Go over your child's homework. Ask review questions *Jeopardy* style. You give the answer; she needs to come up with the question.

Celebrate with Crafts

Design a family Coat of Arms. Each person draws a fancy crest or shield on white construction paper and decorates it with markers and crayons. Divide your design into 4 segments. In each section draw a symbol representing one of your strengths. It could be a math book for someone quick to learn multiplication tables. Someone else might draw a soccer ball symbolizing their soccer skills. Display and discuss your Coat of Arms.

Celebrate with Food

Set out some pizza dough. Have everyone work together making the shape of your state (or if you are really ambitious, the shape of the U.S.). Use olives, cheese, and pepperoni to create geographically correct mountains and rivers. Enjoy eating your state!

Statistics show that children who eat a healthy breakfast do better in school. Mix up a batch of homemade granola. In a saucepan, melt ½ cup honey and ¼ cup oil. Pour into a bowl with 5 cups rolled oats, ½ cup wheat germ, 1 cup raisins, ½ cup sunflower seeds, ½ cup oat bran, and ¼ cup finely chopped nuts. Mix well. Spread granola on baking sheet. Bake at 300 degrees for 15–18 minutes. Let cool. Store in a covered container.

National Thank You Day

Many people help us out in life: family members, friends, neighbors, and others. Take time today to let these people know how much you appreciate them.

Celebrate with Fun

- Begin with the people closest to you. Encourage family members to thank each other throughout the day. At first it may seem awkward to say, "Thanks for making my lunch, Mom," or "Thanks for finding my soccer ball, Shawn." Try to make it a habit to thank each other regularly.

- Brainstorm with family about people who have been an influence. What about that high school teacher who encouraged you to try out for the school play or the ballet teacher who inspired your daughter? Think of ways to thank those people. They'll be shocked to hear from you!

- The next time your children receive a gift from a relative, take a picture of them holding or wearing the gift. Glue the picture on cardboard and send it as a thank-you postcard.

- Even though it's a May Day tradition, kids love knocking on someone's door and running away. Make a card or fill a basket with flowers and write a thank-you note to a neighbor. Sneak to their front door, leave the gift, knock, and run away before they answer.

Celebrate with Crafts

Make a set of homemade thank-you cards to keep on hand. Get sheets of plain, high-quality paper. Pour some red paint on a paper plate. Cut an apple in half horizontally to reveal the "star" shape in the center. Gently press the cut apple in the paint and then onto the paper. You'll get a great design to decorate your thank-you note cards.

Celebrate with Food

Make your favorite sugar cookie dough. Roll it out. Have your child put her (clean!) hand on the dough. Use a knife to trace around her hand, creating a handprint cookie. After baking the cookie, use frosting to write a person's name on it. Give it to the recipient and say "Trina—you deserve a big hand for being a great sister!"

National Snow Day

Bring out the snowsuits and mittens! It's time to celebrate winter fun. If you live in Florida, turn up the air-conditioning and pretend it's snowing.

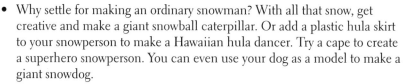

Celebrate with Fun

- Why settle for making an ordinary snowman? With all that snow, get creative and make a giant snowball caterpillar. Or add a plastic hula skirt to your snowperson to make a Hawaiian hula dancer. Try a cape to create a superhero snowperson. You can even use your dog as a model to make a giant snowdog.

- Set out an assortment of plastic bowls and funnels to use for snow molds.

- Do your children know how to make snow angels? Demonstrate the art of falling on your back, then sliding your arms and legs back and forth to make snow angels.

- Use chalk to draw a giant bull's-eye on the garage door. Let kids throw snowballs at the target. (Obviously this works only if there are no windows nearby.)

- Is there an elderly neighbor who has difficulty shoveling snow? Surprise her by removing the snow from her sidewalks.

- Use snowballs to shoot baskets. Who can make a three-pointer? Pack some more snowballs to play broom hockey.

- If you live in a warm climate, ask your local ice skating rink for a few buckets of shaved ice that they get from smoothing the ice. Let children make minisnowmen.

Celebrate with Crafts

Make a giant snowperson or snowcreature. Decorate your creation with edible jewelry for the birds. String popcorn for a giant necklace. Use apple slices for facial features. Sprinkle birdseed on the snowperson's head.

Celebrate with Food

Try making some snow ice cream. Collect 4 cups clean snow in a large bowl. Add 2½ Tbs. evaporated milk, ⅓ cup sugar, and ½ tsp. vanilla. Mix well. It won't taste like the premium ice cream your children are used to, but it was quite a treat in the days of *Little House on the Prairie*.

If you have a shaved ice machine, go outside and make shaved ice cones. Pretend the ice is actually snow!

National Frisbee Day

Check out your garage or toy box. You'll probably find several forgotten Frisbees. Bring them out and enjoy these activities.

Celebrate with Fun

- Before Frisbees were invented, college students threw pie pans back and forth. (They really should have been studying!) Collect a few lightweight aluminum pie pans and try tossing them to each other.
- Using traditional Frisbees, practice fancy catches and throws. Take turns demonstrating your skill at standing on 1 leg while singing the National Anthem as you throw a Frisbee.
- If your dog loves catching Frisbees, let him join in the celebration. Throw the Frisbee to him until he actually gets tired. With some dogs, this may take a while!
- See how many times you can toss a Frisbee back and forth to a partner without dropping it. Now try it with 2 Frisbees at the same time.
- Set up a Frisbee Skill Course. Toss Frisbees at a specific target, through a hula hoop, or into a wastebasket. Ask a person to be a moving target walking back and forth between 2 points. Try to toss your Frisbee to hit the target person (but not in the face).
- Contact your local Parks and Recreation department and ask if they sponsor the "Catch and Fetch" contest. Many departments organize this contest in which dogs and their owners display feats of skill catching and throwing Frisbees. Start practicing now so you can enter with your dog.
- Check if your community has a Frisbee disc course. The course is usually laid out with metal stands that serve as targets. Many towns set aside a portion of a park for flying disc fans.

Celebrate with Crafts

Give everyone a plain-colored Frisbee. Purchase glow-in-the-dark paint to decorate your Frisbees. As soon as it gets dark, go outside and toss your glowing discs to each other.

Celebrate with Food

Okay, this is not your traditional food tip, but it does help you celebrate National Frisbee Day. Make sure everyone has their own Frisbee. Wash them well and use them as your plates for dinner!

National Volunteer Day

JANUARY 14

Jesus frequently tells us to help others. Children quickly learn that volunteering is rewarding and is a natural way to help people and give time to worthwhile causes.

Celebrate with Fun

- Volunteer to help some animals. Create a backyard wildlife sanctuary. Ask neighbors to get involved too so more animals have a natural habitat. Put out bird feeders and birdbaths. Plant flowers to attract butterflies.
- Read *You Can Change Your World!* by Sondra Clark. This 14-year-old author gives over 200 ideas for kids and adults on volunteering.
- Pick up trash in your neighborhood. Recycle any cans or bottles you find.
- Begin now to collect hats and gloves to give to low-income children this winter. See if stores offer clearance prices on leftover winter items.
- If your middle school or high school has been involved with a volunteer project, have them apply for the Prudential Spirit of Community Award. Applications are available at www.prudential.com/community.
- Another organization that recognizes youth involved in volunteering is the Nestle Very Best in Youth Awards. Details on how to enter are on their website under "What's New": www.nestleusa.com.
- Do you know a child or adult who has made a significant contribution to the community by volunteering? Nominate him or her for a Daily Points of Light Award. Apply online with the Points of Light Foundation at www.pointsoflight.org.
- Does your family have a membership to a children's museum? Often your membership includes several guest passes for free membership. Donate those passes to a women's shelter. You might just give a child the opportunity to go to a museum for the first time.

Celebrate with Crafts

Ask a local children's hospital if you can bring in colorful wall decorations. Have your children make bright tissue paper flowers or paper "snowflakes" to hang from the ceiling.

Celebrate with Food

Invite the family to go on a loose change hunt. Scour the house to collect as much loose change as possible. Check coat pockets, under seat cushions, and the car's ashtray! Purchase canned goods for a local food bank with the money. Store food in a closet. Every month, repeat your change hunt until you have a sizable donation to give a food bank.

Take a Missionary to Lunch Day

(In honor of Albert Schweitzer's birthday)

Albert Schweitzer was born in 1875. He became a writer, missionary, humanitarian, and even a Nobel Prize winner. Take time to honor other well-deserving missionaries today.

Celebrate with Fun

- Celebrate the most obvious way—take a missionary to lunch! Better yet, take their whole family out to lunch or dinner. Call your church or local Christian organizations to see if any missionaries are home on furlough.

- Can't find any missionaries to take to lunch? Put together a "lunch basket" to send to missionaries overseas. Include a variety of items they may not be able to get in India or Africa. Let your children pick out their favorite snack to send to missionary children.

- We often think of missionaries as people who serve God only in remote third world countries. Show children how they can be missionaries in their community. Find a way to share the gospel with a neighbor or an unsaved relative.

- Ask your church or denomination for the addresses (or e-mail addresses) of missionaries with children close in age to your children. Start a correspondence with them. Ask about their hobbies, daily schedule, and new experiences. Ask how you can pray for them.

- Read a book about Albert Schweitzer's life.

- Ask a missionary how your family can pray for him or her this coming year. If the missionary is in a third world country, can you help by sending school supplies to his or her children? Find a way to stay in contact with the missionary's family.

Celebrate with Crafts

Design a "Getting to Know You" scrapbook. Give family members sheets of paper that will fit in a photo album. Everyone designs several pages with photographs and descriptive captions. Include brochures from your hometown. Compile the scrapbook and send it to a missionary family.

Celebrate with Food

Along with taking a missionary to lunch, consider giving missionaries living in the U.S. gift certificates to restaurants. They'll appreciate being able to take their family out to eat on a limited budget. Throw in some gift certificates to McDonald's for fun!

Martin Luther King Jr.'s Birthday

Martin Luther King Jr. was born in Atlanta in 1929. He actually started college when he was 15, later going on to become a minister and social rights activist.

Celebrate with Fun

- Have children try memorizing a section of Martin Luther King Jr.'s famous speech: "I have a dream that my four little children will one day live in a nation where they will not be judged by the color of their skin, but by the content of their character."
- Ask children, "What is your dream?" Try to get beyond their dreams about a new video game. Do they have a dream to be a missionary in a foreign country? Do they have a dream to help homeless children? Discuss the steps they can take now to start making their dreams come true.
- Buy a dozen white eggs and a dozen brown eggs. Show your children the 2 colors of eggs. (Many children don't know brown eggs exist.) Let them crack open several white eggs and then several brown eggs. The lesson should be obvious—we may look different on the outside, but we're the same on the inside.
- Sing "Jesus Loves the Little Children, All the Children of the World" with your family.
- Martin Luther King Jr. won a Nobel Prize for his peace efforts. Award your children prizes for outstanding behavior or acts of kindness, for example, "Outstanding Award for Helping Grandpa Work in the Garden" or "Service Award for Sitting Next to the New Girl in Sunday School."

Celebrate with Crafts

Make a rainbow hand wreath in honor of Martin Luther King Jr.'s birthday. Trace around your children's hands on various pieces of colored construction paper. Cut out the hands. Glue the hands in a circle, overlapping the fingertips of 1 hand with the heels of the next. Make 1 large wreath or several smaller ones, symbolizing that we can all work together no matter the color of our skin.

Celebrate with Food

Most of us enjoy eating our meals while in the company of family and friends. Help your family experience the isolation many African Americans felt when they had to sit in the segregated areas of restaurants. Serve everyone their meal for dinner, then split up and eat alone in separate rooms. (Naturally young children will be with an adult.) What does it feel like to be an outcast?

National Nothing Day

Harold Pullman Coffin was a journalist who felt he had too much to do. As a result, he created this uneventful day to do nothing and celebrate nothing.

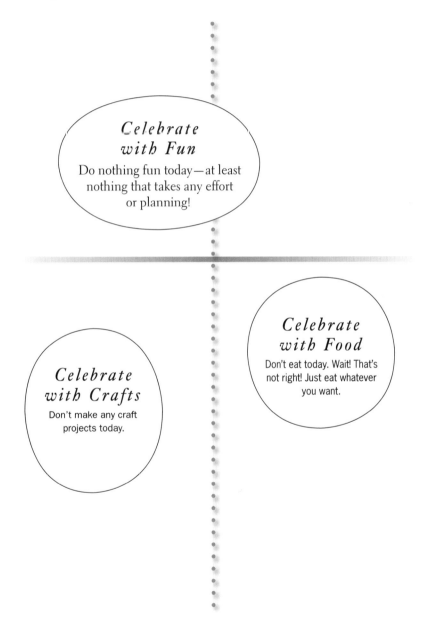

Celebrate with Fun

Do nothing fun today—at least nothing that takes any effort or planning!

Celebrate with Food

Don't eat today. Wait! That's not right! Just eat whatever you want.

Celebrate with Crafts

Don't make any craft projects today.

Shari Lewis's Birthday

Remember Shari Lewis and her beloved sock puppet Lamb Chop? Shari entertained millions of people through the use of puppets. Try to entertain at least 3 or 4 people with your own homemade puppets.

Celebrate with Fun

- Rent a video to see Shari Lewis in action. Can you see her mouth move as she makes Lamb Chop talk? Practice being ventriloquists. Put on a big smile, clench your teeth, hold your lips steady, and say, "It's time to go to bed." (Your children will pretend they don't understand you.)
- Watch *The Sound of Music*. In one scene Maria and the children stage an elaborate marionette show. Don't be discouraged by how complicated it looks. There are many ways to enjoy puppets without trying to maneuver wooden handles and strings.

Celebrate with Crafts

Make a jellyfish marionette. Fold a paper plate in half. Cover with aluminum foil. Paint the foil, creating a shiny jellyfish. Let dry. Punch 5 or 6 holes in the straight edge of the jellyfish. Attach sparkly ribbons to the holes. Punch a hole on each edge of the straight side and attach 18-inch pieces of yarn. Make your shiny jellyfish "swim" through the water by gently pulling up and down on the yarn.

Make a simple wooden spoon puppet by drawing on the "bowl" of the spoon. Make a face, then add yarn or ribbon hair for a sturdy puppet.

Use a paper cup to make a flower pop-up puppet. Cut a flower out of craft foam. Glue it on the end of a wooden craft stick. Draw flower stems on a paper cup. Cut a slit in the cup's bottom. Gently put the wooden stick inside the cup and out through the cut. Hold the cup in 1 hand. Push up on the stick to make the flower "grow" out of the cup.

Glue a large fuzzy pom-pom on top of an empty toilet paper roll. This forms the basis for your clown head. Attach small wiggle eyes to the clown's face, along with a smaller red pom-pom for the clown's nose. Wrap colorful paper around the tube to create the clown's shirt. Slip your middle 3 fingers inside the roll to manipulate.

Celebrate with Food

Slip your hand into a clean sock puppet. Select a "volunteer" to be fed by the puppet. See if the puppet can pick up pieces of fruit, bagel, and cheese and feed the human volunteer. Pull off some string cheese strips to represent the strings of a marionette!

Winnie the Pooh Day

Celebrate the antics of Winnie the Pooh and his lovable friends Piglet and Eeyore. Today is the birthday of A. A. Milne, author of *Winnie the Pooh* and *The House at Pooh Corner*.

Celebrate with Fun

- What does Tigger like to do best? Bounce! Have children be little Tiggers and bounce around the house. Set up a series of activities they must do while bouncing: Bounce on 1 foot. Bounce backward. Bounce holding hands with a partner. Bounce while balancing a pillow on your head.

- Winnie the Pooh's best friend is Piglet, who likes exercising in the morning. Get a lively exercise video and do some aerobics before breakfast. If it's good for Piglet, it's good for your family!

- Winnie the Pooh also frequently says, "Think, think, think." Give children a series of thinking activities: How many animals can you name that begin with S? What would you do if your teddy bear started talking? What is a female whale called? (A cow) What vegetable is used to make sauerkraut? (Cabbage)

- Piglet likes to hum. See if children can guess which songs you are humming. Start by humming a few bars of a popular song. Whoever guesses the song gets to be "It" and hum the next song.

- Christopher Robin enjoys playing with balloons. Blow up several balloons and toss them in the air. Keep batting them so they don't touch the ground. Give everyone a magazine to use. Wave the magazines under the balloons to keep them in the air.

Celebrate with Crafts

Make a beehive to help Winnie the Pooh get some honey. Each child needs a piece of yellow construction paper. Find some bubble wrap (the kind that makes a great "pop" when you break an individual bubble). Cut the bubble wrap into the shape of an upside-down U to look like a beehive. Glue the bubbly beehive to the yellow paper. Use black markers to draw honeybees flying all over your beehive. The bubble wrap looks like the small cells of honey in a honeycomb.

Celebrate with Food

Winnie the Pooh's favorite food is toast with honey, so it's only appropriate to serve toast with honey as a snack. Trim the crusts off bread and cut into fun shapes with cookie cutters. Spread some butter and honey on your toast for a sticky but delicious snack.

Tin Can Day

In 1825 the tin canning process was invented. Just think how messy it would be to buy tomato soup or tuna fish in a plastic bag!

Celebrate with Fun

- Make a tin can pinball machine. Using a wall as 1 side, mark out an area 6 feet long and 3 feet wide with masking tape on the floor. Set out 6–7 tin cans in a random pattern. Sitting at a narrow end, roll a ball to the opposite end, trying to get around the tin cans.
- If you normally don't recycle, start this week. Sort your trash into metals, paper, and food scraps.
- Bring out cans from the cupboard. See who can make the tallest tower of stacked cans. Watch out for toes as the tower tumbles!
- Collect an assortment of empty tin cans. (Check for sharp edges.) Stack them in a pyramid shape similar to a carnival game booth. Use balls to try to knock down the cans.
- Buy some unusual canned foods. Did you know you can buy peeled potatoes, grapefruit slices, and even canned chicken? Compare the taste of fresh cherries with the taste of canned cherries.

Celebrate with Crafts

With an adult's help, make tin can stilts. Use 2 empty 15–16 oz. cans. Turn them upside down so the open end is on the floor. Have an adult drill or poke 2 holes in the "top" (actually the bottom) of each can. Insert a sturdy rope that runs through both holes and make a loop about 3 feet long. (Children stand with a foot on each can while holding on firmly to the ropes.) Begin walking slowly on your tin can stilts.

Make tin can storage containers. Set out a variety of empty tin cans. Check that there are no sharp edges on the tops. Decorate cans by covering them with contact paper or fabric. If you have colored tape, use that to make a striped or plaid design. Store pencils or crayons in your personalized cans.

Celebrate with Food

Set out a variety of canned food items. (No canned dog food though!) Blindfold family members as they hold and shake the various cans. After they select one mystery can each, remove the blindfold. Make a meal out of all the selected mystery can foods.

National Popcorn Day

What puts the "pop" in popcorn? A tiny packet of water is in each kernel. As the water gets hot, it bursts through the outer shell to form this tasty snack.

Celebrate with Fun

- Set out a cupcake or muffin pan. Using masking tape, label each section with a point value such as 5, 10, -2, etc. Take turns trying to toss popped popcorn pieces into the pan. First person to accumulate 50 points gets to eat a bowl of popcorn. (Your kids may not even catch on that they are doing math!)

- Play a game of "Popcorn Baseball." Give the batter a wooden craft stick. Toss a piece of popped popcorn and see if he or she can hit a home run. The dog can eat all the fly balls.

- Fill an empty film canister with unpopped popcorn. Have family members guess the number of kernels inside. Winner gets to help pop and eat the popcorn.

- The Pilgrims ate popcorn with milk and sugar. See if you can get your family to substitute their breakfast cereal for popcorn Pilgrim style.

- Here's a fact: 1 oz. (2 Tbs.) unpopped popcorn makes 1 quart popcorn. Have children figure out how much unpopped popcorn it takes to make 3 quarts popcorn for a class party.

- See if a nearby specialty store sells popcorn that is still on the cob. The ordinary-looking corn on the cob goes in the microwave for 1 minute. Suddenly the kernels start popping off to produce tasty popped popcorn.

Celebrate with Crafts

Many craft projects involve making necklaces. Now you can make a giant necklace for the birds. Pop a batch of popcorn and let it sit out overnight. (It's easier to string that way.) Thread a blunt-nosed needle and "sew" through a kernel of popcorn. Next thread on a raisin, bit of apple, more popcorn, etc. Drape the necklace around a tree for the birds to enjoy.

Draw a snow scene on paper. Use popped popcorn to represent giant snowflakes.

Celebrate with Food

Want to serve a snack in a special way? Get clear plastic gloves (the kind deli workers wear). Drop a red gumdrop in each finger. Fill the glove with popped popcorn and tie shut. You now have a "handful" of popcorn.

Chinese New Year

(Starts the first new moon of the New Year, usually between January 21 and February 14)

This holiday is a celebration of change as a new year begins. Try some of these customs to help your family focus on the many opportunities a new year brings.

Celebrate with Fun

- This doesn't sound like much fun, but is probably needed— clean the entire house! Dust, vacuum, and straighten a few closets! Get the family involved in at least a 60-minute cleanup. Write chores on small pieces of paper. Slip the papers into balloons and blow up the balloons. Get family members to pop the balloons, no hands allowed! It's fun watching people try different techniques to pop their balloons. Look for the paper as your balloon pops. Everyone then does their assigned chore before popping another balloon.

- Wear red clothing as often as possible. Red is a bright, happy color, and it symbolizes that the wearer will have a sunny and bright future.

- During Chinese New Year, children receive crisp dollar bills in red envelopes.

- Check the newspaper for listings of upcoming Chinese New Year events. Many communities sponsor parades and festivities with authentic costumes and foods.

Celebrate with Crafts

Children enjoy making large Chinese dragons out of boxes. Give each child a box large enough to place over their head. Have an adult cut 2 large eye holes in the box. Make a wild-looking dragon. Paint or cover the box with paper. Cut and curl paper strips to form "hair" for your creature. Embellish the box with outdated and shiny CDs. Hang strips of crepe paper from the edge of the box. Use chenille stems as large eyelashes around the cutout eyes. When complete, put the box over your head and race around as a moving Chinese dragon.

Celebrate with Food

It's traditional to celebrate Chinese New Year by eating a whole fish. This represents togetherness as a family. If you make spaghetti, leave the noodles uncut. This shows you will have a long life. Set out a traditional tray that offers 8 types of dried fruits. No matter what you serve, the key is to have an abundance of various types of food.

Polka Dot Day

Clowns wear big polka-dotted shirts to create a feeling of fun. Celebrate this day with a variety of "dotty" activities.

Celebrate with Fun

- Encourage everyone to wear polka dots today. How about a subtle tie with tiny dots for Dad? Is your teenager brave enough to wear a polka-dotted shirt?

- Have a dot hunt throughout the house. Purchase a bag of small fuzzy pom-poms. (Or if you are ambitious, cut out hundreds of small dots.) Hide the pom-poms throughout the house on every ledge or nook and cranny. Part of the fun is hiding hundreds of pom-poms. Let your family try to find as many as possible. (You'll be finding pom-poms in corners for months afterward!)

- Bring out the Frisbees and set up a game of Frisbee golf. Cut 10–15 large polka dots out of paper and attach them to trees, swing sets, bikes, etc. outside. Use the Frisbee (which is really a plastic polka dot) to try to hit the dotted targets.

- Cut sheets of newspaper into 10–15 circles the size of a large pizza. Number each dot. These are your polka-dot stepping stones. Place them in a circle for your dotted cake walk game. Everyone stands on a dot. As lively music plays, walk from dot to dot until the music stops. Call out a number. The lucky person on that dot gets a small prize.

- Walk through the house to see how many dots or circular items you can find. You'll be amazed at how many polka dots are in broad view!

- While looking for polka dots, play some lively *polka* music.

Celebrate with Crafts

Have everyone draw a simple picture or design on plain construction paper and embellish the picture by gluing dots on all the lines. To make dots, use a hole punch to punch out as many paper dots as your hand can handle. Use the dots to make your polka-dot picture.

Many dollar stores sell BINGO dotters to use for marking BINGO cards. Purchase several different colors so children can make pictures using their own "polka dotters."

Celebrate with Food

Make a batch of cupcakes and frost with vanilla frosting. Give everyone a cupcake and let them create a polka-dot masterpiece. Set out small bowls of "dots" such as M&M's, Smarties, and other round candies.

39

National Pie Day

Take a break from the dreary days of winter by baking and eating your favorite pie. Get creative and try a new kind of pie. Some restaurants serve grape pies. How about a kiwi pie?

Celebrate with Fun

- Celebrations always need some noise! Collect a number of aluminum pie pans. Fill a pan with 2 tsp. unpopped popcorn. Spread a layer of glue on the rim of the pie pan and place a second pan on top, upside down. Let the glue dry. For extra reinforcement, tape the edges together. Shake your pie pan tambourine for some real celebratory noise.

- Go to a bakery thrift shop and buy a number of low-cost pies. Hold an old-fashioned pie eating contest. See who can eat their pie in the least amount of time.

- Do your children know about "pi"? Remember how you learned that pi equals 3.14? (Everyone needs some mathematical humor in their lives!)

- Feeling brave? Fill an aluminum pie pan with whipped cream. Go outside so your children can attempt to throw the pie in your face. Better yet, see if your children will let you throw a pie at them.

Celebrate with Crafts

Make some salt-dough clay by mixing 1 cup flour with 3/8 cup salt. Pour in 3/8 cup hot water. Stir well. Place on a floured surface. Knead the dough 5–8 minutes, adding yellow food coloring while you knead. Use to make great clay sculptures. The color is a natural look-alike to pie crust. Collect some bottle caps and look at them closely. See how they resemble tiny pie pans? Roll out the clay and carefully fill the bottle caps with the dough. Shape extra dough to look like cherries or apple slices, then paint. Display the mini-pies for all to see.

Celebrate with Food

How else could you celebrate National Pie Day except by eating pie? Make a pie together, with everyone helping roll out the dough and prepare the filling. Or keep it simple by buying a pie from your favorite bakery.

Get with a partner and create a new flavor of pie. After making (or purchasing) the crust, see what type of filling you can create. How about a peach, apple, and blueberry pie? Or try a pie with meat and vegetables, like a shepherd's pie. Come up with a creative name for your pie. Ask others to sample and rate your culinary masterpiece.

TV Game Show Day

Today celebrates the birth of Mark Goodson in 1915. He created popular game shows such as *The Price Is Right, Family Feud,* and many others.

Celebrate with Fun

- Begin the day by waking your children with loud cries of "Alison—Come on down! Mark—Come on down!" Be sure to use your best game show voice.

- At breakfast, make a game out of selecting cereal. Cover the boxes of cereal on the table. Ask your children, "Do you want cereal number 1, number 2, or number 3?" Whatever box they pick, that's their cereal for breakfast.

- When making lunches, wrap sandwiches in aluminum foil or brown wrapping paper. Write a note on the sandwich that says, "Congratulations! You are a winner! Your prize is inside this wrapping paper."

- Check if you have board games modeled after a game show. If not, borrow one from a neighbor and play the home version of *Let's Make a Deal* or *What's My Line?*

- Help your children with their homework by playing *Jeopardy.* You give them the answer while they answer in the form of a question. Example: "Jeff. The liquid that comes from a cow." Jeff's brilliant reply is, "What is milk?" You can even play this with math by giving your children a number, like "12." They answer, "What is 3 x 4?"

- Make up your own game show. Invite friends over to play the all-new, all-popular *The Johnson Family Game Show.* Award silly prizes to the winners.

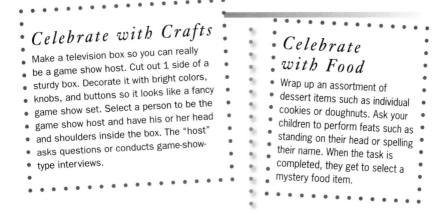

Celebrate with Crafts

Make a television box so you can really be a game show host. Cut out 1 side of a sturdy box. Decorate it with bright colors, knobs, and buttons so it looks like a fancy game show set. Select a person to be the game show host and have his or her head and shoulders inside the box. The "host" asks questions or conducts game-show-type interviews.

Celebrate with Food

Wrap up an assortment of dessert items such as individual cookies or doughnuts. Ask your children to perform feats such as standing on their head or spelling their name. When the task is completed, they get to select a mystery food item.

A Room of One's Own Day

Even if you share a room with someone, you can still celebrate having your own personal space. This is also a good day to clear out some clutter.

Celebrate with Fun

- Celebrate your room by cleaning it! No, it doesn't sound like fun, but a clean room helps you enjoy the things you have. Label 4 large boxes with "Donate," "Discard," "Can't Decide," and "Keep." Go through clothes, toys, and all your "junk," sorting each item into a box. This simple form of elimination gives you more breathing room.

- Play a few rounds of "Cross the Room" in your uncluttered room. Have everyone stand on 1 side of a room. Taking turns, 1 person at a time crosses the room in a different way. This means people crawl, jump, or even pirouette across the room. When everyone is on the opposite side, keep the game going by crossing back to the original side. Remember, each person must come up with a new way to cross the room.

- Set out old magazines, scissors, and glue. Design your perfect room by cutting out furniture and accessories and gluing them on paper. Wouldn't it be great if we could all have hot tubs in our bedrooms?

- Help your children rearrange their rooms. Sometimes just having the bed in a different position makes the room seem entirely new. Moving the furniture is a great opportunity to find those lost socks and get rid of dust bunnies.

- Does your room need a decorating boost? Try adding a simple wallpaper border. Many home improvement stores sell outdated borders at a discounted price. Even children can dip the borders in water and then transfer the paper to their walls.

Celebrate with Crafts

Have an adult use a screwdriver and remove the plastic light-switch plate in your room. Use permanent markers, paint, or stickers to decorate the plain-looking plate. After it's dry, have an adult screw it back on the wall. Try using glow-in-the-dark paint so the switch plate acts like a small night-light.

Celebrate with Food

Order room service! Pick a room where everyone will eat dinner. One family member acts as a hotel staff and serves everyone their meal in the special room. Don't forget to leave a tip!

National Bubble Wrap Appreciation Day

Never take bubble wrap for granted again! Use this day to celebrate different ways of using this lightweight package filler. Get popping!

Celebrate with Fun

- Lay pieces of bubble wrap on the floor. On "Go!" family members create indoor firecracker sounds by popping the bubbles with their heels.

- On pieces of bubble wrap with extra-large bubbles, use a fine-tipped permanent marker to label some "bubbles" with things that bother your family. Some might be labeled "Need to fix lawnmower" or "Sarah has a bully at her bus stop." As a stress reliever, read each statement, then "pop" it while you come up with a solution to the problem.

- Many computer stores have large amounts of bubble wrap. Ask for a donation of several sheets with large bubbles. Wrap and tape bubble wrap around your child's body. (Keep her head uncovered.) Watch and listen as your plastic child rolls across the living-room floor.

- Wrap a raw egg in several layers of bubble wrap. Tape shut. Go outside and drop the egg from 2 feet high. Did it break? Now drop it from 4 feet! Keep experimenting. How many layers does it take to protect your egg when dropped from a 12-foot ladder?

- Cut up bubble wrap with large bubbles so you have a piece with 3 bubble rows across and 3 rows down. Play Tic-Tac-Toe by marking an X or O on the bubble, then poking it with a sharp item.

Celebrate with Crafts

Use bubble wrap to make modern-art flower paintings. Draw the outline of a tulip or daisy on construction paper. Color the stem and petals. Pour a little paint on a paper plate. Wad up some "tiny bubbles" bubble wrap into the size of a Ping-Pong ball. Dip the bubble wrap in paint, then dab inside your flower outline. This gives your flower a distinctive design. Add different colors for a multicolored flower.

Celebrate with Food

Try a "Popping-Good" snack. Track down an old-fashioned self-contained popcorn popper. Place an old sheet on the floor. Ask family members to sit around the edges while the popcorn popper rests in the middle of the sheet. (Be sure no one trips over the electrical cord.) As the oil and popcorn heat up, remove the lid from the popcorn. Let people try to catch the popcorn as it flies out of the popper and onto the sheet.

More ideas: www.sealedair.com/products/protective/bubble/bubble_fun.html This site even has virtual bubble popping!

National Activity Professionals Day

Many professional activity directors plan fun activities at nursing homes or for other groups of people. At home, show off your activity planning skills for family fun.

Celebrate with Fun

- You can play balloon dodgeball indoors or out. Blow up several balloons to use as your balls. Stand several family members against a wall. The person who is "It" gets to throw the balloons at people against the wall. You need several balloons since they move more slowly than the people you are trying to hit.

- Plan a book party. Select a family favorite and read the book together. Then give everyone 15–20 minutes to dress up as a character from the book. If you're really creative, dress as part of the scenery or a prop from the story.

- You probably sang "The 12 Days of Christmas" last December. Adapt the same song to your family. Your song might begin with "On the first day of Activity Professionals Day, my true love gave to me three bouncing beach balls, two games of Scrabble, one jump rope . . ."

- Make a shooting rocket in the backyard. Tie a sturdy string around a tree. Slip a straw onto the string, then wrap the loose end of string tightly around another tree about 10 feet away from the first. (After you get the hang of shooting your rocket, you can use trees farther apart.) Blow up a long narrow balloon. Firmly hold the end shut. Slide the straw to 1 end of the string. Still holding the air in the balloon, tape the balloon to the straw. Release the end of the balloon and watch the air push the balloon forward on the string. Set up 2 parallel sets of string so you can race the balloons against each other.

Celebrate with Crafts

All great activity directors know how to make pasta necklaces. Set out 3–4 paper cups. Pour ½ cup rubbing alcohol and 1 tsp. food coloring in each cup. Now add some tube-shaped pasta to each cup and stir well. Drain the pasta and let dry on a paper towel. Use the pasta to make colored necklaces.

Celebrate with Food

Pretend it's the middle of summer. Hang up yellow streamers to represent the sun's rays. Put a gingham tablecloth on the floor and have an indoor picnic. Plastic ants are optional.

National Puzzle Day

Puzzles provide challenges! From toddlers with their 3-piece wooden puzzles to adults working on a 1000-piece reproduction of the Mona Lisa, everyone enjoys the intricacies of connecting the pieces.

Celebrate with Fun

- Go to the store and look at the variety of puzzles available. Buy a new puzzle that the family can work on together. Are you brave enough to try a 1000-piece puzzle?

- Try a puzzle piece hunt. Select 1 person to hide the pieces of a 25-piece puzzle around the house. (To make finding the pieces feasible, make sure the pieces are in sight.) The rest of the family looks for the pieces and then tries to assemble the puzzle.

- Find a wooden 7–10-piece puzzle. (If you don't have one, borrow one from a neighbor with young children.) Have each family member look at the completed puzzle. Mix up the pieces. One at a time, blindfold someone and let him or her try to put the chunky pieces back together again. Time each other to find the "Blindfolded Puzzle Champion."

- Keep a complicated puzzle on a coffee table where people can work on it whenever they want. Many meaningful conversations take place between parents and children while putting the puzzle together without making eye contact.

- Do you have an abundance of puzzles you've completed? Plan a puzzle exchange with friends. Everyone is happy to trade in their completed puzzle for a "new" one.

Celebrate with Crafts

Make your own puzzles. Find a picture you like from a magazine. Spread glue on the back, then glue the picture on a piece of construction paper. Let dry. On the solid paper side, draw random interconnecting lines to form puzzle pieces. Carefully cut along the lines, creating your own puzzle. Try the same technique on photographs. Send to a friend who'll have to put the photo puzzle together.

Celebrate with Food

Toast 6–8 pieces of bread. Cut off the crusts. Use different cookie cutters to cut shapes out of the toast. Mix up all the pieces. Put your edible puzzles back together again, then enjoy.

Inspire Your Heart with Art Day

From ancient times, art has inspired people to contemplate how they live their lives . . . hopefully for the better. Use this day to experiment with various forms of art.

Celebrate with Fun

- Visit a local art gallery to view various forms of art. Take time looking at paintings or analyzing sculptures. Which artwork inspires your heart?
- Check out oversized art books from the library. Take time to look at different artists to see what inspires them and their art.

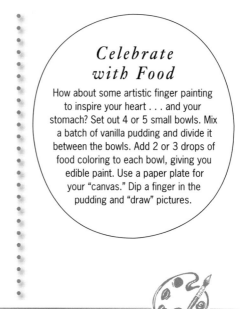

Celebrate with Food

How about some artistic finger painting to inspire your heart . . . and your stomach? Set out 4 or 5 small bowls. Mix a batch of vanilla pudding and divide it between the bowls. Add 2 or 3 drops of food coloring to each bowl, giving you edible paint. Use a paper plate for your "canvas." Dip a finger in the pudding and "draw" pictures.

Celebrate with Crafts

You'll feel very inspired as you make a "smooch picture." Put lipstick on your children. (At least attempt to put lipstick on your son!) Ask children to give a big "kiss" to a piece of paper. Now it's up to them to draw a picture incorporating the lips. Perhaps the lips are a skirt for a person. Of course, the lips could simply be lips, and children could add eyes and a nose.

Decorate ordinary shoelaces to create designer laces. Place shoelaces on a flat surface, taping the ends so the laces stay taut. Use a toothpick dipped in paint to decorate the laces. Try tiny stripes or miniflowers.

Every refrigerator needs a few more magnets. Find a picture in which your child's face is at least the size of a 50-cent piece. Cut out his or her face and glue onto a piece of construction paper. Have your child draw a body to go with it. After the clothes, arms, and legs are added, cut out the entire body. Attach a magnet to the back and display on your refrigerator.

Make a few flexible art sculptures. Set out a number of colored chenille stems, along with small ½-inch and 1-inch Styrofoam balls. Ask children to create a sculpture by poking the chenille stems into the balls. Hint: To cut chenille stems, use an old pair of nail clippers. That way you won't ruin your scissors.

FEBRUARY

Wild Bird Feeding Month
National Cherry Month
Library Lovers' Month
Responsible Pet Owner's Month
Black History Month

Weeks to Celebrate

2nd Full Week • Random Acts of Kindness Week
Last Full Week • Friendship Week
6–14 • Smart Sitters Week

Days to Celebrate

Usually 1st Wednesday • National Girls and Women in Sports Day
3rd Monday • Presidents' Day
Tuesday before Ash Wednesday • Pancake Day

- 1 Be an Encourager Day
- 2 Job Shadow Day
- 2 Groundhog Day
- 3 Norman Rockwell's Birthday
- 4 Halfway Point of Winter
- 6 Pay a Compliment Day
- 8 Boy Scout Day
- 9 100 Days of School (approximately)
- 14 Turn Off TV Day
- 14 Valentine's Day
- 19 Solar System Day
- 20 Love Your Pet Day
- 23 Tootsie Roll Anniversary
- 29 Leap Year Day

Wild Bird Feeding Month

North America is home to over 800 bird species. You won't find all of them in your backyard, but spend this month attracting birds native to your area.

Celebrate with Fun

☃ To attract the most birds to your feeder, avoid generic seed from a discount store. It contains mostly junk seeds that few birds eat. Instead, go to a local specialty pet store to purchase higher quality seeds.

☃ As you watch the birds, record which birds like to eat from the feeder. Some would much rather eat directly from the ground.

☃ Use binoculars for a close-up view. Observe colors and markings, then sketch your favorite feathered friends. Use water colors for a professional look. Display sketches near your viewing window for comparison.

☃ In the Bible, ravens fed Elijah (1 Kings 17:24). Cut out some paper birds and act out the story. Let birds "fly" to Elijah and bring him food.

☃ Encourage children to closely observe a bird. What shape is its beak? Does it have wing bars or eye rings? Are wings round or pointed? Does the bird stay with a group or keep to itself?

☃ Subscribe to *Audubon Adventure,* a magazine put out by the Audubon Society for Kids. Call 212-979-3000.

☃ The World Wildlife Organization offers a website filled with educational and fun activities. Kids can play games while learning about saving endangered animals. www.worldwildlife.org

Celebrate with Crafts

Want to get a close-up view of birds? Make a bird blind. Professionals spend hundreds of dollars to construct these camouflaged structures. Your family can make one for under a dollar. Cut several 3″ x 6″ slits in a refrigerator box at various heights. (Local appliance stores will gladly save a box for you.) Cover the box with leafy branches or evergreens so it blends in with the surroundings. Stay in the bird blind and watch the birds close-up.

Celebrate with Food

Instead of you eating something, celebrate by preparing some homemade bird food. In a saucepan mix 2 quarts water and 1 cup margarine. Boil. Add 4 cups cereal like cornmeal, rolled oats, or grain. Mix in 1 cup peanut butter and 1 cup chopped fruit like raisins or dates. Pack mixture firmly in several plastic containers. Let cool. Set bowls outside so birds can enjoy their homemade pudding.

More ideas: www.birdfeeding.org

National Cherry Month

Thanks to the legend of George Washington and the cherry tree, this month is set aside to celebrate juicy cherries. Even though they are out of season, purchase a few cherries as a special treat.

Celebrate with Fun

- After enjoying the taste of juicy cherries, organize a pit-spitting contest. Set up cans so people can spit their cherry pits for accuracy. See who can spit the pits the farthest.
- Tell your children the (made-up) story about George Washington cutting down the cherry tree. When his father asked if he did it, George answered, "I cannot tell a lie. I cut down the tree." (The legend doesn't tell what motivated him.) Discuss lying with your children. Is lying ever appropriate? What does the Bible say about lying?
- Play "Pin the Cherry on the Tree." Sketch a tree with several branches on a large sheet of paper. Tape it to the wall. Cut out paper cherries and attach tape "doughnuts" to the backs. Blindfold a person and spin him or her around 3 times. Can he or she place a cherry on a tree branch?
- The saying "Life is just a bowl of cherries" is commonly seen on inspirational posters. What does it mean? Come up with various explanations about the true meaning of this popular saying.
- We associate cherries with bright red. Pick a day this month to dress in as much red as possible. Get out your red shirt and add some red socks.
- Surprise your children by giving them a dollar bill as a reminder that George Washington always told the truth.

Celebrate with Crafts

We always see black silhouettes of George Washington's face. Make your own family silhouettes. Tape white paper on the wall and stand your child 2 feet from the paper. Shine a bright light so the shadow of your child's head is on the paper. Trace the shadow, then cut out the shape. Place the white silhouette on top of a black piece of paper. Carefully recut the face out of black paper—just like George's!

Celebrate with Food

Purchase cherries fresh, frozen, and even canned. Set them out in bowls and let your family sample the various forms of cherries. How about sampling dried cherries? Don't forget to make a cherry pie.

More ideas: www.cherrymkt.org

49

Library Lovers' Month

Anyone who likes to read enjoys going to a library. Just looking at the stacks of books makes the avid reader's heart beat faster. Visit the library as often as possible this month.

Celebrate with Fun

- Plan a scavenger hunt to help children feel comfortable with the library. Give them a list of items to find: (1) an autograph from a librarian; (2) a magazine about animals; (3) a globe; (4) a computer game; (5) a newspaper from another state.

- Ask a librarian for a personalized tour of the library. More than likely, she'll be glad to show you there's more to the library than checking out books. You might discover the library offers a chance to check out paintings or even toys. Ask to see the storage area for books needing repair, or ask if there is an old card catalog somewhere. Perhaps you could show your children how flipping through those cards helped you find the books you needed in elementary school.

- Visit a library other than your local public library. If a college is nearby, visit their library. Some colleges have separate libraries featuring information on specific topics such as music or law. Children are amazed to discover that so much information is available on one topic.

- Spend time in the oversized book section with your children. The large books filled with breathtaking pictures let children see books on their favorite subject in a new way.

Celebrate with Crafts

Make a thank-you card book for the library staff. Staple 8–10 pages together and cover with construction paper. Have children decorate the pages while also writing notes of thanks to library employees. Thank the custodian for keeping the building clean. Acknowledge people who shelve the books. Thank the reference librarian for answering all those difficult homework questions. Use shiny stickers and glitter glue to give the card an extra-sparkly effect.

Celebrate with Food

Make a bookworm cake. Bake a rectangular cake. Frost the sides with a cream-colored frosting to resemble the pages of a book. Use a darker color frosting for the top "cover." Write the title of your favorite book on the top with gel frosting. Stick a few gummy worms halfway into the book.

This month, spend extra time with your pet. Make sure your beloved hamster, dog, or lizard has what it needs to live comfortably at your house.

Celebrate with Fun

- Read some "Clifford" books, which tell about a girl who owns a very large red dog. In honor of Clifford, wear red clothes while reading the books. Discuss what it would be like to own a dog who fills an entire garage.

- Read a book about your pet's care. Can you improve its living conditions? Does the doghouse need a new rug? Is the aquarium filter working properly? Are the cat's food bowls kept clean?

- Some people own exotic pets. Find someone nearby who owns a parrot or a rare breed of dog. Visit them to see how they take care of animals with unusual needs.

- Pledge to give the dog more exercise this month. Ask children to go along, and take the neighbor's dog so you can form a pet parade. The dogs will love the extra attention. (Exercise is wonderful for humans also!)

- If you have the space and supplies, ask a local animal shelter if you can provide a foster home for young puppies or kittens needing extra attention.

- Play "Roof, Roof—Meow, Meow." Get a group of at least 10 people together. Divide into "dogs" and "cats." Have the 2 groups mingle. Ask everyone to close their eyes and begin barking or meowing. When a "dog" hears another dog barking, they hold hands and go off to find another dog. See which team gathers all their members together the fastest.

Celebrate with Crafts

Purchase a cardboard frame to hold your favorite picture of your pet. Decorate the frame according to the pet. A picture of your dog could be surrounded by small dog biscuits glued to the frame. Put plastic water lilies around a picture of your fish.

Celebrate with Food

Here's a tasty treat for your dog, not for you! In a medium bowl, mix together 1½ cups flour, 2 Tbs. powdered milk, 1½ cups wheat flour, 1 egg, and ½ cup cornmeal. Slowly stir in 1–1½ cups beef or chicken bouillon. Mix well. Knead for several minutes until dough is smooth and pliable. Roll out to about ½-inch thick. Use any shape cookie cutter to cut out your doggy biscuit shapes. Bake at 350 degrees for 45–60 minutes on a greased pan. Let cool and give Bruno his homemade dog biscuits.

Black History Month

This month was started by Dr. Carter Woodson to raise the awareness of the contribution African Americans have made to U.S. history.

Celebrate with Fun

- If possible, visit an African American church. Notice the different styles of worship. This can be a big culture shock if your family usually goes to a quiet, conservative church!

- Historically, African Americans suffered many hardships. Give children 8 and older a gentle exposure to discrimination. "Segregate" family members, perhaps based on the color of their hair or eyes. You might say, "Tonight, only people with curly hair will get dessert." Later on, state, "Whoever has blue eyes can stay up a half hour after bedtime." There will be cries of "But that's not fair!" Go on to explain how many people face discrimination on a daily basis.

- Learn more about African American inventors. In 1897 Alfred Cralle invented the ice-cream scoop. In 1899 J. A. Burr invented the lawnmower. In 1923 Garrett Morgan invented the traffic light.

- Read or explain to your children how Rosa Parks changed history by her refusal to give up her seat on a bus to a white person. Arrange several rows of kitchen chairs to represent bus seats. Act out what it would be like to be forced to sit in the back of the bus because you were African American.

Celebrate with Crafts

Martin Luther King Jr.'s famous "I Have a Dream" speech inspires us all. Make a mobile sharing your dreams. From an 8½ x 11 piece of construction paper, cut out a large "cloud" shape. Punch 4 or 5 holes on 1 edge. Write "I have a dream . . ." on your cloud. Cut out 4 or 5 paper stars, writing one of your dreams on each star. Punch a hole in each star and use embroidery floss to attach the stars to your cloud.

Celebrate with Food

Since a rainbow is a symbol of peace and hope, make a rainbow cake. Bake a regular round layer cake in your favorite flavor. Frost half the cake with green frosting to look like blades of grass. Use M&M's to create a rainbow curving over the grass. Divide the candy so you have curved rows of red, orange, yellow, green, and blue M&M's to make a crunchy rainbow.

More ideas: www.asalh.com

Random Acts of Kindness Week

This week, make a concentrated effort to surprise others by doing something nice for them. Try to do a few secret good deeds also.

Celebrate with Fun

- Purchase a number of inexpensive coupons for ice-cream cones. Throughout the week, leave the coupons in unexpected places for family members. Make sure everyone has 1 coupon by the end of the week.

- Send an e-mail card to your pastor. Comment positively about some aspect of his or her ministry.

- Help children figure out acts of kindness by listing ideas on strips of paper. Let them reach into the jar for an idea when they need inspiration.

- Tell your children the story of Lifeboat number 14. On April 15, 1912, the "unsinkable" luxury liner Titanic sank after hitting an iceberg. Only 20 lifeboats were available for 2,000 people. The few lifeboats tried to get away from the sinking Titanic, even though people in the water were drowning. Lifeboat number 14's passengers made a brave decision to go back and rescue whomever they could. According to a witness, "A precious few people were saved." They performed a very courageous act of kindness. When considering a random act of kindness, ask your family, "What would the people in Lifeboat number 14 do?"

- Mother Teresa helped the "poorest of the poor" in India. People often contacted her, wanting to come help her. She always told them, "Calcutta can be found all over the world if you have eyes to see." She told people to stay home and perform acts of kindness for the people in their own community. Read some books about foreign missionaries to inspire your family, while also showing them how the principles of service apply to everyday life.

Celebrate with Crafts

Create a chain of kindness. Every day this week, ask children if they did or saw a random act of kindness. Write down the situation on a slip of paper. Make a chain from all the strips of paper. See how far you can get the kindness chain to reach.

Celebrate with Food

This is the perfect time to organize a food drive for a local food bank. Many food banks collect large amounts of food during the holidays, but their cupboards are bare after the holiday season. Ask classmates and coworkers to donate nonperishable food.

More ideas: www.actsofkindness.org

53

Friendship Week

Think about the friends in your life. What makes them special? Use this week to celebrate the joy of friendship.

Celebrate with Fun

- Throw a party celebrating friendship for all your friends! Send out invitations 2 weeks in advance in the shape of cutout paper dolls holding hands.

- When people arrive, ask them to make crazy name tags. Set out an assortment of scrap paper, scissors, glue, tape, stickers, and glitter. People can be creative and make name headbands or name tags with folded pop-up letters. Announce that there is a prize for the most creative name tag. Hand the winner a paper and markers kit so he or she can continue making cute name tags.

- Play "People Bingo." Print out sheets of paper with 9–12 squares. On each square list a category like: A person who went to college in Ohio. Someone who has a pet lizard. Someone who likes peanut butter and celery sandwiches. A person who sleeps with a teddy bear. Everyone goes around trying to get the names of people who fit that category.

- Discuss with your kids why you invited friends over. Share how Margie helped out when all 3 kids had chicken pox and how Dave always lets you borrow his tools! Encourage children to share about their friendships.

- Try a home swap with your friends. Move into their house for the weekend while they move into yours. Your family will feel like they are on vacation by living in another house. Even if you are just a few miles from your home, the entire atmosphere is unique as you eat in a different kitchen and sleep in a different bed.

Celebrate with Crafts

Show your friendship by making a friendship heart wreath. Using your favorite 2 colors of construction paper, cut out 10 hearts 3 or 4 inches high. Glue 1 edge of a heart to another edge, overlapping about a heart to another edge, overlapping about ½ inch. Continue overlapping in a circular shape so you have a wreath. Add a ribbon bow on top before giving to a friend.

Celebrate with Food

At your friendship party, serve refreshments in various parts of the house: pretzels and chips in the family room, veggies and dip in the kitchen. This helps people mingle as they move from room to room getting food. Ask each guest to bring a batch of their favorite cookies. Then you can all enjoy eating "friendship cookies."

Smart Sitters Week

Do you ever use babysitters? Do you have any children who babysit for others? This is the week to get some tips on how to make the babysitting experience positive for everyone involved.

Celebrate with Fun

- Invite potential babysitters to come over for an hour or so as a "mother's helper." He or she can play with your children while you observe from a distance.
- If your son or daughter wants to earn extra money babysitting, sign them up for a babysitting class. Preteens gain valuable skills in child care and handling emergencies. Still hesitant to allow your children to babysit for others? See if they can volunteer in the church nursery. Your child gains experience in a structured, controlled setting.
- Purchase a few toys or puzzles at a garage sale. Keep them in a special place to use only when the babysitter arrives. Children will play longer with toys they normally don't use.
- Negotiate the hourly rate with your babysitter before she begins her job. This avoids miscommunication and hard feelings later.

Celebrate with Crafts

Young children enjoy making simple craft projects. Babysitters can bring along a few crafts to help pass time until parents return home.

Cut strips of paper into various lengths and widths. Fold each end of the papers under by ½ inch. Make arches and bridges with the papers by gluing the folded sections to a piece of cardboard.

Paper bag puppets are always a hit. Set out lunch bags for children to decorate with markers and stickers. Tell them you are looking forward to seeing a puppet show when you get home.

Have older children use watercolors to paint on sheets of aluminum foil. The results are shiny, mosaiclike paintings. Young children enjoy tearing paper. Let them tear tissue paper to glue on construction paper. The thin paper tears easily and quickly sticks to the glue.

Celebrate with Food

Always leave clear instructions with your sitter about what children can eat. Inexperienced babysitters could inadvertently give toddlers food like hot dogs or peanuts, which pose a high risk for choking. Post a list of appropriate snacks. Set out a special snack for your sitter to enjoy when children are asleep.

More ideas: www.babysittingclass.com

55

National Girls and Women in Sports Day

USUALLY 1ˢᵀ WEDNESDAY IN FEBRUARY

Today celebrates the passage of Title IX in 1972. This law guaranteed gender equity in federally funded school programs. This meant girls suddenly had many more athletic opportunities available to them.

Celebrate with Fun

- Get moving! Today's the day to participate in a sports activity. Play tennis, shoot some hoops, or toss a foam football.

- Girls today assume they can participate in any sport available. Share examples of how your school had few, if any, sports opportunities available for girls. In 1896 the first intercollegiate female basketball game took place between the University of California at Burbank and Stanford. The girls wore dresses with bloomers—and no men were allowed to watch the game.

- Read an autobiography of a female athlete. Gertrude Ederle was the first female to swim the English Channel. She also broke the male's record for crossing time! Find out how tennis sensations Venus and Serena Williams got their start. These athletic role models might inspire your daughter.

- Ask your daughter about a sport she'd like to try. If she's not already participating, arrange for a few lessons. Would your daughter like to play basketball? Ask a girl on the high school basketball team if she would come over and give a minilesson to your daughter.

- Take your children to a high school or college women's athletic event. The strong, athletic girls on the playing field serve as positive role models.

- Check out the Girl Scouts website for an entire section on the importance of girls in sports. www.girlscouts.org

Celebrate with Crafts

At a used bookstore, buy some back issues of children's and teen magazines that are at least 25 years old. Ask your children to look through the ads at how girls were depicted. Make a "Then and Now" poster. Glue pictures from the magazines under "Then." Glue today's ads showing girls in a variety of athletic activities under "Now."

Celebrate with Food

Reverse the traditional roles of cooking. Before Title IX, boys were encouraged to participate in sports while girls were told to bake cookies and sew their own clothes. Tonight while your daughter is busy with a sporting activity, have the males in your family make dinner and clean up afterward.

More ideas: www.aahperd.org/ngwsdcentral

Presidents' Day

Today is the day we celebrate the birthday of 2 presidents, George Washington and Abe Lincoln. Since many children are home from school today, be sure to dress in red, white, and blue as you celebrate.

Celebrate with Fun

- Ask children what they would do if they were president. Go beyond vague answers such as "Make world peace." Encourage children to think about specific changes they'd make. Then ask the hard question: How would they implement those changes?

- Bring out the coins and hundred-dollar bills in your house. Look at the various presidents on each. Who is on the thousand-dollar bill?

- Since you have coins handy, try some presidential rubbings. Place a piece of tracing paper over a coin. Rub a pencil or crayon over the coin to make circular portraits of presidents.

- Do your children have nicknames? How did they get those nicknames? Why is George Washington called "The Father of our Country" and Abraham Lincoln called "Honest Abe"?

- Pretend someone in the family is president. Make a sign over your door that says "1600 Pennsylvania Avenue, The White House."

- Sing as many patriotic songs as possible (at least the first verses). Try "God Bless America," "You're a Grand Old Flag," and "Yankee Doodle."

Celebrate with Crafts

Transform a half-gallon milk carton into a president's log cabin. Thoroughly wash and dry the empty carton. Use duct tape to flatten the spout end so you have a rectangle as the base of your log cabin. Cut 5 or 6 large paper bags into strips the length of 1 side of the rectangle (about 8 inches long). Roll the paper strips around pencils to form logs. Tape or glue the ends to keep from unrolling. Glue first log at base of milk carton. Continue making logs and gluing them to the carton. Use extra logs to form a pitched roof. Make doors and windows by gluing paper cutouts in the proper locations.

Celebrate with Food

It's traditional to serve cherry pie for Presidents' Day. Let children make this easy cherry recipe. Purchase a packaged graham cracker crumb crust. Pour in one 16 oz. can cherry pie filling. Top with a decorative spray of whipping cream from a can. Serve to future presidents of the U.S.

Pancake Day

The lowly pancake . . . easy to make, often taken for granted. Today's the day to look with new eyes at an ordinary pancake.

Celebrate with Fun

- Make up a poem involving pancakes. Here's an opening line for you: "I think that I shall never make, a thing so lovely as a pancake . . ."
- How many names can you come up with for different versions of pancakes? (Hint: flapjack, griddle cake, crepe, blintze . . .)
- When making pancakes for breakfast, save 1 or 2 for later in the day. Go outside and use the pancakes as flexible Frisbees. Toss back and forth to each other.
- Communities across the country offer special events in honor of Pancake Day. If nothing is happening in your town, plan your own pancake events. (1) See who can run the farthest balancing a pancake on a spatula. Set up obstacles for participants to go over and around. (2) Plan a race in which people hold a (cold) frying pan containing 1 pancake. They must keep flipping the pancake as they run. If it drops, it's back to the starting line. (3) Try a pancake throw for accuracy. Attach a paper plate target to a tree. Try to toss the pancake so it hits the target. (4) Cut a hole in the middle of a pancake. Use it as a ring toss as you throw it over a bottle of syrup.

Celebrate with Crafts

Create fluffy pancake characters. Mix up your regular pancake recipe. Pour the batter into the pan in varying amounts to form different-sized circles. Everyone gets 8 or 10 pancake circles. Lay out the circles on your plate to make a person, animal, or abstract design. Give a title to your pancake design before eating it.

Celebrate with Food

Make a batch of your favorite silver dollar pancakes. See who can stack the largest pile before they topple over.

Plan a "Make Your Own Pancake Bar." Use your favorite recipe to make stacks of pancakes. Set out a variety of toppings to eat with pancakes—bowls of fresh fruit, chocolate chips, peanut butter, whipped cream. Try different-flavored jams and syrups. Anyone for salsa on a pancake?

Pour pancake batter into a plastic squirt bottle. Heat the pan as you would for normal pancakes. Instead of ladling a spoonful of batter, squirt the bottle in a random design full of squiggles. Eat as you would an ordinary pancake.

More ideas: www.pancakeday.com.au

Be an Encourager Day

It's all too easy to be negative with the people in our lives. Set aside this day to make a strong effort to encourage everyone you see.

Celebrate with Fun

- Using a permanent marker, write a positive statement about each family member on a deflated balloon. The short statements can say, "Jordan has a great sense of humor" or "Emily can tie her shoes!" Let everyone blow up their balloons and read the personalized messages. Tie balloons shut and hang throughout the house.

- Some people call negative thoughts "ANTS"—"Automatic Negative Thoughts." Demonstrate to children how to be an encourager instead of a discourager. When they feel like saying "Jeremy is such a bad speller," show them how to look for a person's positive traits. Perhaps Jeremy is a great soccer player or always feeds the dog on time.

- Buy a batch of decorative postcards. As a family, send short words of encouragement to relatives and friends who will be delighted to get an unexpected positive note.

- Plan a family "Mutual Admiration Society" get-together. Corny as it sounds, take turns telling wonderful things about each other.

- Take turns sharing a time you had a problem or were discouraged and someone encouraged you. Find some Bible verses that talk about lifting people up by praying for them and encouraging them.

Celebrate with Crafts

Since the stores are selling thousands of boxes of those hard candy hearts that say "Hug Me" or "You're Cool," buy some early. Take 4" x 6" index cards and fold them in half to make place cards for the dinner table. Ask each person to write their name on a card and glue their favorite candy sayings on it. Use the cards for the rest of the month. It's fun to eat dinner looking at your name card with candy heart sayings on it.

Celebrate with Food

Before you bake a batch of cupcakes, take time to write a message of encouragement with a permanent marker on the inside of the cupcake liner. After the cupcakes are baked, tell your children they have a special message hidden in the cupcake.

More ideas: www.lizcurtishiggs.com

Job Shadow Day

Many high schools now require students to explore various careers by "job shadowing" people in the community. Take part in this national program by having family members learn more about possible careers.

Celebrate with Fun

- Describe your ideal job! Where would it be? Would you set your own schedule? How much money do you want to earn?

- Plan a family field trip to a community business. It usually just takes a phone call to arrange a behind-the-scenes look at a bakery, radio station, or fire department.

- If you have teenagers, start now to find a short-term internship for them this summer. It's a good opportunity to explore different careers.

- Look up www.jobshadow.org and see the wide variety of programs available to learn more about career options. If your child is interested in a specific career, try to arrange a job shadow. Contact a person in that particular field to ask if your child can follow them on the job for a few hours.

- The library is a wealth of information on careers. Check out books describing what it is like to be a marine biologist or park ranger.

- Write the names of various occupations on individual pieces of paper. Some of these could be: veterinarian, writer, teacher, producer, computer programmer. Take turns selecting an occupation and acting out what is done on the job. Other family members try to guess the job.

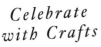

Celebrate with Crafts

Set out an assortment of paper along with markers, stickers, glitter, and scissors. Make cards of appreciation for people in your community. How about a thank-you card for the trash collector or a note of thanks to your pastor? You'll make people smile as they receive your unexpected cards.

Celebrate with Food

Do you have friends with interesting or unique jobs? Invite one of them over to share details about their work. Prepare their favorite dessert!

For Job Shadow Day, serve some shadow foods. Hold up different fruits and other foods behind a piece of paper. Shine a light so the shadow of the food shows through. Have everyone guess the food.

More ideas: www.jobshadow.org

Groundhog Day

Everyone waits anxiously on Groundhog Day to see if Punxsutawney Phil sees his shadow. If he does, that means 6 more weeks of cold wintry weather.

Celebrate with Fun

- Watch local newscasts as media from around the country head to Punxsutawney, Pennsylvania, to watch the world's most famous groundhog come out of his hole. Clap along if Phil's prediction is for the end of winter.

- Set up your own shadow theater. Hang a white sheet from the ceiling in the middle of the room. Put a bright light about 8 feet from the sheet. While the audience watches, take turns standing between the light and the sheet to create shadow figures. At first children will simply want to prance around. As they practice, they'll develop fun ways to use props and slow movements to develop more intricate shadow designs.

- Since your shadow theater is set up, use it to make "tableaus" in which people "freeze" in one place while the rest of the family guesses what their shadow shows. Write down several scenes for children to depict, like 2 people playing basketball, the Last Supper, or a person riding a horse.

- Form living-room couch cushions into a "groundhog den." Children take turns going into the den. As they poke out of the den, shine a flashlight on them so everyone sees the groundhog's shadow.

- Play "Shadow Tag." If you're lucky enough to have sun, go outside to play. A person becomes "It" if someone steps on his or her shadow.

- What's the difference between a groundhog and a flea? (A groundhog can have fleas, but a flea can't have groundhogs!)

Celebrate with Crafts

Make some minigroundhogs. Decorate the top half of a wooden tongue depressor to look like Punxsutawney Phil. Draw shaggy brown fur with markers. Cut a slit in the bottom of a small paper cup. Slide your wooden groundhog through the inside of the cup. Use your puppet to pop up out of the cup to look for his shadow.

Celebrate with Food

Using your shadow theater, hold up various food items. As your family looks at the shadows, they can easily guess the shape of a banana, but what about an orange, a bagel, or a piece of bologna?

More ideas: www.groundhog.org

61

Norman Rockwell's Birthday

Anyone looking at a Norman Rockwell painting can't help but long for the "good old days" when life was simple and innocent. Relive the world of Norman Rockwell with some down-home fun.

Celebrate with Fun

- Get a book of Norman Rockwell paintings. Take time looking at the details of each one. Ask children to tell you what happened before and after the situations in the paintings. How did the little girl get her black eye? Who stole the clothes when the boys were skinny-dipping in the pond?

- Look at the pictures depicting the Four Freedoms. Give each family member one of the paintings. Take turns pretending to be a museum curator and giving a "lecture" about your particular freedom.

- Rockwell's paintings convey a warm fuzzy feeling about family. Create a new family tradition. Do something today that starts a once-a-year ritual. Maybe you'll go out to dinner at a '50s diner or buy a new birdhouse. Whatever you do, try to do it every year on Norman Rockwell's birthday.

- Play "statue" with some of Rockwell's paintings. Show a painting to your children. Give them 20 seconds to quickly put themselves into the same position as the characters in the painting. Have them hold the pose for at least a minute so you can enjoy your stationary children.

- Visit a used bookstore to look at Rockwell's paintings on *Saturday Evening Post* magazines. He painted over 332 magazine covers for various publications.

Celebrate with Crafts

Try your hand at a Norman Rockwell–style sketch. Distribute paper along with colored pencils. Select a family member to be the model. Dress her up in a gingham dress with some traditional props. Sketch what you see in a realistic style. Any budding artists in your family?

Celebrate with Food

Rockwell's depiction of a perpetually happy family enjoying a Thanksgiving dinner is one of his most famous paintings. The food is perfect, the children are perfect, the world is perfect. As a family, cook a simplified Thanksgiving dinner. Don't worry about making Aunt Louisa's complicated oyster mushroom stuffing. Let your 10 year-old make stuffing from a package. Roast a turkey, make instant potatoes, and buy a pumpkin pie. Ask a neighbor to come over and photograph your family in the same position as in Rockwell's painting.

Halfway Point of Winter

No matter what Punxsutawney Phil decided 2 days ago, winter is still with us. Have fun today knowing you are at the halfway point of winter.

Celebrate with Fun

- Bring out a tray filled with 10–15 winter items like a mitten, thermometer, and bare tree branch. Have children stare at the items for 20 seconds. Cover the tray. See how many items they can remember and write down. Play the game again, adding a few different items. Watch how children stare intently at the tray. After 20 seconds, leave the room. They'll expect to write down the items. Instead, stay in the other room and tell them, "Write down in detail what I was wearing while I held the tray." That's one way to test their powers of observation!

- Look forward to the coming days of spring. While eating dinner, dress in shorts and tank tops. Give each other pedicures to get your feet ready for walking barefoot in the grass.

- Is there snow on the ground? Get out squirt guns, supersoakers, or ordinary spray bottles. Fill with water and add a few drops of food coloring. Spray the colored water on the snow. Write your names or make a multicolored snowman.

Celebrate with Crafts

Make designer snowballs. Most snowballs are plain white. See if your family can create beautifully ornate ones. Give everyone a white paper circle. Use sequins and glitter to decorate the snowball. Use markers to make intricate designs.

Bring out a package of inexpensive white paper plates. Punch holes in 2 opposite sides of each plate. Connect the plates in a long chain with paper fasteners. Use markers to make banners with winter sayings such as "Snow Is Sweet." Write 1 letter on each plate. Hang across doorways to help brighten up gloomy winter days.

By now many stores are carrying paper doilies for Valentine's Day. Purchase packages of 2 different-sized white doilies. Glue 2 of the larger doilies to form the body of your snowman. The smaller doily is the head. Use actual buttons for eyes. Add a fabric or paper scrap hat and shawl.

Celebrate with Food

Mix a batch of easy spiced cider. Heat apple cider. Pour into cups and stir with a cinnamon stick. For another type of flavor, drop in a peppermint hard candy left over from Christmas.

Pay a Compliment Day

FEBRUARY 6

Think back to the last time someone told you, "Thanks for making my favorite meal." You felt pretty good, didn't you? Use this day to encourage family members to compliment each other.

Celebrate with Fun

- Exaggeration can be a great learning tool. Make a point of exaggerating family compliments. They can be as silly as "Susan, I like how you parted your hair," or "Mike, it's wonderful how you breathe through your nose." After exaggerating, give some sincere compliments too.

- Encourage children to practice good manners along with complimenting others. At dinner, pass out 5 tokens or pennies to each person. The goal is to catch someone doing something positive and give them a token. You might say, "Lizzie, thank you for passing the gravy to me." Lizzie then gets a token from the "complimenter." The object is to find people with good manners and compliment them.

- As you drive to school or soccer practice, ask children which people they could compliment today. How about the school cafeteria workers? Or a shy student? Or the soccer coach who taught them a new skill? Your children will see the smiles that come when a person is complimented.

- Do your children ever say rude or inconsiderate things to each other? Never? If they ever do, try the movie director's approach: If an actor flubs his lines, the director says, "Take 2," and the scene is repeated. Teach children that if they are being mean, you'll say, "Take 2" and expect them to repeat their statement with more respect.

Celebrate with Crafts

Purchase spring-type clothespins for each family member. Decorate each pin with glitter and markers. Add a few beads or shiny jewels for a sparkly effect. Attach a magnet to the back of the clothespin. These are now your "Compliment Holders." Place the clothespins on the refrigerator. Get in the habit of writing short notes to each other and attaching them to the appropriate clothespin. It's a great feeling to walk by the refrigerator and see a note to you that says, "Thanks for French braiding my hair, Mom."

Celebrate with Food

Select the person in your family who cooks the least. (To make this activity work, they should be at least 4 years old.) Help that person cook dinner. Naturally, other family members will compliment the young chef.

More ideas: www.complimentday.com

Boy Scout Day

Way back in 1910, the Boy Scouts of America obtained their first charter. At that time, the president of the U.S. was the honorary head of the agency. Today boys in more than 80 nations enjoy the benefits of scouting.

Celebrate with Fun

- Ask your children these Boy Scout riddles: (1) What steps should a Boy Scout take if he meets a bear in the forest? (Very long ones) (2) Where do Scouts sleep when they are dog tired? (In pup tents)

- Boy Scouts enjoy exploring. Try this color exploration activity. Lay a white coffee filter on a flat surface. Place a coin in the center and trace around it with a green marker (not permanent). Now stretch the coffee filter over a cup. Drop a few drops of water in the coin outline. Watch the water spread the green marker, separating the ink into different-colored rings of yellow, green, and blue. Try different-colored markers. Surprisingly, a black marker produces yellow, red, and blue circles.

- Boy Scouts are honest and trustworthy. Play 3 Truths and 1 Exaggeration. The first person tells 4 personal statements. Three are true, while one is a made-up exaggeration. Dad might say, "I won the fifth-grade school spelling bee. My first car was a '67 Mustang. My favorite flavor ice cream is pistachio. I met your mom in the college library." Can the family guess which statement is made up?

Celebrate with Crafts

Boy Scouts see many animals on their outdoor expeditions, so make some giant fireflies. Wash and dry a plastic soda bottle. Use craft foam to cut out wings and eyes. Glue onto the bottle. When it's dark, insert a glowstick inside the bottle. Help your firefly fly though the night.

Boy Scouts make craft projects at their den meetings and camps. Make these unusual gourd planters. Buy a gourd with a narrow "neck." Help your child cut off 1 inch on the gourd's narrow end. (Allows water to drain from the planter.) At the gourd's wider end, cut off the top to create an opening. Fill the wide end with dirt and a few flowers. Stick the narrow end in the ground for an all-natural flower planter.

Celebrate with Food

Teach boys that cooking can be easy. Make "Soccer Bread." Preheat oven to 400 degrees. Grease a bundt pan. Cut refrigerated biscuits into 4 pieces each. Roll each section into a ball and then roll into cinnamon sugar. Drop "soccer" balls into bundt pan and bake for 10–12 minutes.

More ideas: www.scouting.org

65

100 Days of School

Almost every elementary school celebrates the day children have attended 100 days of school. Continue the theme at home by seeing what you can do with the number 100.

Celebrate with Fun

- Give each child two rolls of pennies (100) to spend. How would they spend a crisp $100 bill? Go to the 100-cent (dollar) store and buy 2 100-piece puzzles. Mix up the pieces. Have fun putting together the 2 individual puzzles.

- Have children find 100 of the same item to display in your "100-Day Museum." Encourage each child to creatively figure out how to display the items as well as to write a description for others to read. Someone might bring in 100 buttons glued onto a pillowcase. Another child might make a model using 100 pieces of Legos.

- See how many ways you can count to 100. How about counting backward by 2s, by 5s, by 10s? Go outside and count off 100 steps. How many sets of 100 steps does it take to get to the bus stop?

- What was life like 100 years ago? Talk about daily life without television and video. Is there someone 100 years old in your community? Ask if you can drop by for a short visit.

- Watch the movie *101 Dalmatians*. (Well, that's close to 100 items!)

- Get everyone moving—do 100 exercises: jumping jacks—10, curl ups—10, knee lifts—10 . . . Try doing 10 sets of 100 exercises for a real workout.

- Use a tape measure to visualize the length of 100 inches or 100 centimeters. Find something in the house that measures exactly 100. Look at a map to see where you'll end up by driving 100 miles north.

Celebrate with Crafts

Make a "100 collage." Children select from yarn, stickers, buttons, colored popcorn, or any items they want, as long as there are 100 of them. The picture could include 100 pieces of yarn with 100 gold stars at each end or 100 flowers using buttons as the centers.

Celebrate with Food

When children ask for breakfast, tell them they have to count out 100 pieces of cereal for their bowls. Later in the day, give children 10 bowls to fill for snacks. Each bowl must contain 10 pieces of a food item. One bowl could have 10 apple slices, while another bowl has 10 chocolate chips. The snack pieces total 100.

More ideas: www.members.aol.com/a100thday

Turn Off TV Day

Studies show the average family has the TV on 7 hours a day. Think what your family could do with that extra time. Turn off the TV and spend the day having fun together.

Celebrate with Fun

- Instead of sitting passively in front of the TV, build a fort in the living room. Move furniture around, drape sheets over tables, and crawl inside. Tell jokes while squashed in your comfy fort.
- Take the dog for an extra-long walk. If you don't have a dog, borrow the neighbor's dog.
- Share some TV-related statistics with your family:

  The average child watches 1,500 hours of TV per year.

  That same child spends 900 hours in school.

  In the U.S., 66 percent of Americans watch TV while eating dinner.

  By the time a child finishes elementary school, he'll have seen 8,000 TV murders.
- Listen to a radio show like *Adventures in Odyssey* or to a National Public Radio broadcast. Experience using your imagination while listening.
- See if your community is sponsoring a free concert or low-cost play. Attend an event you normally would overlook in favor of watching a *Seinfeld* rerun.
- Plan a family talent show. Everyone has to participate, even if it means your toddler demonstrates how she can jump up and down. Applaud enthusiastically anyway!

Celebrate with Crafts

You'll probably feel the house is too quiet with the TV off. This is the perfect time to make some crazy face noisemakers. Give everyone an empty milk jug or plastic soda bottle. Make self-portraits on the bottles by cutting pictures of eyes, a nose, and a mouth out of magazines. Glue the facial features onto the bottles. Add hair by using ribbon or even paper strips. When the jug heads are complete, add 1 tsp. unpopped popcorn to the container. Put the cap back on, shake, and bring back the noise to your house!

Celebrate with Food

Purchase a package of Fig Newtons. The shape should remind you of your TV set. Using black gel frosting, make an X on each cookie as a reminder of "No TV today."

Valentine's Day

Get mushy! Today is the day to go all out and let the people you love know they are special.

Celebrate with Fun

- Announce to your family that you're setting up an official kissing booth. You'll get some groans, but with any luck, some takers. Cut the bottom out of a large box and set it on a table. Decorate the box and sit behind it like you're on a pretend TV. As family members approach, ask them a trivia question. If they answer correctly, they get a kiss—a real kiss or a chocolate kiss—you decide.

- If the weather is snowy in your area, make a valentine for the birds. Mold a section of snow into a heart shape. Fill the heart with seeds, bread crumbs, and tiny fruit pieces for your feathered friends.

- Give this Valentine's test to family members and see how well you know each other. Change a few key words if necessary to make it apply to your family: Who loves to give hugs? Likes to snuggle while reading a book? Says kind things when someone is sad? Blows kisses the most often? Likes to rub noses? Knows how to give a butterfly kiss? Is the kindest to animals? Makes funny noises while kissing?

- Take time to read John 3:16 and discuss how God loved us so much that he sacrificed his Son.

- Have everyone make a "minicarnival" booth out of small boxes. Draw clown faces on the boxes and cut holes for the mouths. Throw candy hearts instead of beanbags! Take turns participating in a tabletop carnival.

Celebrate with Crafts

Make perfect hearts with fingerprints. Press index finger into red ink pad, then on paper. Put another fingerprint next to first, joining at the bottom. Put fingerprint hearts on napkins, kid's lunch sacks, even the bathroom mirror. Have fingerprint hearts everywhere!

Celebrate with Food

Since Valentine's Day is full of sweets, go all out and make a candy pizza. Roll out sugar cookie dough in the shape of a large circle. Bake on a cookie sheet. When cool, spread frosting on the cookie. Top with an assortment of chocolate chips, coconut, candies, and nuts. Eat, then brush your teeth!

Use your heart-shaped cookie cutter to make heart-shaped sandwiches. Cut thin cheese slices into heart shapes. Be really creative and cut cookie dough into heart-shaped cookies.

Solar System Day

We've all looked at the night sky and been in awe at God's creation. Take today to gain a greater awareness of the solar system.

Celebrate with Fun

- Craters form when asteroids hit a planet. Children love making their own craters. Fill a dishpan with flour and smooth the surface. Let children stand on a chair and drop small rocks onto the flour "planet." Craters form! What happens when you drop a huge "asteroid" orange?

- Want to quickly learn all the planets? Simply memorize the following:

My	(Mars)	Served	(Saturn)
Very	(Venus)	Us	(Uranus)
Educated	(Earth)	Nine	(Neptune)
Mother	(Mercury)	Pizzas	(Pluto)
Just	(Jupiter)		

- If it's a clear night, go outside and look at the stars. Find a sky chart and try to look for the Big Dipper and other constellations.

- Jupiter is known for its swirling gases. Make some swirled designs by pouring ⅔ cup milk in a pie pan. Add 2 drops red food coloring on 1 edge of the pan. Also add 2 drops yellow, blue, and green, spacing the dyes as far apart as possible. Gently spin the pie pan. The colors blend to look like swirling gases on Jupiter. Impress your family—tell them Jupiter is so big that if it was hollow, all the other planets could fit inside it.

Celebrate with Crafts

Use a wire coat hanger as the basis of a star mobile. Cut 5–7 various-sized stars out of cardboard. Cover with aluminum foil. Punch a hole in each star. Tie dental floss or thread to each star, then tie stars to hanger. Vary the threads' lengths so stars hang in a random pattern.

Celebrate with Food

Turn breakfast into an edible solar system. Serve children a bowl of thick oatmeal. Set out a picture of the solar system. Children can place raisins, banana slices, and even a chocolate chip or two on their oatmeal to represent the planets. A glass of orange juice represents the sun. Later, bake star-shaped cookies and sprinkle with shiny sprinkles.

Love Your Pet Day

Some people have a houseful of pets, while others are content with a single goldfish. Whatever pets you have, make them feel loved on their special day.

Celebrate with Fun

- Spend extra time with your pet today. How about taking your dog for a run in the park or giving your cat a massage? (Don't laugh—there are books available on pet massage techniques.)
- Keep an updated photo of your dog or cat in case your pet gets lost and you need to make a "Lost Pet" poster.
- Take a portrait of family members with your pets. Have it enlarged and display in a location where everyone can see your adorable creatures.
- Sing "For He's (or She's) a Jolly Good Fellow" to make your pet feel special.
- In the spirit of animals, play "Animal Cracker"—with your pet watching, of course! Let each family member select a cookie from a box of animal crackers. Don't let anyone see your animal. Taking turns, act out the animal you selected as other people try to guess what you are. Eat any leftover cookies.
- Even though you may have had your pet for years, read a book or magazine article to update yourself on its nutrition and health needs.

Celebrate with Crafts

Get your pet a customized feeding dish. Purchase a new bowl for your hamster, iguana, or St. Bernard. Using permanent markers, decorate the bowl with hearts and the name of your pet. If you have an aquarium, draw a border around the outside glass to liven up your fish habitat.

Celebrate with Food

This is slightly messy, but your cat will thank you. Whirl 1 can of your cat's favorite cat food in the blender till smooth. Pour this mixture into a heavy-duty Ziploc bag. Squeeze the mixture to one corner and make a small cut in the bag. Squeeze mixture into small kiss shapes onto a wax paper–lined cookie sheet. Bake at 300 degrees until dry—about 15–20 minutes. Let cool before giving your cat this yummy treat.

Tootsie Roll Anniversary

In 1896 an Austrian named Leo Hirschfield developed the recipe for Tootsie Rolls. Back then he made the candies by hand. That wouldn't be possible today because 49 million Tootsie Rolls are made *daily*!

Celebrate with Fun

- Have you ever had the dentist make a mold of your teeth? He or she probably used "professional" material to make the mold. Some dentists use Tootsie Rolls to make impressions of their patients' teeth! Bite into a Tootsie Roll and look at the shape of your teeth. What other unusual uses can you come up with for Tootsie Rolls?

- Here's a question to ponder. How many licks does it take to lick to the center of a Tootsie Pop? Students at Purdue University actually made a "Licking Machine" to determine the scientific number of licks. Their result was 364 licks to reach the Tootsie Pop's center. Try your own family experiment. Give everyone a Tootsie Pop. Begin licking and counting until you hit the chocolate center.

- Purchase a bag of the wrapped miniature Tootsie Rolls. Practice now for Easter by having a "Tootsie Roll Hunt." Hide the candy all over the house and yard. Just for fun, hide 1 extra-large Tootsie Roll for some lucky winner. After finding and eating all the candy, don't forget to brush your teeth!

- Use small Tootsie Rolls to play tabletop football. Sit at 1 end of a table, with your fingers making a goalpost. Another person sits across from you and tries to "flick" a Tootsie Roll through the goalpost.

Celebrate with Crafts

Use Tootsie Pops to make some flying angels. Cover a Tootsie Pop with a white tissue or a piece of shiny paper. Use a ribbon to tie a knot under the round part of the sucker, keeping the paper secure. Add small wiggle eyes to the "head," along with yarn for your angel's hair. Use sparkly chenille stems to form wings that attach to the Tootsie Pop stick. Let your angel fly through the air before she's eaten.

Celebrate with Food

Use Tootsie Rolls to make an edible sculpture. Unwrap several small Tootsie Rolls, leaving them on their individual wrappers. Place in microwave for approximately 60 seconds. Remove from microwave and start working with your pliable, edible clay. Shape into animals or other fun designs. Let harden, then eat!

More ideas: www.tootsie.com

71

Leap Year Day

This holiday only happens every 4 years, so celebrate while you can! Wonder why we have a leap year? Our calendar has 365 days in nonleap years, but an astronomical year (the time it takes for the earth to go once around the sun) is 365.25 days. A leap year every 4 years gives us 366 days and keeps our seasons from going off course and into the wrong months.

Celebrate with Fun

- When was the last time you played leapfrog? It's good exercise to crouch down as other family members leap over your back. Try playing in slow motion, then speed up to double time.
- Ask children what other animals make leaps. Act out kangaroo, grasshopper, and cricket leaps.
- People born on February 29 only get a birthday party every fourth year. Have an honorary birthday party for them, pretending that all the leap-year birthday people are there. Wear silly party hats, blow party streamers, and sing "Happy Birthday."
- Have a leaping contest. Measure who can jump the farthest. Go to a high school or community track and use the sandpit for the long jump. Children leap their longest leap and land in the sand. Measure leaps.
- Play a game of "Leaping Lizards." Cut out 10–12 tissue paper lizards. Divide the group into 2 teams. The first 2 people in each line put a straw in their mouth and "suck in," holding a tissue lizard at the end of the straw. Run to the finish line, drop your lizard, and have the next person in line use their straw to get another lizard to the finish line.

Celebrate with Crafts

Make a diorama of a "leaping" animal in its habitat. Go beyond decorating an ordinary shoe box. Find a wooden apple crate or an empty ham can to use as the "home" for your plastic frog, kangaroo, or cockroach. Use small stones, twigs, moss, plastic flowers, and other figurines. Create an environment so your leaping animal feels right at home.

Celebrate with Food

Have fun with some leaping pancakes. Make your favorite pancake recipe. After pancakes have cooled on 1 side, use only the pan to get them to "leap" over to the other side. For safety, have adults flip the actual frying pan. Children can leap their pancakes using a completely cooked pancake in a small cool frying pan. Give a "flip" to try to turn the pancake completely to the other side.

More ideas: www.leapyeardayproject.com

MARCH

National Peanut Month
National Women's History Month
National Craft Month
Music in Our Schools Month

Weeks to Celebrate

1st Week • Newspaper in Education Week
3rd Week • American Chocolate Week
4th Week • National Clutter Awareness Week
1–7 • Write a Letter of Appreciation Week
40 Days before Easter • Mardi Gras (sometimes in February)

Days to Celebrate

3rd Thursday • Absolutely Incredible Kid Day

1 National Pig Day
2 Dr. Seuss's Birthday
3 I Want You to Be Happy Day
12 Girl Scouts Anniversary
14 National Kids' Craft Day
17 St. Patrick's Day
20 Big Bird's Birthday
20 World Storytelling Day
21 World Poetry Day
21 National Teenager's Day
22 National Goof Off Day
23 Dixie Cup Anniversary
24 Harry Houdini's Birthday
26 Make Your Own Holiday
28 Children's Picture Book Day
29 Fish Day
30 Van Gogh's Birthday

National Peanut Month

Did you know peanuts are not nuts? Technically they are considered a legume. Over 75 percent of American homes have at least 1 container of peanut butter in their cupboards.

Celebrate with Fun

- Set out a bag of peanuts. See who can shell the most peanuts in 30 seconds. Declare that person the "Peanut Sheller of the World." Their prize? A peanut butter sandwich!

- Find the hidden nutcracker in the back of your kitchen utensil drawer. Many children have never used one. Purchase an assortment of nuts in their shells. Let children experience the different force it takes to crack open a walnut or a pecan. Compare the tastes of each nut.

- Walk through a park and look for remnants of nuts. Find the acorns the squirrels overlooked. Ask children if they know how peanuts grow. On bushes? On vines? (Hint: They grow underground like potatoes.)

- Write a point value on each of the 12 compartments in an empty egg carton. Set it on the floor. Have children stand 6 feet away and let them collect points tossing small nuts like pistachios into the compartments.

More ideas: www.peanutlovers.com

Celebrate with Crafts

How about making peanut people? Use peanuts in their shells to form the basis of peanut bodies. Cut chenille stems into 3- or 4-inch pieces. (Use an old pair of nail clippers to avoid ruining your scissors.) Wrap the chenille around the peanuts for arms and legs. Permanent markers can be used to draw cute faces.

Don't be selfish with your peanut butter. Share some with the birds! Tie a piece of yarn about 12 inches long on the end of a pinecone. Spread smooth peanut butter in and around the pinecone. (Very messy job!) When the pinecone is saturated, roll in a layer of birdseed. Use the string to hang your bird feeder outside.

Celebrate with Food

Make open-faced sandwiches by spreading peanut butter on 1 side of bread. (For easy spreading, use frozen bread. It thaws quickly.) Top with fillings such as raisins, banana slices, chocolate chips, or thin apple slices.

Make some homemade crunchy peanut butter. In a blender or food processor, pour 1 cup shelled peanuts (salted or plain, according to your taste). Mix on low speed with ¼ cup peanut oil. Spread your fresh peanut butter on crackers or toast.

National Women's History Month

In 1987 Congress approved this month to honor the role women have played in America's history. Help your family understand the importance of women as explorers, educators, and scientists.

Celebrate with Fun

- Look through your children's history books. If the book describes few women, find supplemental material to read to your children.
- Girls and boys both love Laura Ingalls Wilder's books depicting life as a pioneer. She wrote, "It is still best to be truthful and honest. To make the most of what we have, to be happy with simple pleasures and to be cheerful and have courage when things go wrong." Reread a Little House book and point out the courage of Laura and her family.
- Harriet Tubman risked her life to lead 300 slaves to safety between 1850 and 1860. Some communities stage evening activities during which people pretend they are slaves looking for safety on the Underground Railroad. It's an eye-opening experience for children to be out in a field at night, trying to avoid being "caught" by their master.
- Marie Curie stated, "Nothing in life is to be feared. It is only to be understood." Ask children how they can overcome their fears.
- Nellie Bly was a famous journalist who pretended to be insane and went undercover to expose the cruelty taking place in mental hospitals. She also traveled from New York around the world, breaking Jules Verne's record of 80 days—all when women were supposed to be doing embroidery! Have children write a newspaper article on a controversial topic. Stick up for the underdog! Stand up for your beliefs!
- Read a book about Helen Keller. How would your children communicate with someone who is deaf and blind? Blindfold a child and put some cotton or earplugs in her ears. What is it like to eat or simply walk from room to room when you have lost two of your senses?

Celebrate with Crafts

Make a paper doll of your favorite woman in history. Design a contemporary outfit and dress your doll as she would look today.

Celebrate with Food

Teach children to take risks, just like women in American history. Go to an Italian restaurant and ask for a hamburger or taco. It's scary, but you may get what you asked for.

More ideas: National Women's History Project, 707-838-6000 or www.nwhp.org

National Craft Month

Even if you feel artistically challenged, celebrate this month with your children. They'll love being creative and making a mess!

Celebrate with Fun

- Start the day by giving a craft-related present to your child at breakfast. Wrap up a new box of markers or scallop-edged scissors.

- Try a craft project you've never done before. Check the library for information on origami, soap carving, or scrimshaw and try it!

Celebrate with Food

Make a squishy marshmallow sculpture. Provide an assortment of toothpicks and miniature marshmallows. Poke toothpicks into marshmallows to make an interconnecting sculpture.

Celebrate with Crafts

Mix up a great batch of smelly play clay. (Good smelling, that is!) Mix 1 cup sifted flour, ½ cup salt, 3 Tbs. oil, and 1 small package unsweetened Kool-Aid. Have an adult add 1 cup boiling water. Knead and stir until mixture is smooth. Store in a covered container. The Kool-Aid adds great color and smell to the clay.

Give everyone a variety of chenille stems to make whatever they want. You'll be amazed how creative you can be with these flexible wires.

How about making some Hawaiian leis? Fold 4 or 5 paper cupcake liners in half. Cut scallops around the edges. Cut plastic straws in 2-inch sections. Thread embroidery floss through a straw, then through the center of the cupcake paper "flower." Repeat the pattern of straw/liner/straw/liner until the lei is done.

Silly Spoons are easy for children to make. Pass out plastic spoons for children to transform into people. The "bowl" of the spoon forms the face. Use fabric scraps to make clothes for your plastic people.

Pop bottles make great wind chimes. Remove the label from a plastic pop bottle. Have an adult cut bottle about 4 inches from the top. Tie a string around the top so you can hang your wind chime. Use paint or permanent markers to decorate the plastic. Punch 5 holes around the cut edge of your bottle. Tie various-length pieces of yarn to each hole. Find nonbreakable items to attach to the yarn to complete the wind chime. Try using small bells, plastic spoons, or old keys. Hang outside so your "chimes" hit each other to create a unique sound.

More ideas: Hobby Industry Association, www.i-craft.com

Music in Our Schools Month

In 1985 music educators began this holiday to increase awareness of the importance of music in our schools. Continue the celebration by enjoying musical activities at home with your family.

Celebrate with Fun

- Put together a band! Who cares if no one has an instrument? Go through the house and look for anything that makes noise. Try hitting chopsticks on a football helmet for a unique instrument. When you have your instruments, select a bandleader. Follow the leader and march around the house making music—well, maybe just making noise!

- Rent a musical such as *Singing in the Rain* or *The Music Man*. Children unfamiliar with musicals have difficulty understanding how 2 people can be having a normal conversation and then suddenly burst out in song. After watching a musical, try making up your own songs. In a regular voice, tell children that it's getting close to bedtime. Then, to catch them unaware, begin singing (very enthusiastically) about brushing their teeth and the joy of taking a bath. Ignore your children when they question your sanity!

- Play "Name That Tune." Use a CD or tape to play the first few bars of various songs. See who can guess the name of the song first. You can also simply hum the beginning of songs while children guess.

- Attend a professional or amateur musical event this month. A local theater may be putting on a musical or the high school may present a concert.

- If you are in an elevator or office building, make your children aware of Muzak playing in the background.

- If your school doesn't have a music teacher, get other parents to help you begin a music enrichment program.

Celebrate with Crafts

Make a unique instrument by gluing 2 paper plates together topside to topside. Punch 4 holes around edge. Tie 4-inch pieces of yarn to holes. At yarns' other ends tie jingle bells or wooden beads. Flip instrument back and forth; bells or beads echo off the paper plates.

Celebrate with Food

Make up a meal menu using musical names for ordinary foods. Play music in the background as you eat! Try Polka Potatoes, Harmony Ham, Country Western Corn, Operatic Olives, or Barbershop Bananas.

More ideas: www.menc.org

Newspaper in Education Week

The Newspaper Association of America Foundation uses this week to publicize the educational value of newspapers. Celebrate by using your ordinary newspaper for family-friendly newspaper activities.

Celebrate with Fun

- Give each person $10,000 to spend in the stock market. Okay, use Monopoly money, not your savings account. Show children how to read the stock market page. Pretend to purchase shares of stock and track the ups and downs daily. How much money did you make as the stock market fluctuated this week? Who made the most money on investments?

- Take out an ad highlighting your child's accomplishments in the classified section. Your children will enjoy reading "Congratulations to Jessica for an amazing soccer goal on Saturday!"

- Read the comics as a family. Have each person cut out their favorite comic and paste it on paper. Then have them draw their own version and glue it on the same paper. Can you tell which is the original?

- Read one day's local newspaper thoroughly, both individually and reading some sections out loud together. Afterward, pick a topic you all feel strongly about and write a family letter to the editor to express your opinions. Check the paper to see if your family letter gets published.

- Look at the newspaper advertisements. Which ads stick out the most? Does color draw attention to an ad? Pick an ad and rewrite it. Come up with a new slogan and advertising claims. Look at the sports page. Do females get equal coverage? What's the most unusual sports article?

- Show kids how to press Silly Putty on newsprint to copy a picture or article.

Celebrate with Crafts

Have a newspaper fashion show. Give people a stack of newspapers and duct tape. Work with a partner to design a gorgeous (or outrageous) outfit, dressing up 1 person in the crinkly "clothing."

Celebrate with Food

Restaurant critics can make or break a restaurant. Read several restaurant reviews so children understand how critics evaluate the food and ambiance. Prepare and serve dinner to your own restaurant critics. Afterward, ask family members to write a review describing the smells, tastes, and atmosphere of your "restaurant." Give a rating of 1–5 stars, with 5 being excellent. Read the reviews and compare impressions.

More ideas: www.naa.org

American Chocolate Week

The third week in March is set aside to honor everyone's favorite treat—chocolate. Naturally you'll want to celebrate chocolate all year, but here's one week to go all out!

Celebrate with Fun

- Buy several types of chocolate candy bars. Blindfold family members and have a taste test to see if they can distinguish between a Snickers, Mars, or Heath bar. Purchase 1 higher-priced chocolate bar along with a regular Hershey bar. Can family members distinguish between "quality" chocolate and "household" chocolate?

- Give everyone strips of paper that say, "I love chocolate because . . ." Make up songs or poems beginning with those words. Perform for the rest of the group.

- Design your own chocolate bar and draw a wrapper that describes the contents, like caramel, cherry chips, and marshmallows. Try to "sell" your chocolate treat to other family members.

- Play a regular board game with a chocolate twist. Instead of using game pieces to designate each player, use different-colored M&Ms.

Celebrate with Crafts

Chocolate bowls are a great edible craft. Melt 12 oz. chocolate chips (or peanut butter chips) with 2 tsp. shortening in microwave for 20 seconds. Stir and microwave another 20 seconds until smooth. Pour into shallow pie pan. Blow up small balloons and tie ends. Holding tied end, dip bottom half in chocolate, coating to form a "bowl." Cool on waxed paper. Carefully remove balloon and eat the bowl!

Celebrate with Food

Chocolate-dipped foods are a creamy, rich treat. Melt 12 oz. semisweet chocolate chips with 4–5 oz. shortening in the microwave for 60–90 seconds. Stir and melt longer if chips are still too firm. After chocolate melts, use as dip for fruits, cookies, or even pretzels. Coat foods in chocolate. Let cool on waxed paper. Treats are ready to eat after an hour.

In 1930 Ruth Wakefield owned the Toll House Inn in Massachusetts. While making her favorite cookies, she ran out of chopped nuts, so she cut a chocolate bar into pieces and added them to the cookie dough. Instead of melting, the chocolate pieces stayed intact. She named the new cookies "Toll House Cookies." Grab a bag of chocolate chips and make a batch of these popular cookies. Eat warm for best flavor!

National Clutter Awareness Week

Is your house a showplace with white furniture, toys stored in color-coordinated containers, and clear countertops? Probably not! Celebrate Clutter Awareness Week with a few tips to reduce the "messes" in your home.

Celebrate with Fun

- Every night, designate a "Trash Dash" through the house. Everyone races to quickly toss away loose papers and pick up misplaced items.

- We've all carried the plastic containers of Tic Tac breath mints in our pockets. When the container is empty, use it to store small items such as seed beads, sewing needles, safety pins, or buttons.

- If you are short on storage space for your bathroom or children's room, hang up a 3-tiered wire basket. It's handy for storing extra washcloths or your child's favorite small stuffed animals.

- Teach children to undress next to their clothes hamper. This makes it easy to toss in their dirty socks and underwear.

- Make a group project of cleaning out a few closets. Set out 3 boxes labeled "Toss," "Donate," and "Keep." Pull items out of the closet and place in one of the boxes. Hopefully you'll have fewer items to put back in your uncluttered closet.

- Speaking of closets, are your children's closets set up so they can easily reach the clothing rod? Are there shelves available at their heights?

Celebrate with Crafts

Okay, it's not that much fun to clean closets and pick up musty socks. Give everyone a medium-sized cardboard box. Decorate the boxes with scrap paper and stickers. Keep the boxes in the garage or some out-of-the-way place. On a daily basis, when you find shoes and books lying around, toss them into the owner's box. They'll probably soon get tired of looking for their items in a jumbled box. Instead of putting everyone's items away, save yourself work by dropping their things in the appropriate boxes.

Celebrate with Food

Your pantry is probably a jumble of cans, boxes, and cake mixes. After straightening out the shelves, pull out 5 or 6 cans. Remove the labels. Ask family members to guess the contents by shaking the cans. Decide what order to eat the contents in by the sound. You may have a dinner of peaches, stewed tomatoes, chili, and applesauce!

Write a Letter
of Appreciation Week

Who has made an impact in your life? Write him or her a letter of appreciation. Has someone inspired you? Write him or her a letter of appreciation too. Use this week to let people in your life know they are special.

Celebrate with Fun

- With your family, brainstorm about people who deserve appreciation. Select 2 or 3 people to receive letters from your family. Include pictures from your preschoolers. Decorate the envelope. Make it special!
- Write each family member's name on a piece of paper. Draw names, making sure not to show each other the names. Sometime during this week, write a letter of appreciation to the person you selected and leave it on his or her pillow.
- Instead of a letter, write a limerick to someone. "There was a great teacher from Silver Beach, who taught kids to go beyond their reach . . ."
- Does the person you appreciate take a brown-bag lunch to school or work? Use the computer to generate a cute design with a saying like "Sondra is an outstanding babysitter!" in the middle. Run the bag through your printer to make the recipient feel extra special at lunchtime.
- Make an "Appreciation Tree" for someone. Cut out a number of paper leaves. Punch a hole in each leaf and attach an 8-inch piece of yarn as a "loop." Fill a flowerpot with soil or sand. Insert a small tree branch. Write appreciative notes on each leaf and hang from the tree. Your gift will bring a big smile to the recipient.

Celebrate with Crafts

A creative homemade touch makes your cards even more special. Fold a piece of 6″ x 9″ construction paper in half. Punch holes all around the outside edges of one half, 1 inch apart. Weave a narrow ribbon in and out of the holes. Use a dab of glue to hold ribbon edges in place.

Press your finger on an ink pad, then onto some light-colored paper. Use fingerprints to create personalized cards. Add 6 legs and some antennae to turn the fingerprint into a bug. Draw arms, legs, and a head to make a fingerprint person. Press your fingerprints in a long row touching each other to make a centipede.

Celebrate with Food

Include this "recipe" in your letter of appreciation: "Mix 2 cups of patience, 1 heart full of love, 2 hands full of generosity, a head full of compassion, and a pinch of humor. Sprinkle with kindness and faith, then show to everyone."

Mardi Gras

This loud, colorful celebration marks the beginning of Lent, forty days before Easter. If you can't get to New Orleans, plan your own Mardi Gras party at home.

Celebrate with Fun

- Costumes are an all-important part of Mardi Gras. In New Orleans, some people spend thousands of dollars on elaborate, hand-sewn costumes. For most families, a trip to the dress-up box is more in line with their budget. Plan an evening meal at which everyone wears a costume. Mom might dress up as a pirate, Dad as "The Little Mermaid."

- Party supply stores sell inexpensive gold, purple, and green plastic beads. Wear strings of beads around your neck or drape them from ceiling lamps to add to the Mardi Gras atmosphere—the more the merrier.

- During Mardi Gras parades, participants throw gold-paper-covered chocolate coins to the crowd. Instead of tossing candy, hide chocolate coins through the house and let children look for their treats.

- It's traditional to select a King and Queen for Mardi Gras. Take turns letting family members be King or Queen for the day. That person gets special treatment. How about breakfast in bed or a reprieve from chores? The King or Queen selects the food for dinner—and doesn't have to help with dishes! Find a piece of velvet or satin for the designated royalty to wear as they walk through the house exploring their domain.

- Check if your local community is sponsoring a Mardi Gras event. Perhaps there's a jazz concert nearby. Sometimes high schools offer free concerts with a Mardi Gras theme.

Celebrate with Crafts

Purchase inexpensive, plain half-masks from a party supply store. Decorate the masks using tiny sequins and beads. Glue small feathers around the edges. For Mardi Gras, the gaudier the better! This is an ideal activity for children since they can glue all the colorful items they want onto their masks.

Celebrate with Food

Traditional Mardi Gras food calls for jambalaya, shrimp, rice, and ambrosia. Meals are served with sparkling drinks. Set out various fruit juices, ginger ale, and sparkling waters. Create festive drinks by mixing several of the liquids together. Top each glass with a festive paper umbrella.

More ideas: Find inexpensive Mardi Gras necklaces, banners, and masks at www.ssww.com/holiday

Absolutely Incredible Kid Day

3ᴿᴰ THURSDAY IN MARCH

The Camp Fire Boys and Girls program encourages adults on this day to write a positive note to the children in their lives.

Celebrate with Fun

- Buy some special paper and write a short note to your children telling why they are special to you. Leave the note by their plate for breakfast.
- Find a humorous card to send to your child at school. Send cards to nieces and nephews also. Every child needs to hear how special they are.
- On a roll of adding machine paper or construction paper strips taped together, write a l-o-o-o-n-n-g letter describing why your kid or kids are incredible. Tape it to the ceiling, lamps, and walls. Children will enjoy moving around reading the lengthy note about themselves.
- Spend one-on-one time with each of your children today. Even if they get embarrassed, tell them why you love them.
- Make an acrostic for each of your children. Use the letters from their first name to describe reasons they are incredible.

S—ings remarkably well

O—pen to new experiences

N—ice to her friends

D—oes what she says she'll do

R—eady to help others

A—lways reads her devotional book

- Design your computer's screen saver to say "Ashley Is a Super Soccer Player!" If children get home before you do, leave a message on the answering machine telling them why they are incredible.

Celebrate with Crafts

Place large sheets of butcher paper on the floor. Have children lay on the paper. Trace around them. Children can use markers to embellish their paper body with hair and clothes. Family members can write positive comments on the borders like "Jordan is a great skateboarder!"

Celebrate with Food

Buy a bag of Hershey's Kisses. Cut off the paper "labels" and add your own. On thin strips of paper, write messages like "Jen, your jokes always make me laugh." Glue the paper messages to the chocolates. Hide them around the house and let kids look for them.

More ideas: www.campfireusa.org

83

National Pig Day

The poor lowly pig! People associate pigs with farm animals wallowing in the mud. Show the world today just how cute pigs can be!

Celebrate with Fun

- Anyone with long hair has to wear it in pigtails today!
- Get together at least 10 people to play Pigs and Cows. Divide the group into "Pigs" and "Cows." Have both groups mingle in the room. On "Go!" everyone closes their eyes and begins "oinking" or "mooing." All the cows try to get the cows on 1 side of the room, identifying each other only by sound. See which group collects their "own kind" first.
- Try some pig latin. Basically pig latin involves moving the initial consonant cluster to the ending of a word and adding "ay." "Ball" become "all-bay," "star" becomes "ar-stay." Instead of saying "summer," you would say "ummer-say."
- Bring out the "pigskin" and toss the football back and forth.
- If you don't own the game of Pig, borrow it from a friend. Instead of rolling dice for the game, you roll 2 rubber pigs. Points are awarded if the pigs land on their sides, backs, or heads.
- Have you ever said, "This room looks like a pigpen!"? Find the messiest area in the house and spend at least 30 minutes cleaning it up. Everyone chips in to straighten up Junior's bedroom or a corner of the garage.
- Place 2 ears of corn (or 2 rolled-up newspapers) on the floor. Pick 2 children to be pigs and push the corn with their noses. See who can get their corn across the finish line first.

Celebrate with Crafts

Collect metal juice can lids to make piggy magnets. Use them as pigs' heads. Glue a small pink pom-pom in the middle for the nose. Wiggle eyes and pink ears complete the face. Attach magnets on the backs.

Make an easy pig snout. Cover a small Dixie cup with pink paper. Punch 2 holes on opposite sides of the top of the cup. String yarn through each hole. Place over your nose and tie yarn around your head.

Celebrate with Food

How about some supereasy pigs in a blanket? Use refrigerated crescent rolls. Carefully unwrap each roll. Place a hot dog on top and reroll dough. Bake on a cookie sheet 15–20 minutes for tasty pigs in a blanket.

Have a "pignic." Serve pigs in a blanket along with corn and chocolate pudding (to symbolize the mud pigs enjoy).

Dr. Seuss's Birthday

Theodor Seuss Geisel was born on March 2, 1904. He sold over 200 million copies of his books. When you feel discouraged, think about the fact that his first book, *And to Think That It Happened on Mulberry Street*, was turned down by 27 publishers!

Celebrate with Fun

- Read *The Foot Book* to your family. Trace around each person's feet to make paper footprints. How many of Dad's paper feet placed end to end does it take to reach from the couch to the refrigerator?

- Try fishing after reading *One Fish, Two Fish*. Make several paper fish 6 or 8 inches long. Slip a paper clip over their "mouths." Find a stick for a pole, attach a string to the end, and on the end of the string tie a magnet. To catch a fish, cast your magnetic hook down on the paper fish. When the magnet touches the paper clip, you can reel in your fish.

- The Cat in the Hat is known for balancing items on his head. Collect a few plastic bowls or unbreakable cups. Walk around the room balancing items on your head. Try balancing a cup topped with a plastic plate on your head. Do deep knee bends while balancing items on your head.

- Try writing your own wacky story, Dr. Seuss style. Develop unique rhyming names for your unusual characters. Get the family artists to make colorful illustrations. When Grandma comes over, read her 2 Dr. Seuss stories and your story. Can she tell which story is the "imposter"?

Celebrate with Crafts

Make "Cat in the Hat" hats from medium-sized brown paper bags. Place the bag on a flat surface covered with newspaper. Paint wide red stripes on 1 side of the bag. Let dry and repeat with other side. After both sides are dry, lightly stuff ⅔ of the bag with crushed newspaper. Use masking tape to hold newspaper inside bag. This prevents your head from being totally inside the bag.

Celebrate with Food

Naturally, you'll serve green eggs and ham sometime today. Scramble eggs, adding a few drops green food coloring. If children won't eat green scrambled eggs, boil several eggs, adding 1 tsp. vinegar and 3–4 drops food coloring to the boiling water. Serve green boiled eggs instead.

Kids will enjoy eating a "One Fish, Two Fish" aquarium. Mix together blueberry Jell-O according to the package directions. Pour into clear bowls or glasses. When Jell-O is partially set, drop in 2 gummy fish. Let Jell-O set firmly before eating your "One Fish, Two Fish" home.

I Want You to Be Happy Day

This day is dedicated to reminding people to be helpful to others and to try to make others feel happy.

Celebrate with Fun

- Don't those bright yellow smiley faces make you feel happy? Decorate your house with smiley faces. (No artistic skills needed to draw that happy little face.) Cut out circles and draw smiley faces on them. Your family can't help but feel happy seeing happy faces throughout the house.

- Get a l-o-o-o-n-n-g piece of paper (tape several pieces together). Make a list of all the things your family is happy about. These can range from being happy your toddler is potty trained to being happy the rain is watering your lawn.

- Play the song "Don't Worry—Be Happy" throughout the day. Have your family sing along or lip-sync to the words.

- Play a game of indoor sock soccer to make everyone feel happy. Roll up a pair of socks into a tight ball. Set up 2 goals (2 boxes) at the end of each room. Divide the group in half and get into the game!

- Stand in a circle and toss a water balloon from person to person. As someone catches the balloon, they say, "I'm happy because . . ." and then toss the balloon to someone else. Keep throwing faster and faster.

- Play "Smile or Pout": Line everyone up against a wall. Select a person as the "Smile Maker" who walks back and forth saying or doing silly things in front of the others, while they try to keep solemn faces. Can the Smile Maker get family members to put on a happy face?

Celebrate with Crafts

Bring out several of your extra photos that show people's faces close up. Cut out the faces. Tape 3" x 1" pieces of paper around your fingers to make rings. Glue the photo faces on to make happy-face finger puppets. With everyone's puppet ready, put on a puppet show. You're sure to feel happy watching and performing with your puppets.

Celebrate with Food

You've probably heard the saying "When life gives you lemons, make lemonade." Make some homemade lemonade as a reminder to be happy when at all possible. Mix 1½ cups sugar with 1 cup water. Stir well and boil for 1–2 minutes. Let cool, then add 1¼ cups lemon juice. Mix sugar-lemon mixture in a pitcher with additional 6 cups water.

Girl Scouts Anniversary

Juliette Low began the Girl Scouts when she was 50 years old. Back in 1912, it was considered outrageous that girls earned badges in electrical work, went camping, and dared to wear bloomers!

Celebrate with Fun

- Know any Girl Scouts? Ask to see their handbook and try some of their activities. Plan an outdoor activity such as a nature hike or a bird-watching trip. Tell a few stories to each other. Go to the local YMCA and try rock climbing. Organize a parent/child soccer game or try building something with hammer and nails.

- "Try-It" badges, which encourage young girls to experiment with various hobbies, careers, and interests, are popular with younger Girl Scouts. Set up some "Try-It" activities with your family: (1) Visit an ethnic restaurant you've never tried. (2) Try a new craft like origami or papier-mache. (3) Listen to a new musical style. Opera, anyone? (4) Get a foreign language dictionary and say a few words in Spanish, German, or Swahili. (5) Sometime during this week, try visiting a church outside of your denomination. Compare worship styles.

- Design a badge representing your family. Work together sketching a badge that depicts your family's interests and beliefs.

- Sing "Kum Ba Ya" at least twice today!

Celebrate with Crafts

Pretend you're at Girl Scout camp—make some craft projects. Purchase inexpensive wooden frames with wide borders. Squeeze glue in a random pattern on the wood; overlap to create a design like a stained glass window. Let glue dry completely. Paint various colors inside the raised glue "borders." Let paint dry, then add your favorite picture.

Celebrate with Food

Girl Scout cookies make tasty desserts. Put 6 or 8 of your favorite Girl Scout cookies in a resealable bag. Use a rolling pin to crush the cookies. Scoop ½ cup vanilla yogurt in a sherbet dish, then add ⅓ cup crushed cookies and ⅓ cup blueberries. Repeat with another layer.

Fill an empty juice can with softened sherbet. Put back in the freezer for several hours. Remove the other end of the can so you can push out the sherbet. Slice the sherbet into 1-inch slices. Put each slice of sherbet between 2 Girl Scout cookies.

More ideas: www.girlscouts.org

National Kids' Craft Day

Studies show children who are exposed to a wide variety of art experiences develop creativity and problem-solving skills. Have fun making these projects.

Celebrate with Fun

- Set up a craft corner so children have the supplies to be creative. Use a silverware tray to hold items like buttons and paper fasteners. Inexpensive plastic bins hold larger items like toilet paper tubes and packing peanuts. Always looking for scissors? Attach a magnetic knife strip to a wall. You'll easily find scissors and hole punches stuck to the magnet. (Not suitable to do if young children are around.)

Celebrate with Crafts

To make personalized door hangers, cut craft foam into rectangles 10" x 4". Punch 2 holes in the top. String yarn through the holes as a loop to hang around the doorknob. Decorate hanger with scrap foam and sequins. Use a permanent marker to write your name.

Need craft projects for a large group, birthday party, or Sunday school class? Check out the group craft products available from S&S Worldwide, www.ssww.com, where you can buy all the supplies needed to make craft projects for 12, 24, or even 50 children.

Create some flowerpot characters by gluing 2 small flowerpots together rim to rim. This forms the body of your character. Glue a Styrofoam ball to the flat surface of one flowerpot as a head. Use paints to add clothes or other embellishments on the body. Plastic wiggle eyes give your character great personality.

Celebrate with Food

Try something more complicated than gluing cotton balls on paper. Let kids make a graham cracker candy house. Give each child a small box the size of an animal cracker box. Using "Glue Frosting" (recipe follows), glue graham crackers to the sides of the box (cut the crackers to fit the dimensions of the box). This forms a sturdy basis for your house. Glue 2 crackers to form a peaked roof. When frosting is hard, glue on small candies and miniature marshmallows. Frosted shredded cereal glued to the roof creates a thatched roof effect.

Glue frosting: Mix together 1 box sifted confectioner's sugar, 6 Tbs. water, and 3 Tbs. powdered egg white. Beat well for at least 6 minutes. Use for gluing decorations to graham cracker house. Eating the house afterward is optional.

St. Patrick's Day

If you can work it into your schedule, head over to New York City for the annual St. Patrick's Day parade. You can join over 1 million other people who watch this 6-hour parade.

Celebrate with Fun

- Be sure to wear something green! If you don't, someone has the right to pinch you!
- Play bagpipe music throughout the day. Dance an Irish jig to add to the St. Patrick's Day atmosphere. Can you get male family members to put on pleated skirts and dance a jig? Don't forget to take pictures!
- Are there leprechauns in your house? Collect small toy action figures or the "Little People" your toddler enjoys. Hide the pretend leprechauns and have a race to find the elusive tiny people.
- Take a walk outside, wearing green, of course! Notice all the different shades of green. The grass is "regular" green, but so are the pale green buds on a tree. Notice the lime green bike in your neighbors' yard or the deep green trim on a house.
- Since potatoes are popular on St. Patrick's Day, set out a potato bar buffet. Bake potatoes. Let people make their own meal by adding sour cream, chives, cheese, salsa, and other toppings.
- Bring out the Mr. Potato Head game and stage a tournament to see who can make the most colorful plastic faces.

Celebrate with Crafts

Shamrocks really aren't hard to make. The shape is basically 3 hearts with their pointed ends together. Make some St. Patrick's Day fuzzy shamrocks. On sturdy cardboard, draw a shamrock and outline with glue and a strip of green yarn. The "fuzzier" the yarn, the more distinct your shamrocks will be. Hang up shamrocks to enjoy as you eat your green dinner.

Celebrate with Food

You have to have green food today! Serve a complete meal using imagination and green food coloring. A salad with lettuce and cucumbers starts the meal. Continue with green mashed potatoes, broccoli, and lime Jell-O. Don't forget to sprinkle parsley over your meat. (Who wants green meat?) For dessert, serve lime sherbet. Get brave and try kiwi juice to drink, or add a few drops of green food coloring to give milk a great green tint.

Big Bird's Birthday

Even if you don't have preschoolers at home, it's fun to honor this feathered friend on his birthday.

Celebrate with Fun

- Wear something yellow, of course!
- Select the youngest family member to be an honorary Big Bird. Dress her in yellow and tape some cutout paper feathers to her body. Everyone sings "Happy Birthday" to miniature Big Bird—and then eats cake!
- Toss yellow feathers (available in any craft store) into the air. Try to keep feathers from touching the ground by blowing on them.
- Visit a pet shop and ask the staff to tell you about the various birds they sell. Which is the most expensive? What is the smallest bird in their store?
- Take a walk and listen for different birds. You can usually hear birds chirping even on a busy street.
- We all know how much Big Bird loves the alphabet. Divide family members into groups of 2 or 3 for a game of "Alphabet Scavenger Hunt." Each group goes through the house with a bag and finds 1 item for each letter of the alphabet; they might find an Apple, a Book, a Catalog, a Dance slipper, and so on. For objects too large for the bag, simply toss in a piece of paper that says "Denise's Door." No sense trying to stuff your St. Bernard into a paper bag!
- Watch a few minutes of Big Bird. Notice his distinctive walk. Who can do the best imitation of Big Bird walking across the room?

Celebrate with Crafts

Kids love the screeching noise this squawking bird makes. Have an adult poke a small hole in the bottom of a plastic cup. String a 12-inch piece of embroidery floss so the floss hangs down through the inside of the cup. Tie a large knot in the top of the string so it doesn't slide through. At the other end of the string, tie a small piece of cotton fabric. Decorate the outside of the cup to look like a bird. Now you're ready to start squawking. Dampen the piece of cotton. Hold the cup in 1 hand. With the other hand, squeeze the cotton around the top of the floss. Slowly pull the cotton down the string. You'll hear a loud screeching sound!

Celebrate with Food

In honor of Big Bird's legendary color, serve a yellow meal: macaroni and cheese, bananas, and lemon cake.

World Storytelling Day

Mom! Tell me another story!" Children beg to hear favorite stories over and over. Use stories to teach a lesson or simply to entertain your family.

Celebrate with Fun

- Give children a story's ending like "And that's why the leopard has spots" or "That's how Grandma got gray hair." They think up a beginning and middle that make sense. Then give children "story starters" and have them finish the tale. Try "It was so funny when . . ." or "I knew it was an answered prayer when I . . ."

- Read and act out Jesus' parables. Have children retell "The Prodigal Son" in a modern-day setting. How about a rich pizza manufacturer whose son, instead of taking over the pizza business, takes his inheritance to start a computer business? When that business fails, the son is forced to work for minimum wage delivering pizzas for his dad's competitor . . .

- Read a short story after dinner. Vary the stories from history to Bible stories to science fiction.

- Glue assorted magazine pictures on index cards. The family sits in a circle. The first person draws a card and begins a story incorporating the card's picture: "Once upon a time, there was a polar bear." They continue describing the bear until they point to the next person, who draws a card and somehow includes their picture of "peanut butter and jelly sandwiches" into the polar bear story. Continue until everyone has a turn and the story is so outrageous it doesn't make sense.

Celebrate with Crafts

Make a Silly Story Book. Pick a general topic like "wild rabbits," "cucumbers," or "clowns." Everyone takes 2 pieces of paper and privately illustrates and writes several sentences about the topic. Randomly collect the pages, staple them into a book, and design a cover. Then read out loud the very disjointed story your family put together on "cucumbers."

Celebrate with Food

Tell the story of stone soup. A poor man comes to town without any money. He convinces the townspeople to add their vegetables to his delicious stone soup. Have children wash 3 smooth stones. Put them in a pot of boiling salted water. Take turns acting out the story as family members bring onions, potatoes, carrots, beans, and broccoli. Add to the pot and cook until tender. Who knew stone soup could taste so good?

World Poetry Day

"Roses are red, violets are blue . . ." Those words form the beginning of a very popular poem. Increase your poetry awareness today.

Celebrate with Fun

- Speaking of "Roses are red," use that line to start your own poems. Have every family member write a conclusion to "Roses are red, violets are blue . . ."

- Collect poetry books and have a "Poetry Reading." Sit on the floor with classical music in the background while reading Shel Silverstein. Burn some incense to convey that beatnik poetry-reading atmosphere.

- The word *poetry* comes from the Greek word *polein*, which means "to make" or "to create." Encourage children to create their own poetry. Bring out a portable chalkboard to encourage budding artists. Or give children their own poetry kits consisting of a small lined journal with a fancy pencil. Plan a poetry celebration in a few weeks where they can read their poems out loud.

- Throughout the day yell, "Poetry Freeze!" Everyone needs to stop whatever they are doing, "freeze," and listen while you read a short poem.

- Give children different poems and ask them to change the endings. It's fun to read a familiar poem and suddenly have a surprise ending.

Celebrate with Crafts

Poetry refrigerator magnets are available in many gift stores. You move the magnets to match up different words. Instead of buying magnets, make your own "Poetry Pebbles." Find 20–30 small smooth stones. Wash off any excess dirt. Use a toothpick for a brush and write words on the rocks. Include adjectives, nouns, and verbs. A collection of pebbles with the words *snow, sun, the, of, on, set, blanket, the, low,* can be arranged to say, "The sun sets low, on the blanket of snow." Simply move the pebbles to create more poems.

Celebrate with Food

Invite everyone into the kitchen to help make dinner. Each person needs to find 2 foods that rhyme. Put the foods on the table to enjoy an unusual rhyming meal. How about:

ham and jam
rice and ice
tomatoes and potatoes
apple and Snapple

More ideas: Check "world poetry day" on your favorite search engine

National Teenager's Day

Teens can be full of life, hope, and a desire to stretch their wings! Give your teen extra attention today. (But not so much that he or she gets embarrassed.)

Celebrate with Fun

- Plan a "rite of passage" day or weekend with your teen. Have Dad take the boys and Mom the girls for a weekend. Discuss important issues like sex, faith, and their hopes and dreams. Help them list goals, then review their list with them each year. Add fun activities too like miniature golf, bowling, and eating hot fudge sundaes for breakfast. Take pictures of your time together!

- Let your teen purchase something at his or her favorite store. The only catch—he or she has to go shopping with you so you can spend time together.

- Communication between teens and parents can be strained. Ask teens to go for a walk with you at night. Often your teen will start opening up as they walk in the dark without having to make direct eye contact.

- Call the parents of your teenager's friends for help in planning a surprise activity. Bring teens to the location of an impromptu party. It's a great time to get to know other parents too.

- Shock your teen by sitting down to listen to their music. Have them play their favorite song. Why do they like it? Do the words have meaning, or do they just like the beat? Give them a new Christian CD.

- Let your teen know you pray for him or her on a daily basis.

Celebrate with Crafts

Teenagers like wacky crafts such as this abstract sculpture. Heat a pan of water until just ready to boil. Drop in a plastic berry basket (that's right, melt a berry basket in a saucepan). It melts into an abstract shape. Pull out your sculpture with kitchen tongs. While it's cooling, string some beads on dental floss or clear fishing line. Attach 1 end of the floss to sculpture and wrap the floss in and out of the sculpture, spreading the beads until the floss runs out. Hang your weird sculpture in the window to be admired by all!

Celebrate with Food

Eating is a favorite teen pastime. Let your teen invite a best friend over for dinner. Prepare his or her favorite meal, even if it means ordering pizza. Bring out sparkling cider to "toast" the teens.

National Goof Off Day

Parents often take life too seriously. Today, forget about all your to-do lists and appointments. Spend some time relaxing and goofing off.

Celebrate with Fun

- Keep the camera handy today and take spontaneous pictures of your family making silly faces (that shouldn't be too hard!) whenever you stick the camera in front of them.

- Do something totally silly. Go for a bike ride before breakfast. Take a chocolate cake to the office to celebrate the day. Put on your pajamas as soon as you get home.

- Eat dinner while watching TV. Why bother having a pleasant dinner-table conversation? This is a day to goof off and eat TV dinners if you want.

- Ask each family member to come up with a goofy activity. Be prepared for standing-on-your-head contests, burping demonstrations, and other wacky events.

- Have everyone chew a saltine cracker at the same time—then see who can whistle first.

- Here's a goofy game. Get a stopwatch or a 1-minute egg timer. Designate a "hot seat" and have 1 person sit in it and continuously talk about him- or herself for 60 seconds. If they stop talking before 55 seconds or talk longer than 65 seconds, everyone gets to throw pillows at them. The idea is to get as close to 1 minute as possible.

- Make brown paper floppy "goofy" ears to tape to your head. (Ignore the pain when removing them!) It's hard not to feel goofy wearing floppy ears.

Celebrate with Crafts

Since you are goofing off all day, goof off by making a "lick and stick sculpture." Collect a box of biodegradable packing peanuts. (Ask local stores to save them for you, or check packing boxes.) These peanuts are made out of cornstarch so they are gentle on the environment. They also make unique sculptures. Just lick 1 end of a peanut and stick it to another. It bonds instantly! Continue licking and sticking to create a large sculpture. (If licking the packing peanuts is a bit disgusting to you, then simply dab each peanut on a damp washcloth.)

Celebrate with Food

Hey! It's National Goof Off Day—why bother making anything to eat? Call and order a pizza delivered to your house!

Dixie Cup Anniversary

We've all used the ordinary Dixie cup to get a quick drink of water. Enjoy celebrating the invention of this household item.

Celebrate with Fun

- Did you know "cup stacking" is an actual game with rules and competitions? Look up www.speedstacks.com. The website even has videos of children stacking cups with incredible speed. Keep practicing and you might end up in the World Championships. Cup stacking involves stacking 12 plastic cups in predetermined sequences. Organizers say the process improves concentration and increases manual dexterity.

- Make an old-fashioned telephone from 2 Dixie cups. Get a cotton string or piece of embroidery floss about 6 feet long. Poke a small hole in the bottom of each cup. Pull the string through each hole and tie a knot. You should have both ends of the string tied to the cups. Get a partner. Hold 1 cup to your ear. Have your friend walk the length of the string so it is taut and talk into her cup. You'll hear her clearly!

- Set up an indoor bowling alley with Dixie cups as the pins. Use a small ball to try to knock down the Dixie cup pins. Or place several Dixie cups on the floor and have children try to throw pennies into each cup from various distances.

- Use your Dixie cups to make some noisemakers. Put several teaspoons of unpopped popcorn or uncooked rice in a cup. Place another cup on top and tape together. Decorate your shaker with stickers and sequins.

Celebrate with Crafts

Make Dixie cup puppets. Turn the cup over and glue a Ping-Pong ball or fuzzy pom-pom to the bottom. This forms the head of your puppet. Use scrap fabric or paper to decorate the cup "body" of your puppet. Stick pipe cleaners into the Dixie cup for arms. To bring your puppet alive, simply place your hand inside the upside-down cup.

Celebrate with Food

Use Dixie cups to make creamy homemade popsicles. Mix up a batch of instant pudding with milk as directed on the package. Pour the mixture into Dixie cups. Stick a wooden craft stick or plastic spoon in the middle of each cup. Freeze for 3–4 hours. Peel sides of cup to remove popsicle.

Harry Houdini's Birthday

MARCH 24

While Harry Houdini was known for escaping from straightjackets and underwater coffins, you can celebrate today with some simple (and safe) magic activities.

Celebrate with Fun

- Make your children shimmery magicians' capes to wear today. Purchase ½ yard of fabric per child. The easiest cape is simply fabric pinned at 2 corners to your child's shirt shoulders. If you're more ambitious, fold the narrow edge of fabric under 2 inches. Sew or glue a casing. Slip a 24-inch ribbon through the casing and tie around your child's neck.

- Libraries often stock "How to Perform Magic" videos. Check one out to watch some tricks performed and then learn the sleight of hand.

- Purchase various inexpensive magic tricks at a party store. Lay out your own pretend store and pass out Monopoly or play money throughout the day as kids do chores. Before bed, let kids shop in the magic store.

- Amaze your children with this trick: Ask a volunteer to select 1 crayon. Hold it behind your back. Don't look at the color! Make up some "patter" about how you can tell the crayon's color by feel. Have the volunteer take the crayon from you. Bring your hands forward, gesturing as you say, "The color of the crayon was—green!" Repeat with another color and guess correctly again. Amazing! (Here's the trick: Behind your back, dig your fingernail into the wax. When you bring your hands forward, glance at the color of crayon under your fingernail.)

Celebrate with Crafts

Write a secret message with lemon juice. Use cotton swabs to dip in the juice and write messages such as "Meet me in the kitchen at 7:30 for ice cream." Let the paper dry. To reveal the words, hold the papers close to a lightbulb (under adult supervision). The lemon juice turns brown.

Celebrate with Food

Let children help make a "Magic Drop" cake. In a bowl, mix 1½ cups flour, 1 cup sugar, 3 Tbs. cocoa, 1 tsp. baking soda, and ½ tsp. salt. Pour into an 8" x 8" baking pan. Make 3 holes in the dry mixture. In 1 hole pour 1 tsp. vanilla, in another hole pour 1 Tbs. vinegar, and in the last hole pour 6 Tbs. oil. Pour 1 cup water over the mixture and stir gently with a fork. Bake 25–30 minutes at 350 degrees. Children will be amazed at how their "dropped" ingredients turn into a tasty cake.

Make Your Own Holiday

Why stick to celebrating traditional holidays? Make up your own holiday by celebrating something your family enjoys!

Celebrate with Fun

- Brainstorm with your family about the new holiday you'll create. Vote on your favorite idea. Examples: "No Chores Day," "Pizza for Breakfast Day," "Sleep in the Family Room Night," or "Family Games Night."
- Decide how to celebrate your special day. Make banners and add to the festivity by putting up balloons, no matter what your holiday.
- Invite friends over to celebrate. Send out invitations to the new "national" "Eat All the Desserts You Want Day." Your friends will be delighted to help you celebrate this untraditional day. Ask them to come dressed in a holiday-related costume or bring a food-related treat.
- Adapt games to tie in with your holiday. For "Doughnut Day," play "Pin the Sprinkles on the Doughnut" or make a giant doughnut piñata.
- Celebrate by making a sparkling storm in a bottle. Find a narrow plastic bottle with a resealable cap. Pour in 1 cup rubbing alcohol, then add vegetable oil almost to the top. Add 1 tsp. shiny objects like beads, glitter, or tiny pieces of aluminum foil. Replace cap tightly and shake gently. The oil and alcohol don't mix!
- This little magic trick is suitable for any holiday: Pack a small baby food jar with uncooked rice. Press down firmly on the rice. Use a plastic knife to "jab" into the rice 15 or 20 times. Announce to your children you will now lift the entire jar of rice with the knife. Quickly poke the knife into the rice. Lift straight up and the jar should remain attached to the knife because of friction.

Celebrate with Crafts

Since this is sure to be an annual holiday event, make some reusable holiday decorations. Set out an inexpensive plastic tablecloth and permanent markers. Decorate and date the tablecloth to use annually when you celebrate your family's special day.

Celebrate with Food

If your holiday centers around pizza, desserts, or tacos, it's easy to celebrate by simply eating your favorite food. If your holiday is "nonedible," celebrate it with a cake. Purchase or make a plain cake. Select a family member to decorate the cake in honor of your new annual celebration.

Children's Picture Book Day

When children are little, we sit them on our laps and read picture books to them. Check out the latest picture books at the library. Many are geared for 8–10 year olds and have longer story lines and brilliant pictures.

Celebrate with Fun

- Have a Library Night during which each family member selects a picture book according to their interest. Don't worry, picture books are available on subjects ranging from tractors to quilt making.

- Read a picture book and have family members act out the story.

- Have fun with the story *There Was an Old Woman Who Swallowed a Fly* by Bonnie Rose. Cut out flannel-board pictures of all the items she swallows. Let children take turns reading the book and placing the appropriate items on the flannel board.

- Children enjoy reading *The Man Who Didn't Wash His Dishes* by Phyllis Krasilovsky about a man who was too lazy to wash dishes. He ends up putting the dirty dishes in his truck and letting the rain wash them. Set a few dirty dishes aside until it rains. Have children place the dishes outside to see if rain can really clean them.

- The classic story *Millions of Cats* by Wanda Gag delights children as they envision living with millions and millions of cats. Before reading the book, collect all the stuffed animals in your house. Place them around you as you pretend to be surrounded by cats while reading the book.

- Learn a few Spanish words by reading *My Dog Is Lost* by Ezra Jack Keats. Ask children how they would feel if they were in a foreign country and no one understood them.

- Ask friends with similar-aged children if they'd loan you some of their family's favorite books.

Celebrate with Crafts

Make your own unusual family picture book. Cut out magazine pictures of famous people or people in unique settings, like exploring the North Pole. Now cut just the faces out of the pictures. Next find extra family photographs. Cut out the faces of your family and insert them under the cutout pictures of the president or a rock star. Use the pictures to make a very original picture book about your family.

Celebrate with Food

What better way to enjoy reading picture books than serving hot chocolate and cookies?

Fish Day

If there are holidays for cows, dogs, and even popcorn, then there should be a holiday for fish. Celebrate today with fish crackers and a fishing book.

Celebrate with Fun

- Get out the cards and play a game of Go Fish.
- Plan a "Fish Masquerade Party" using the new giant-sized goldfish crackers. Each person designs masquerade costumes for their fish crackers. Use dabs of peanut butter, raisins, cream cheese, jelly, or salsa to "disguise" fish. Offer prizes like "Best Use of Cream Cheese" or "Best Fish Disguised as a Princess."
- Create a giant fishing booth with a spring tension rod across a doorway. Drape a sheet over the rod to make your carnival booth. Have children make fishing poles using sticks, string, and clothespin "hooks" at the ends. Let children "fish" in several ways: Children cast and "catch" a paper stating their chores for the day. Children catch a treat at the end of their lines. If it's allowance day, they can catch their allowances.

Celebrate with Crafts

Fish scales often glisten in sunlight. Make your own sparkling fish: Outline a fish on lightweight cardboard. Wad up pieces of different-colored crepe paper, dip each paper ball in water, then press on cardboard fish. The paper dye bleeds onto the cardboard. Keep using crepe paper until entire fish is decorated. Use glue to outline your fish. Sprinkle glitter on the glue to complete glistening fish print.

Try your hand at Gyotaku, the Japanese art of fish printing. Buy the cheapest whole fish available, or if you have a fisher in your family, use one of their catches. Place fish on flat surface. Paint gills and fins with a paintbrush. Paint the body another color. When fish is painted, gently press a piece of plain-colored paper on fish. Press with fingers over fish so all paint is transferred to the paper. Lift up paper to reveal reverse fish print. Wash off fish and make several more prints as you paint it different ways.

Celebrate with Food

Is your family brave enough to try sushi? Many grocery stores sell small packages of sushi. This is a low-cost, low-risk way to see if your family enjoys raw fish.

Make tuna fish sandwiches. Be sure to cut the bread in the shape of a fish.

Serve tomato soup with little fish crackers floating on top.

Van Gogh's Birthday

MARCH 30

The Dutch painter Vincent Van Gogh was known for his bold and powerful use of color. He used dabs of paint to show light and various textures. Spend today demonstrating the artistic side of your family.

Celebrate with Fun

• One of Van Gogh's most famous paintings was *Starry Night*, depicting an evening sky. Purchase glow-in-the-dark stars to stick on your children's ceiling. They'll enjoy looking at the glowing stars while falling asleep.

• Go to an art gallery to look at posters of famous paintings by Van Gogh. If you live in a city with an art museum that has actual Van Gogh paintings, be sure to visit!

Celebrate with Crafts

Van Gogh painted many self-portraits. Have children make a thick paint to do their own self-portraits, Van Gogh style. Mix 2½ cups water, 1 cup white flour, ¼ cup sugar, and 1½ Tbs. salt. Cook over medium heat until thick and mixture bubbles. Cool. Separate "paint" into 3 or 4 small containers. Mix in different liquid watercolors or food coloring. Use cotton swabs or wooden craft sticks as paintbrushes. Dab the paint on with bold strokes, creating an impressionistic self-portrait.

Van Gogh's *Sunflowers* shows a field of bold yellow sunflowers. Let children make their own sunflower picture from finger paints. Mix 2 parts liquid laundry starch with 1 part powdered paint. Stir well. Make several batches in different colors. Spread the colors on paper using fingers. Make your own paintings of colorful flowers.

Many of Van Gogh's paintings incorporate swirls or circular lines. Use a salad spinner to make your own swirly picture. Cut a piece of paper to fit in the bottom of a salad spinner. Drop a marble in a small container of paint. Use a spoon to remove the paint-covered marble and place it in the salad spinner. Snap on top. Spin the salad spinner, causing the marble to make a circular painted picture. Repeat with other colors of paint-covered marbles. (You're not using the salad spinner for anything else, are you?)

Celebrate with Food

This evening use the dinner meal as a "paint pallet." Serve food in small circles around the plate so it looks like a pallet of paint. Scoop out white mashed potatoes, orange squash, brown meatballs, green cucumber slices, and red beets.

More ideas: www.vangoghgallery.com

APRIL

Month of the Young Child
Mathematics Education Month
National Poetry Month
Keep America Beautiful Month
National Garden Month
National Kite Month
Bedtime Story Month

Weeks to Celebrate

1st Full Week • National Week of the Ocean
3rd Week • National TV-Turnoff Week
3rd Week • Young People's Poetry Week
3rd Full Week • National Volunteer Week
Week of Earth Day • National Wildlife Week

Days to Celebrate

Palm Sunday • (sometimes March)
Easter • (sometimes March)
Mid-April • National Youth Service Day
Mid to Late April • National Teach Children to Save Day
4th Thursday • Take Our Daughters and Sons to Work Day
Last Friday • Arbor Day
Last Saturday • National Day of Puppetry

  1 April Fools' Day
  2 International Children's Book Day
  3 National Circus Day
  6 National Twinkie Day
 10 Encourage a Beginning Writer Day
 14 International Moment of Laughter Day
 16 National Stress Awareness Day
 20 International Astronomy Day
 21 Kindergarten Day

 21 School Librarian Day
 22 Jellybean Day
 22 Earth Day
 24 Spring Cleaning Day
 25 Penguin Day
 26 National Bird Day
 27 Tell a Story Day
 30 International Walk Day

Month of the Young Child

Preschoolers are filled with energy. They love being with adults and are always ready for fun. Enjoy these activities with a young child.

Celebrate with Fun

- If you don't have any preschoolers in your family, borrow one! Offer to babysit a neighbor's young child for a few hours. You'll have a chance to play on a playground, play Duck, Duck, Goose, or finger paint. Your young friend's parents also have the opportunity for a few hours of quiet.

- Preschoolers enjoy simple games. If you want to relax and your child wants to play, try playing "Bring Me." Ask your child, "Bring me something I could put on my feet." It's up to your child to bring you socks, shoes, or slippers. Then ask, "Please bring me something I use if I'm cold." Your child uses creative thinking as he or she runs through the house, gathering items. All you have to do is sit in your favorite easy chair!

- Ask preschoolers to contort their bodies into various shapes. See if they can use their body to: Look like a long board. Make the shape of a doughnut. Make a frame for their face. Get as tiny as possible. Get as huge as possible!

Celebrate with Crafts

Go out of your comfort zone and try these preschool-pleasing crafts: Spray shaving cream on a nonpermeable surface. Let your children spread the cream on the table. Add a few drops of tempera paint and watch how much fun it is to play with colored shaving cream. Have children "draw" a picture in the shaving cream with their fingers. Place a piece of paper over their design and press gently. When you lift the paper, you'll have a reverse print of their picture! Now get really brave and do the same thing with pudding! (They can even eat it from the clean surface once they are done with their artwork.)

Celebrate with Food

Young children enjoy helping in the kitchen. Let them demonstrate their culinary skills by making banana pops. Smash 1 ripe banana in a bowl. Add ½ cup vanilla yogurt and mix well. Slowly add ½ cup milk. "Smoosh" everything together. Pour mixture in Popsicle trays. Insert wooden craft sticks. Freeze overnight. You can also pour mixture in an ice cube tray and use wooden craft sticks for handles.

More ideas: www.naeyc.org

Mathematics Education Month

How often have you heard, "But why do I *have* to learn math? I'll never use it!" Use this month to demonstrate how math affects us on a daily basis.

Celebrate with Fun

- All month, involve children with mathematical situations. How many pizzas should you order for the soccer party if 12 teammates will eat 2 pieces each? Are they clamoring for expensive new shoes? Have them call several stores to get the best prices and check for sales. They can decide which is a better deal, $49.99 shoes at 25 percent off or the same pair for $38.95.

- Send your children on a "Tape Measure Scavenger Hunt." Give them this list: "Find something 8½ inches long. Find something with a diameter of 22 inches. Find something with a radius of 3 inches. Find something with a circumference of 12 inches." Then vary the list by asking: "How high is the kitchen table? How long is Dad's Bible? How long is the car? How long is the slide? How high? Find a worm 4½ inches long."

- Ask your children, "What weighs more—a pound of feathers or a pound of rocks?"

- Here's a tip to help everyone with "9" multiplication tables. To figure out 3 x 9, place both hands on a table. Curl the third finger underneath. Count the straight fingers to the left—2. Count fingers to the right—7. The answer—27! Practice the trick until it becomes natural.

Celebrate with Crafts

Make math fun with personalized flash cards. Give children 4″ x 6″ index cards. On each card, write a math problem, with the answer on the back. Let children decorate their flash cards with colorful designs. They can use markers, stickers, and stamps.

Celebrate with Food

Set out assorted foods that require children to use math skills. Give your 3 children 2 ice-cream sandwiches, for example. How can they divide them evenly? Set out a handful of M&M's. How will they divide them equally? A recipe needs a pint of strawberries. You have a 1-cup measuring cup. Can they figure out the correct amount of berries? Double their favorite cookie recipe, but let them double the amounts. What do they do when the recipe calls for ⅔ cup sugar?

More ideas: www.nctm.org or 703-620-9840

National Poetry Month

"I think that I shall never see, a poem lovely as a tree . . ." Maybe you'll never be as eloquent as this poet, but you can enjoy various forms of poetry.

Celebrate with Fun

- Begin your month as a poet by writing simple free-form verse. This requires no rhyming, no set line lengths, and no specific subject. Just write about something—anything—in short sentences or phrases. Give children a broad topic such as "animals" or "things I like at school."
- Attend a local poetry reading. These casual events give poets a chance to read their poems to a receptive audience.
- Get silly—try limericks, 5-line poems telling a story. The first, second, and fifth lines rhyme; the third and fourth lines rhyme between themselves.
- Tongue twisters aren't exactly poetry, but try writing some. Writing them is easy—saying them is difficult! For inspiration, try these: She sells sea shells by the seashore. Soldier's shoulders. Blow big blue bubbles.
- Place cutout magazine pictures in a box. Have each family member select a picture and immediately make up a poem about the picture.

Celebrate with Crafts

Make a background for your Haiku poetry. On a sheet of tan paper, drop 3–4 drops of thin black paint. Use a straw to give quick "blows" to the paint, creating an abstract calligraphy type look to the paper. Write your Haiku around the black paint designs.

Celebrate with Food

How many foods can you eat that are parts of made-up rhymes? Make up some silly rhymes and then prepare food to go with your poetry. Here are some ideas: Eat bananas while wearing bandanas. Eat potatoes with tomatoes. Do flips eating chips (for the gymnast in your family).

More ideas: www.poets.org/npm

Keep America Beautiful Month

Think how beautiful our country would be if everyone did their part picking up litter and making an effort to recycle. This month spruce up your own environment.

Celebrate with Fun

- Clean up your neighborhood by making a "Litter Monster." Lay out a large piece of newsprint in the garage or on the sidewalk. Have an adult walk children around the neighborhood as they collect scraps of paper and small litter. When they return, outline a "Monster" on the paper. Spread glue all over it and stick on the litter collected by the children to create litter "fur." Display for a few days as a reminder of how little effort it takes to have a cleaner neighborhood.

- Purchase a few early season plants like primroses. Plant them in a flower box or by the sidewalk so passersby can enjoy their bright colors.

- Make a conscious effort to beautify your environment. Help improve a trail in your local park or deliver a flower basket to a nursing home. Plant some wildflower seeds in a patch of dry grass.

- Plan a "1-Hour Cleanup" campaign. Designate 1 hour for everyone in the family to take on a home beautifying project. Rake last year's dead leaves, wash the trash cans, clean the doghouse, or plant a tree.

Celebrate with Crafts

Put empty boxes to good use by making "big mouth" puppets. Collect 2 pudding boxes per puppet. Cut the flaps off 1 end of each box. Stack boxes on top of each other, open ends facing same direction. Create a mouth by taping boxes together in the middle of their open ends. Slip your thumb in bottom box and your 4 other fingers in top box. Open and close your fingers—the puppet moves its large mouth! Decorate with paint or contact paper. Glue on recycled button eyes. Use other odds and ends to give your puppet personality. Put on a puppet show featuring ideas about how to keep America beautiful.

Celebrate with Food

Plant a small indoor herb garden. Many stores sell complete kits so you can easily grow fresh mint, basil, and even parsley. Not only do the fresh herbs taste great, they add a touch of natural beauty to your windowsill. Have children compare the smell and flavor of fresh herbs to that of dried herbs from a jar.

More ideas: www.kab.org

National Garden Month

The gloomy days of winter are behind us. Set aside a day this month to start celebrating with gardening fun.

Celebrate with Fun

- Do you have a bird feeder that attracts a large number of birds? Place one part of your old baby monitor next to the bird feeder and bring the other part inside. You'll get to eavesdrop on the birds!

- Start some seedlings. Put potting soil in clear plastic sundae containers from fast-food restaurants, then add seeds. Place in a sunny location until the seeds poke out of the soil. Transplant to your outdoor garden. You can also plant seeds in eggshells. When you make scrambled eggs, save the eggshell halves. Set them in the egg carton so they don't tip, and fill them with potting soil. Add seeds and water. When seedlings appear, dig holes in the garden and plant the entire eggshell container!

- Start some pumpkin seeds indoors. When they are sturdy enough, transplant outdoors. As soon as you see small pumpkins forming, collect a few clear plastic milk jugs. Place a milk jug on the ground and insert the tiny pumpkin. As it grows, it takes the shape of the milk jug. Have an adult carefully cut the jug away from your unique pumpkin in the fall.

- Check if your community offers tours of local gardens. Seeing what other people have done is sure to inspire your family.

Celebrate with Crafts

Create a garden "Welcome" stepping stone. Buy a small bag of mortar and mix according to directions. Pour mix into an old baking pan (or several pans if you have them). Let harden slightly until pudding consistency. Decorate stepping stone by gently placing twigs, small stones, or even plastic jewelry on top of mortar mix. Use the end of a stick to write "Welcome to My Garden" or another greeting. Let dry overnight. Have an adult remove the stepping stone from the pan. Careful! It's heavy! Place the stone at the entrance to your garden, or make several as actual stepping stones to form a path.

Celebrate with Food

Prepare a "Before and After" meal. Buy various seed packages like carrots, broccoli, lettuce, and radishes. Display a few of the seeds on top of their respective packages. Place the actual developed food by each package. It's amazing how tiny seeds grow into great-tasting foods. Eat and enjoy!

More ideas: www.nationalgardenmonth.org

National Kite Month

With springtime weather and gentle breezes, April is the perfect month to fly kites.

Celebrate with Fun

- Begin the day by pretending to be Mary Poppins and singing "Let's Go Fly a Kite." When children ask if they can watch TV, sing "Let's Go Fly a Kite." When they bicker, sing "Let's Go Fly a Kite." Get the idea?
- If you can't find last year's kite, buy another from a discount store. If kites are on sale, buy one for each family member.
- Play "Find the Kite." Place a trail of string throughout the house. Children start at one end and follow the trail to discover their prize—a new kite!
- Call the local Parks and Recreation department to see if they know of any kite clubs in the area. These groups meet and fly kites, most incredibly more complicated than yours! They welcome visitors to watch them fly kites with elaborate designs and numerous strings.
- Stage a minikite race. Cut straws into 6-inch sections. Glue a kite-shaped piece of paper to the straws for your minikites. Partners stand facing each other about 10 feet apart. Slip a straw minikite over a piece of string held taut by each set of partners. Slide the straw directly in front of 1 partner. On "Go!" each team wiggles their string to see who can get their minikite to the opposite partner first. Using the same concept, have partners hold their minikites in front of them. Select another person to blow their kite to the opposite end of the string.
- If there's no wind today, use chalk to draw kites all along your sidewalk.

Celebrate with Crafts

Make decorative paper kites. Cut 11″ x 18″ pieces of construction paper into kite shapes. Using the paper scraps, decorate kites by adding stars or stripes. Tape kites to ceilings throughout the house.

Make a homemade kite to fly. Library books contain easy-to-use patterns.

Celebrate with Food

Try some kite-shaped snacks today. Heat a bowl of refried beans. Place Doritos or other triangle-shaped chips on top in the shape of kites.

Toast several pieces of bread. Cut the bread into kite shapes. Decorate by spraying designs with spray-on cheese in a can. Go ahead, splurge for a can so children can squirt out orange cheese designs on anything edible!

More ideas: www.nationalkitemonth.org

Bedtime Story Month

You have probably read *Goodnight Moon* to your children hundreds of times at bedtime. It's a cozy, reassuring ritual to cuddle in bed with a parent reading a familiar book. This month expand your child's repertoire of stories.

Celebrate with Fun

- Read a favorite story to your children, substituting their names for the characters. They'll be delighted to hear, "Then Kevin began building an ark and collecting animals."

- Has your child outgrown certain books? Update your library with a "Bedtime Story Swap." Invite families over in the early evening with books they'd like to exchange. Ask people to come in their jammies for atmosphere. When people arrive, stand up the books on several tables so they are easily seen. Invite people to browse and select "new" books to take home. Before everyone leaves, read a bedtime story to the group as they eat graham crackers and milk.

- Purchase a colored lightbulb for your child's bedside lamp. Story time has a different feel when the room is bathed in a soft pink light.

- The next time you read *Velveteen Rabbit*, add to the story by forming bunny shadow ears on the wall. Try to make a shadow character from each story you read to your child.

Celebrate with Crafts

Design a special bedtime story with your child. Fold 10 or 12 pieces of typing paper in half. Punch 5 or 6 holes in the fold. Weave thin ribbon in and out to bind book together. On the first page write a caption like "Kyle likes to _____ in the summer." On the opposite page write, "Dad likes to _____ in the summer." Fill in the blanks and add illustrations. Fill book with topics like favorite color, favorite vacation place, best friend, favorite foods . . . Read as part of your child's bedtime routine.

Is your child afraid of the dark? Have him or her use puff paint or stickers to decorate a plastic spray "Monster-Go-Away" bottle. Fill bottle with water and add a few drops of vanilla or other scent. Let your child spray away any monsters that might bother him.

Celebrate with Food

Does your child continually ask to get out of bed for a drink of water? Leave a sippee cup or water bottle by her bed. That's the allotted amount of water she can have. Children soon learn to regulate how much they drink.

National Week of the Ocean

Even if you live in a landlocked state, it's fun to pretend you're spending a sunny day at the beach. Celebrate this week with waves, sand dollars, and minioceans.

Celebrate with Fun

- If you can't visit the ocean, make your own "Ocean in a Bag." Purchase a jar of light blue hair-styling gel. Pour 1 cup gel into a resealable sandwich bag. Drop in several small plastic fish or gummy fish. Remove excess air and double-seal the bag with duct tape. Squish your ocean in a bag to make fish "swim." Afraid to let children play with gooey hair gel? Substitute a blue piece of paper that fits inside the bag. Add ½ cup oatmeal "sand." Now add plastic or gummy fish to your mini-ocean.

- Visit a science museum that sells sand dollars and buy one so you can discover the surprise inside. After looking at it and shaking it, break it open. Legend has it 5 small doves will come out, symbolizing hope and joy. See if you can find the doves inside the sand dollar.

- Help children understand the length of some ocean creatures. Using chalk and a tape measure, mark out the length of the following whales and sharks on your sidewalk: Blue whale—110 feet long. Whale shark—46 feet. Goblin shark—11 feet. Spiny Dogfish shark—4 feet. Spined Pygmy shark—7–8 inches.

- Make some ocean waves. Sit a child in the middle of a blanket on the floor. Family members hold on to the blanket's edges and shake them up and down—your child is swimming in ocean waves!

Celebrate with Crafts

Decorate real-looking sea creatures with breakfast cereal. Cut out just the body shapes of sea creatures with tentacles (like an octopus or starfish). Paint bodies light pink or yellow. After paint dries, make tentacles by gluing on colored fruit ring cereal.

Celebrate with Food

Starfish biscuits make tasty ocean snacks. Roll out your favorite biscuit dough ½-inch thick. Cut out starfish shapes with a star cookie cutter. Gently "pull" on the starfish legs before baking, lengthening them. Bake according to recipe. Remind your children that starfish are actually called sea stars. They'll be impressed.

More ideas: Week of the Ocean, Inc. 954-462-5573; www.national-week-of-the-ocean.org

National TV-Turnoff Week

Each year, communities and schools across the nation encourage families to turn off the TV for a full week. That's right—no TV for a week. See how much more time your family spends together when the TV is off!

Celebrate with Fun

- Hold a ceremony celebrating the start of 7 "family fun" days. Put colorful cloths over all your TVs, then reveal a new game or craft supplies. Emphasize fun things you'll do this week, rather than moaning and groaning about no TV.

- Brainstorm about things to do during TV-turnoff week. Write ideas on pieces of paper. Do 2 or 3 a day: Ride bikes, play Clue, and wrestle. Wonder why you ever watched TV?

- Give family makeovers. Let kids update Mom and Dad—you may find Mom looking like a teenager in a miniskirt and short top with her belly button showing.

- Invite friends to an "Invent a Game Night." Hand each family a bag full of assorted items like balls, Frisbees, hula hoops, and empty soda bottles. Everyone has 15 minutes to invent a new game using the items. Then play the very unusual games!

- At week's end, evaluate your "experiment." Did your family enjoy being TV free? Will you cut back or eliminate the TV after this week?

Celebrate with Crafts

In your spare time, make interesting pictures using homemade puff paint. Mix 1 cup flour, 1 cup water, and 1 cup salt. Divide mixture into 3 or 4 squeeze bottles. Add a few drops food coloring to each. Mix well. Squirt out paint pictures on paper. Let dry into puffy, shiny designs.

Have balloon relay races. Each person blows up a balloon and holds the end shut. Stand on a starting line. On "Go!" release balloon to splutter around. Run to where your balloon lands, blow it up, and release again. Keep following your balloon until you cross the finish line.

Celebrate with Food

In most families, dinner is rushed because people want to watch their favorite TV shows. Since you have more time now, plan a "roving dinner." Serve light hors d'oeuvres in the family room. Walk around the block, then eat salad in the kitchen. After another short stroll, eat the main course in the garage or a child's bedroom. Enjoy dessert outside—even if it's cold!

More ideas: www.tvturnoff.org

Young People's Poetry Week

Expand your literary knowledge by reading poetry this week. Find a rhyming dictionary when children want to know what rhymes with *orange*.

Celebrate with Fun

- Show off your poetic skills by including a poem in your child's lunch box. (Tuck a poem in your spouse's pocket also.) Don't worry about form or style — just be funny:

  My dear sweet Madeline
  I think you are so fine,
  Your voice is like a very loud boom
  Today I'll help you clean your room!

- Read the Psalms to your children so they can discover poetry from the Bible.
- Give younger kids a taste of high school studies by reading aloud part of a classic poem like "Beowulf" or "The Charge of the Light Brigade." Younger children may not understand it, but can gain an appreciation for poets beyond Shel Silverstein.
- Select a humorous poster or magazine picture. Show everyone, then have them write a poem about it. Read the poems aloud and laugh at your different interpretations.
- Tongue twisters are short poems. Make up new tongue twisters or recite classics like "She sells sea shells by the seashore" or "Blow big blue bubbles." First recite tongue twisters at regular speed, then go faster and faster until your tongues are truly twisted.
- Plan a poetry party. Ask everyone to memorize 1 poem. Dress to reflect your poem or use a prop during your dramatic interpretation of "The Day I Fell in the Mud."
- Each night this week, read a poem along with the usual bedtime stories.

Celebrate with Crafts

Make a "ransom note" poem. Cut words and phrases from a magazine and place on a table so everyone can see them. Glue words on a piece of paper to form a poem made from a hodgepodge of fonts.

Celebrate with Food

Set up a "beatnik" poetry reading party. Dress up in eccentric clothes while dimming the lights to create a coffeehouse atmosphere. Serve soft drinks with pretzels and chips as people read poetry from various sources. Act very mellow and low-key, trying to be avant-garde.

More ideas: www.cbcbooks.org

National Volunteer Week

This week honors people who volunteer through community service. Over 488,000 volunteers participate each year by volunteering during this week.

Celebrate with Fun

- Know someone who is an outstanding volunteer? Nominate him or her as a Points of Light honoree. Go to www.pointsoflight.org to find out how to apply. It's also inspiring to read about other people's efforts to make the world a better place.

- Call your church to see if volunteer opportunities exist. Can your family fold church bulletins? Are there storage closets just waiting to be organized? Offer to cut out craft projects for a busy Sunday school teacher.

- Need inspiration for more volunteer possibilities? Read *You Can Change Your World!* by teenager Sondra Clark. She describes over 200 practical ways families can volunteer.

- Since this is a week-long "holiday," there's time to get others involved. Select a project like a neighborhood cleanup or children's book collection. Have children design and distribute flyers. Contact the local newspaper. Get people excited about volunteering!

- Police and fire departments urge people to make sure their house addresses can be clearly seen from the road. Check into the possibility of volunteering to paint addresses on the curbs in front of homes. Call your local police or fire department community relations staff person for details.

Celebrate with Crafts

Meals on Wheels is a nationwide program delivering meals to shut-ins. Offer to put together a few "We Care" items to include with meals. Purchase inexpensive vases and decorate with puff paint. Make napkin rings out of wrapping paper tubes. After decorating the rings, slip colorful napkins inside. Purchase sturdy plastic silverware and decorate the handles with permanent markers. Take the items to the Meals on Wheels program to include with their deliveries.

Celebrate with Food

Want to see your money for food go a long way? Purchase a "Survival Pak" from Childcare International (www.childcare-intl.org). For $25, Childcare will purchase beans, rice, powdered milk, and other staples to help an impoverished family. Depending on the country, a Survival Pak can provide: food for a family of 4 in Haiti for a month; breakfast for 10 children in Peru for a month; supplementary food for 10 children in India for a month.

More ideas: www.pointsoflight.org

National Wildlife Week

With more and more land being taken over for development, wildlife is being forced into suburbia. It's becoming more common to see deer and raccoons in heavily populated areas.

Celebrate with Fun

- Look for wild animal tracks outside. Hopefully you won't find any lion tracks, but you might spot bird, raccoon, or possum prints. Even if you don't live in the country, walk through your neighborhood and look for birds, bugs, and other signs of wildlife. Perhaps you'll see a scampering squirrel or some tiny minnows in a pond.

- Look for tadpoles in a small pond. These squirmy creatures are easy to spot. They look like chubby black exclamation points. Scoop them into a clear container for a closer look. Instead of taking them home, return the tadpoles to their home. Come back in a few weeks and look at the tadpoles' physical changes. When they change into frogs, say good-bye with a loud chorus of "Ribbit-ribbit."

- Play a quick game of animal charades. Have children cut out magazine pictures of animals. (Sometimes libraries have "swap shops" where people can donate or pick up extra magazines.) Glue the animal pictures onto index cards. Now it's time to play. A child selects a card, but doesn't let anyone see it. He or she acts out the animal on the card until someone guesses correctly. Try playing by using pantomime only—no loud animal roars allowed.

- Visit a nearby wildlife sanctuary. Many communities have facilities for wildlife rehabilitation.

Celebrate with Crafts

Get your family up early in the morning to look for spiderwebs. They are easiest to find in a park or field. Make sure no spider is on the web before making this craft, then lightly spray the spiderweb with dark-colored spray paint. Gently press a large piece of light-colored cardboard to the painted spiderweb. You'll have an authentic spiderweb to frame and display at home.

Celebrate with Food

S'mores are a traditional food to eat when you are outside. Roast marshmallows over a campfire. When the marshmallow is golden brown, place on a graham cracker. Cover with a piece of thin chocolate and another graham cracker. Enjoy your sticky, sweet treat.

More ideas: www.nwf.org/nationalwildlifeweek

Palm Sunday

On the Sunday before his crucifixion, Jesus rode into Jerusalem on the back of a donkey (Matt. 21:5–9). Use today to prepare for Easter.

Celebrate with Fun

- Reenact Palm Sunday. Use newspaper or pieces of green construction paper to cut out palm leaves. Select someone to read from the Bible as other family members wave palm leaves and cheer for Jesus.

- Tell your children today's story from the donkey's perspective: A young donkey was eating hay when a man came and led him to the main street in town. The donkey felt someone get on his back. As he began walking, he noticed people waving palm branches and smiling at him. "This is great!" he thought. "All these people came to wave to me." He loved the attention. The next day, the donkey thought, "I liked those people clapping and cheering for me. I'll walk down the street again." He went to the same street where he had carried Jesus. This time, though, no one looked at him. No cheering people waved palm branches. Dejected, he returned to the stable and told his mother how disappointed he was. His mother gave him advice that can be a lesson to us all. She said, "You're nothing unless Jesus is with you."

- Make a time line of major events in Jesus' life, including Palm Sunday and his crucifixion, and ending with his resurrection from the dead.

Celebrate with Crafts

Make a palm sun catcher to celebrate Palm Sunday. Place a clean margarine lid on a flat surface. Carefully pour in white glue, almost to the rim. Cut several blades of grass with nail scissors to resemble palm branches. (Yes, you'll feel silly cutting slits into a piece of grass!) Place the miniature palm leaves in the glue. Sprinkle some glitter on top. Let dry 2 or 3 days. Peel flexible opaque sun catcher off margarine lid. Have an adult poke a hole in the top, and thread with ribbon or string so you can hang sun catcher in window.

Celebrate with Food

Make some ice-cream eggs from plastic Easter eggs. Line each half egg with plastic wrap, making sure plastic hangs over the edges. Pack with softened ice cream. Press 2 halves firmly together and freeze overnight. Carefully remove the plastic eggs and plastic wrap to enjoy some ice-cream eggs.

More ideas: annieshomepage.com/palmsunday.html

Easter

THE SUNDAY FOLLOWING THE FIRST FULL MOON
AFTER THE VERNAL EQUINOX!

APRIL

Easter is a "moving" holiday. It can come as early as March 22 or as late as April 25. Celebrate today by having a traditional egg hunt along with other activities that emphasize Christ's resurrection.

Celebrate with Fun

- After boiling and dying eggs, hide them as usual. When children have collected the eggs, select a child to hide the eggs again. That's the fun part—looking for eggs. Keep hiding and finding eggs until children lose interest or the eggs are totally cracked!

- President Madison began the tradition of rolling eggs in front of the White House on the lawn. Boil eggs and pretend you're a special guest at the White House. Roll the eggs from one end of the lawn to the other.

- Set out jellybeans and ask children to eat the colors you mention as you read this poem found on www.annieshomepage.com/jellybeanprayer.html:

> Red is for the blood He gave.
> Green is for the grass He made.
> Yellow is for the sun so bright.
> Orange is for the edge of night.
> Black is for the sins that were made,
> White is for the grace He gave.
>
> Purple is for the hour of sorrow.
> Pink is for the new tomorrow.
> Give a bag full of jellybeans, colorful and sweet,
> Tell them it's a prayer, it's a promise,
> It's an Easter treat! (Shirley Kozak, 1990).

- Make a growing centerpiece for your Easter table. Fill a shallow pan with dirt (a new kitty litter container works well). Sprinkle grass seed over the top and keep watered. When grass begins growing, have children make a cross from twigs outside. Stick cross in dirt.

- When assembling Easter baskets for your children, purchase extra candy and goodies. Let children help put together several small Easter baskets to be delivered to a children's shelter.

Celebrate with Crafts

Make tiny yellow chicks to decorate your house this Easter. Dip your fingertips in yellow paint. Press down on paper. Let dry. Use fine-tipped markers to embellish the body with legs, eyes, and a beak.

Celebrate with Food

As Christians we teach our children that Christ disappeared from the tomb to rise again. Make "disappearing" biscuits: Roll refrigerator biscuits so each one is flattened and wraps around a large marshmallow. Dip each biscuit in melted butter, then cinnamon sugar mix. Bake as directed. Let cool. When children eat the biscuit, they'll find the marshmallow is gone!

115

National Youth Service Day

Youth Service America focuses on helping youth get involved in volunteer activities. Every year, several million youth take part in worthwhile volunteer opportunities.

Celebrate with Fun

- Brainstorm various ways to set up a Youth Service Day with your family. Think big! Can you start a pet food bank or collect and clean donated strollers to give to low-income moms? Use this holiday to start your family volunteering. Carry on the holiday's spirit by volunteering on a regular basis.

- Let your children know about these volunteer-related facts: (1) Teenagers volunteer 2.4 billion hours annually. (2) Youth volunteering is up 12 percent over the last 10 years. (3) Youth who volunteer are more likely to do well in school, graduate, vote, and be philanthropists.

- Plan a fund-raising event so you can donate the money to a favorite charity. Ideas include: A bake sale at a soccer game or other place. A letter to family and friends that asks for a donation along with a tea bag. (The letter can explain why you want a donation. Be sure to say, "Please make yourself a cup of tea, relax, and send in your donation.") A talent show charging admission of cash or donations of canned foods. A youth art exhibit at which young participants pay a fee to show their artwork.

- Many homeless people feel strong loyalty to their pets. Purchase some cans or small bags of dog food to keep in the trunk of your car. The next time you see a homeless person with a dog, stop and give some food to the pet.

Celebrate with Crafts

Decorate a plastic container to hold craft supplies for a women's/children's shelter. Collect good-quality supplies of construction paper, markers, and stickers. Purchase additional supplies to add, and donate the kit to provide fun to needy children.

Celebrate with Food

Today, try to be a vegetarian. Eat more fruits and vegetables, which means fewer animals will be killed for your consumption. Donate the money you'd spend for meat to a charity.

More ideas: www.ysa.org/NYSD

National Teach Children to Save Day

Have you ever told your children, "Money doesn't grow on trees"? Yet many children assume money simply comes out of ATM machines 24 hours a day. Take this day to teach children to develop lifelong money skills.

Celebrate with Fun

- Help children see how quickly money "disappears." In the morning, hand them envelopes of $200 Monopoly or play money. This is their spending money for the day. At breakfast begin your plan. Do they want cereal? Great! That's a dollar. Milk too? Another dollar. A ride to school? Mom's Taxi Service is $10.50 plus a tip. Charge for electricity, water, school lunches, laundry, homework assistance, and bed tucking-in service. They'll be shocked at how quickly their money disappears.

- Set up a 401(k) savings plan for your children. No, they won't need to have a full-time job for this plan. "Match" their savings dollars with a certain amount—maybe you'll put in 50 cents for every dollar they save. When a sizeable amount is reached, purchase some stocks or a bond.

- Find a chart that graphically depicts the power of compound interest. Show children what happens if they invest $1,000 every year for 25 years. At 9 percent interest, your child would have $66,184! The Internet offers many websites under "savings calculators" that let children plug in various amounts of money to see how their investment grows.

Celebrate with Crafts

Help children develop a savings plan with 3-in-1 savings cans. Remove labels and sharp edges from 3 empty soup cans. Coat cans with glue. Wind thick yarn top to bottom around each can, covering the metal. Let dry. Use hot glue or craft glue to join cans together like a cloverleaf. Attach 3 labels to cans: SAVE, SPEND, and TITHE. When children receive an allowance or gift money, they put 10 percent in the tithing can. Decide as a family how the other 90 percent is distributed between savings and spending.

Celebrate with Food

At a restaurant, have children keep tabs on what is ordered and on the final bill. A few days later, duplicate the meal at home and compare the costs.

More ideas: www.aba.com

117

Take Our Daughters and Sons to Work Day

Celebrate today by taking your daughter or son to work with you! This nationwide program encourages young people ages 9–15 to visit workplaces around the country. Over 11 million kids participate each year.

Celebrate with Fun

- Ask your children to describe—in detail—what you do at work. More than likely, your children have only a vague idea how you spend your days earning a living. Go through an hour-by-hour account of the various skills and resources you use on the job.

- Arrange to take your children to work with you, at least for part of the day. Since this is such a widely publicized event, employers are usually open to having children at the workplace.

- Encourage your business or supervisor to plan special activities for children visiting today. How about a pizza party at noon? Some businesses print children T-shirts saying, "Jr. Accountant" or "Up-and-Coming Landscape Architect." Rearrange your normal schedule so children observe different jobs and meet as many employees as possible. (Of course, if you work out of your home, simply invite children into your office for a snack. They've probably seen what you do all day!)

- Break the stereotypes about what boys and girls can do—teach your son to sew on a button or have your daughter check the oil in the car.

- If you can't take your children to work with you, arrange a job shadow for them at another time and location. Do you know someone who works at an aquarium? Ask if children can observe her job. Perhaps you know a college professor. Watch how grown-up your children act as they sit in on a college class.

Celebrate with Crafts

Have children make sketches of what they think you do throughout the day. Ask them to add details such as drawing coworkers and your office. Take the sketches along when children come to work with you. Compare their perception with what you really do.

Celebrate with Food

Show children what you normally do for lunch. Enjoy soup in the company cafeteria or grab a hot dog from the usual street vendor. If you brown-bag it at your desk, make another lunch so you can eat your sandwich together while answering the phone.

More ideas: www.daughtersandsonstowork.org

118

Arbor Day

In 1872 Nebraska had a contest to see which community group could plant the most trees. Over 1 million trees were planted, starting the Arbor Day tradition.

Celebrate with Fun

- Pick a tree close to your home and photograph it. Every 3–4 months, take another picture and compare the leaves and color. Does the tree change its appearance? An evergreen tree might look the same all year, while an apple tree changes dramatically.

- Relive your childhood and climb a tree. Have you ever encouraged your children to climb a tree? Find a tree with plenty of sturdy branches and enjoy seeing the world together from an elevated position.

- Feeling really inspired to celebrate Arbor Day? Build a tree house! It's not as hard as it sounds. Several books give tree house directions ranging from basic models to a dwelling complete with electricity and glass windows.

- Give everyone a piece of paper and a crayon. Go outside and place the paper on the side of a tree. Rub the crayon across it firmly to make a rubbing of the tree bark. Repeat on several trees. Try to identify the type of tree from the crayon rubbings.

- Send away for some trees to plant. Write The National Arbor Day Foundation, 100 Arbor Ave., Nebraska City, NE 68410. They'll send trees appropriate to your specific climate.

- Look at the different trees in your neighborhood. Compare sizes of trunks, leaf shapes, and types of branches.

- Play "Tree Tag." Find an open area with a few trees. "It" tries to tag another person. The only way to avoid being tagged is to "hug" a tree.

Celebrate with Crafts

Give everyone a leaf, any size or shape. Glue the leaf onto paper and incorporate it into a picture. The leaf might be a dress or part of an animal. Use paint or markers to embellish the picture.

Celebrate with Food

Crunch away on some bugs on a tree. Cut celery into 4-inch pieces. These are your "trees." Spread peanut butter on the celery and top with a few bugs. (Raisins!)

More ideas: www.arborday.org

119

National Day of Puppetry

Remember when Maria and the children put on an elaborate puppet show in *The Sound of Music*? You can celebrate National Puppetry Day without worrying about tangling your marionette's strings.

Celebrate with Fun

- Any item can be made into a puppet. Let children use small boxes, plastic cups, cardboard, yarn, fabric, and glue to create a puppet.
- At the doctor's office, ask for a few large tongue depressors. (Or buy them at a craft store!) Add wiggle eyes, yarn, and markers to quickly turn the wooden sticks into tiny puppets.
- Make an easy puppet stage. Put a spring-tension curtain rod across a doorway. Drape a sheet or beach towel over the rod. Puppeteers perform on one side while the audience sits on the other. This stage works well with different-sized children—its height is easily adjusted.
- Make simple paper bag puppets. Many stores sell colored lunch bags, which make puppets more colorful. Children slip their hand into the "flap" at the bottom and move it up and down to make the puppet sing and talk. Draw a face on the puppet.
- Give a realistic appearance to stick puppets. Find a magazine picture of a horse, car, or person and glue it onto construction paper. Carefully cut around the object. Glue a craft stick to the back for an instant puppet.

Celebrate with Crafts

A mouse and mouse house will keep kids occupied for hours. Cut the finger off an old glove to make a mouse puppet. Use a permanent marker to draw eyes on the top of the finger piece. Glue on tiny plastic wiggle eyes. Thread a needle with black or brown thread and pull through the tip, the mouse's "nose," for whiskers. Now that your mouse puppet is finished, make her a house. Decorate a shoe-box lid to look like a house. Have an adult cut out several small windows. Children hold the house and poke their mouse puppet out through the windows. Be sure to use a high squeaky mouse voice.

Celebrate with Food

Make an edible puppet! Set out a few small bowls of different-colored frosting. Teddy Bear Graham Crackers are the base for your puppet. Use toothpicks dipped in frosting to add facial features and decorate clothes on the Teddy Bear. Put on a minipuppet show, then eat the puppets.

More ideas: www.puppeteers.org

April Fools' Day

This is a time of year to celebrate all the silly things you normally are too reserved to do. Let loose and play some great practical jokes.

Celebrate with Fun

- Wake up your family by singing a rousing chorus of "What Kind of Fool Am I?" or "April Showers." Make up the words if you don't know them.

- How about the classic whoopee cushion under someone's chair? If this is your kind of humor, go for the "professional" model. Remote control whoopee cushions are now available. Place one under a seat cushion and wait for just the right moment to push the button on your remote control. It releases the sound under some unsuspecting person!

- Add a few drops of food coloring to your children's glass of milk and tell them it came from a rainbow cow. Or see if you can find some dribble glasses, which are great for surprising people. They take a drink out of these ordinary-looking glasses and end up dribbling on their chests.

- When your children come home from school, put "Wet Paint! Do Not Touch!" signs on the front door. See if they can get by without sticking their fingers on the "wet" paint.

- Unscrew all the lightbulbs in your house. As it gets dark, people will wonder why the lights don't work.

- Put out paper place mats. Set the table as you normally would, only use plastic spoons and forks. One difference: Glue the silverware onto the paper place mats.

Celebrate with Crafts

Since you're the one being silly, make a craft using a human being. Select the family member with the biggest belly. Using red paint, draw "lips" around the person's belly button. Use additional paint to draw 2 eyes and a nose on the person's stomach. Gently squeeze the skin around the belly button to make the mouth "move." Talk in a squeaky voice while moving the belly button mouth.

Celebrate with Food

Serve your children a fried egg for breakfast. But wait—this is April Fools' Day! An ordinary egg wouldn't be appropriate. Instead, toast some bread. (This adds to the illusion.) On a small plate, scoop out ½ cup marshmallow cream fluff. Pat it flat so it looks like a fried egg. Dab a teaspoon of yellow pudding in the center as the "yolk." Yell "April Fools!" as they taste the sweet eggs.

International Children's Book Day

APRIL 2

Today's celebration is in honor of Hans Christian Andersen's birthday. He wanted to be an actor, but wasn't successful enough to make a living. To pay the bills, he began writing fairy tales. Today his books have been translated into many languages. In fact, only the Bible has more language translations.

Celebrate with Fun

- Hans Christian Andersen wrote *The Princess and the Pea*. See if your children are sensitive to something underneath them. Lay a thick towel on the floor. Put a small unbreakable toy under the towel. See if your child can guess what the object is when she lays down on the towel. Try the same test using several towels for extra thickness.

- Find a way for your older children to read to preschoolers. Invite friends with youngsters over or visit a nearby preschool. Your children will feel special using their reading skills to bring enjoyment to preschoolers.

- Ask your local library or bookstore to sponsor a Children's Book Day Story Time. They might arrange to have a "celebrity" author read stories to children.

- Read some of Hans Christian Andersen's stories. What lesson can you learn from *The Emperor's New Clothes* or *The Ugly Duckling*? Act out *The Ugly Duckling* so children experience how it feels to be an outcast.

- Write a family fairy tale! Begin with, "Once upon a time . . ." Be sure to end with, "and they lived happily ever after."

- How can you change these stories? *Goldilocks and the Three* _____. *The* _____ *Mermaid. Jack and the* _____.

Celebrate with Crafts

Make circular children's books by using 8 or 10 coffee filters per book. Have an adult iron the filters on low heat to flatten them. Stack the filters on top of each other. Punch 2 holes about 1 inch apart on 1 side. Use ribbon to lace through the holes and tie together. Let younger children dictate their story to an adult and use markers or crayons to illustrate the story.

Celebrate with Food

Celebrate Hans Christian Andersen's *The Princess and the Pea* by serving split pea soup. Have people sit on a few dried peas during the meal. Can they feel them?

More ideas: www.ibby.org/Seiten/04_child.htm

National Circus Day

Peanuts! Popcorn! Candy! Clowns! The excitement of a circus remains in your memory for a long time. If you can't get to Madison Square Garden to see the Ringling Brothers and Barnum & Bailey Circus, have your own circus activities at home.

Celebrate with Fun

- Put a dab of Vaseline on everyone's nose. Have a relay race in which 1 person runs across the room with a red paper clown nose attached to his or her nose by Vaseline. The object is to transfer the red nose to the next person in line. No hands allowed!

- Bring out the hula hoops. Have your ferocious lions jump through the hoops. Add some red crepe paper to the hoops to give the impression of fire. Have children pretend to be different animals trained to jump through the hoops.

- Transform children into clowns having a hula hoop contest.

- Pretend everyone is a sad clown. Put on baggy clothes and use face paint to design a depressed face. Select 1 person to act totally outrageous and try to get the sad clowns to laugh.

- Cut out large cardboard shapes of feet. Use tape or rubber bands to attach the extra-large soles to the bottom of your shoes. Try walking around. You'll gain an understanding of how difficult it is for clowns to perform with oversized shoes.

- Play a recording of lively circus music and marches. Challenge your children to march through the house for 5 minutes, picking up any out-of-place items. Tell them it's better than working at the circus and having to clean up after the elephants!

Celebrate with Crafts

Blow up several very small red balloons. Tie the ends shut. Use a paper plate to draw a clown face. Add arched eyebrows, a goofy smile, and cute dimples. For the traditional red clown's nose, simply cut a small X where the nose should be. Poke the tied end of the balloon in the slit to form a 3-dimensional nose.

Celebrate with Food

Mix up a batch of clown pancakes for breakfast. It couldn't be easier. Make your favorite pancake recipe. Heat the frying pan to cook 1 large round clown face. Let children use jam for hair, banana slices for eyes, and anything red for the nose.

National Twinkie Day

Twinkies may not be the most nutritious food, but they certainly are worth celebrating! Don't you remember the joy of getting a Twinkie in your school lunch box?

Celebrate with Fun

- Set up a minicarnival in your backyard or living room. Instead of using beanbags, use Twinkies! (For less mess, leave the Twinkies in their protective plastic wrappers.)
- Draw a clown's face on the side of a large box. Cut out a hole for his mouth. Have kids try to throw a Twinkie in his mouth.
- Hang a coat hanger from the ceiling. Ask kids to toss a Twinkie through the coat hanger. If you have space outside, simply try tossing Twinkies through the basketball net.
- Stack several plastic cups in a pyramid shape (4 on the bottom, 3 in the next row, then 2, then 1 cup on top). From a designated distance, kids try to knock down the cups using a Twinkie.
- If you are outdoors, have children select partners. Have partners stand about 2 feet apart and begin tossing a Twinkie back and forth just like an egg toss. Take 1 step backward if you catch the Twinkie.
- Freeze several Twinkies in their wrappers. Set up 2 goals in your driveway or other safe area. Have kids play broom hockey using the frozen Twinkies as pucks. If you have in-line skaters, see if they can play hockey on wheels with frozen Twinkies.
- Buy Twinkies at a discount bread store. Unwrap them and place 3 Twinkies in front of each child. See who can eat them the fastest.

Celebrate with Crafts

Add even more sugar to your diet by making "Twinkies in a Sleeping Bag." Set out various bowls of frosting. Unwrap the Twinkie. Use the frosting to decorate ⅔ of the Twinkie with a pattern so it looks like a sleeping bag. The top third is your head, peaking out of the bag. Use the frosting to draw your facial features, and add hair. Eat!

Celebrate with Food

What better way to celebrate National Twinkie Day than by eating Twinkies? For an extra treat, slice Twinkies lengthwise and cover with sliced strawberries. Top with whipped cream.

Encourage a Beginning Writer Day

Most adults dream of writing a best-selling novel. Give a young author the encouragement they need to develop their writing skills . . . and possibly write that award-winning book.

Celebrate with Fun

- Children of all ages enjoy getting a book "published." Help your child write a story. It can be an imaginative tale or an autobiography. Younger children can dictate to you. Be sure to add illustrations or photographs to the best-selling book. Instead of simply stapling the papers together, go to a copy center and have them spiral-bound. It usually costs less than a dollar and creates a very authentic-looking book.

- As a family, write a family newsletter. Encourage children to write short articles about the hamster escaping from his cage, a new haircut, or the latest adventure on the school playground. Be sure to include the child's name as the author of each article. Make copies and send to appreciative relatives.

- Find several samples of stories or poems from your children's schoolwork that display their writing skills. Bind the creative samples together, either with a hole punch and ribbons or staples. Design a cover for the book. Have a "formal" presentation in which you give your child a copy of his or her book. Read the pages together.

- Participate in your library's story hours to expose children to a wide variety of stories.

- Help your child write a letter to his or her favorite author. (Book publishers are glad to send fan letters to their authors.) Imagine your child's surprise if she receives a letter or picture from her literary hero!

Celebrate with Crafts

Bring out your shoe box filled with hundreds of unorganized photographs. Select "unique" photos of Dad squinting or Baby Jacob with spaghetti in his hair. Glue them on 4" x 6" note cards. Have children write silly captions under each photo. You've just made personalized postcards to send out to family and friends.

Celebrate with Food

Select a family favorite book and serve food relating to the story. If reading *Amelia Bedelia*, serve chicken. (Remember when she was told to "dress the chicken" and she put clothes on the bird?) Perhaps you're reading *The Very Hungry Caterpillar*. Munch on an assortment of fruit.

125

International Moment of Laughter Day

Studies show the average preschooler laughs 350 times a day. Adults? Oh, they chuckle an average of 15 times a day. Here's a chance to try to meet preschool standards.

Celebrate with Fun

- Check out several library books of jokes and riddles. Take turns telling them to each other and vote on your favorite. Tell it the next time your family has company.
- Be brave! Let children actually put a whipped cream pie in your face.
- Let children hear about your most embarrassing moment. Share how your braces got caught during your first kiss or how once you raced the basketball down to the wrong end of the court.
- If you have tricycles or "Big Wheels" available, have family members participate in trike races. There's something universally funny in seeing Dad crouched down on a miniscule trike.
- During dinner, make a rule that no talking is allowed! Instead, sing! Even leftovers taste better as family members laugh when Mom sings (in an operatic voice) "Please Keep Your Elbows off the Table."
- Play "Sound Charades." On slips of paper, list various items that make noise like radios, cars, trains, phones, blenders, and barking dogs. Each person gets to select a paper and try to mimic the sound of their item. The first person to guess correctly gets to be the next sound maker.

Celebrate with Crafts

Play with a batch of Slimy Quicksand: In a bowl, mix 2 cups cornstarch with 4 cups water. Stir with your hands. The cornstarch mixture has a unique texture. Squeeze a handful and the mixture gets hard. Wait a few seconds and suddenly the solution oozes through your fingers. Guaranteed to produce laughter.

Celebrate with Food

Purchase frozen bread dough and let thaw. (If you enjoy baking, make your own homemade bread dough.) Give each person a portion of dough to sculpt and mold. Create personalized self-sculptures out of dough and bake as directed. Enjoy a warm snack, laughing as you pull off baked heads and legs.

National Stress Awareness Day

How often do children hear you say, "I'm so stressed out"? Use today to reduce stress in your life so you can enjoy your family more. (Did you notice this holiday is the day after income taxes are due?)

Celebrate with Fun

- When you notice stress entering your life, switch gears by engaging in a physical activity. Take children on a jog or bike ride. Make a chart to ensure that you and your family have daily exercise.

- Even young children feel stress about starting a new school or being bullied. At bedtime, teach children to picture a large blackboard in their mind. Their job is to keep their mind clear by pretending to "erase" any worrisome thoughts. They should keep the imaginary blackboard clean.

- Set up a "mock court" situation the next time family members bicker. Appoint a judge to listen to both sides of the arguments. Let the jury decide who is "guilty" or not. The judge has the final say in determining disciplinary action for the situation.

- Do family members always feel rushed? Take a hard look at everyone's schedule. One of the easiest ways to reduce stress is by reducing the number of organized family activities. Instead of racing from soccer to ballet to art lessons, stay home and enjoy simply hanging out.

- Is there too much background noise at your house? Reduce noise by turning off the TV and radio. Declare the house a "Quiet Zone" for an hour or two each evening. Talking is fine, but no TV or noisy computer games!

- Teach children these ways to reduce stress: Take a hot bubble bath. Do something physically active. Read the Bible and/or pray. Do a relaxing activity such as drawing or working with clay. Drink some warm milk!

Celebrate with Crafts

Give everyone a large piece of construction paper. Decorate a 2-inch border around all sides. On the sheet, write these questions: What makes me angry? What causes me to get frustrated? What do I worry about? Then write the answers. Discuss them. Find ways to help people reduce frustration and stress.

Celebrate with Food

Okay, there's only one way to reduce stress: Eat chocolate!

International Astronomy Day

APRIL 20

(Officially celebrated on a Saturday near the first quarter moon, mid-April to mid-May)

Each year 15 astronomical organizations get together to observe Astronomy Day. Today find out all you can about the wonders of our stars and planets.

Celebrate with Fun

- Planets themselves have no light. We see them because they are hit by the sun's light and it reflects back to us. Lay out several round items in a darkened room. Include a dark basketball, a white soccer ball, and a ball of aluminum foil. Shine a light on each object and compare the reflections.

- Make up your own verses to "Twinkle, Twinkle, Little Star." Try singing, "Twinkle, twinkle, little star, how I want a candy bar . . ."

- Is there a planetarium in your area? Often special family presentations take place on Astronomy Day.

- Pass out pieces of dark blue paper and a box of stick-on stars. Arrange the stars in a pattern to look like a constellation. Make up constellation names such as "Ryan's Bicycle" or "Jennie's Ice-Cream Cone." Go outside to compare the real stars with your pretend star formations.

- Surprise your family with some small astronomy-related gifts. Hand out star-shaped candles, moon-shaped soaps, or glow-in-the-dark stars.

Celebrate with Crafts

Make a sparkly star to display. Mix up a solution of 1 cup very hot water with 4 Tbs. borax (available in the laundry detergent section of your grocery store). Mix well to dissolve borax. Twist 2 chenille stems to form a small star. Tie a string to 1 tip of the star, and tie the other end of the string to a pencil. Place pencil over the jar of diluted borax so the star is completely immersed. Cover and let sit several days. The borax will form tiny crystals on your star.

Celebrate with Food

Set out ordinary glasses to use for decorating with ministars. Beat 1 egg white until frothy. Use a toothpick to draw stars on the glass, using the egg white as paint. Spread ⅛ cup sugar on a paper plate. Roll "painted" glasses in sugar. Let dry. In a darkened room, shine flashlights on the sparkly glasses as you drink juice.

More ideas: www.astroleague.org

Kindergarten Day

In 1837 Friedrich Froebel began the first kindergarten in Germany. He saw the importance of encouraging young children to play games and learn in a stimulating environment. Celebrate his birthday by becoming a kid again. (Or borrow a kindergartner if you don't have one.)

Celebrate with Fun

- Every kid loves crawling through a "giant spiderweb." Get a ball of yarn to make a web. Attach 1 end of the yarn to a table leg or sturdy piece of furniture. Slowly unwind the yarn, wrapping it in and out of objects in the room to create a giant spiderweb. After the web is complete, invite a kindergartner (or any willing child) to crawl through the web. Cleanup is easy. Simply reroll the yarn and your spiderweb is gone.

- Play the "Direction Game" to give your favorite kindergartner the constant movement they need and also practice in following directions—while you simply sit in your favorite chair! The child races through the house. Whisper a basic direction to your child like "Go to the refrigerator and jump up and down 3 times." (Whispering adds to the fun.) Make commands more complicated if the child is older, like "Touch the kitchen table, hop to the couch, then go upstairs and bring me a dirty sock." Children enjoy showing off their ability to follow directions.

- Play "Indoor Baseball" with equipment a kindergartner can help make. Roll a section of newspaper into a tube. Wrap masking tape around it to form a bat. Crumple up a wad of newspaper and you have everything needed to play indoor baseball with your favorite kindergartner.

- Tell your kindergartner why he or she is so special to you.

Celebrate with Crafts

Make a paper plate puppet. Let your child decorate solid-colored paper plates. Scraps of yarn glued around the edges form a mane for a lion. A red-painted nose could be the start of a clown face. When finished, attach a paint stick for a handle.

Celebrate with Food

Freeze several pieces of white bread. Frozen bread makes it easier for your children to spread on peanut butter and jelly. Let them use a cookie cutter to cut the bread in a fun shape. By the time you pour a glass of milk, the bread will be thawed so they can enjoy tasty sandwiches they made themselves!

School Librarian Day

Children simply assume their school library will be stocked with interesting books. Take time to celebrate the hard work of your school librarian.

Celebrate with Fun

- Use the school intercom to announce that it is School Librarian Day. Publicly thank your librarian for his or her work at making the library an inviting place.

- Take children to a high school or college library to see school librarians in a different setting. Most kids will marvel at the size of a college library compared to their school library.

- Gather a group of volunteer parents who offer their services for an hour or two. Your school librarian will be thrilled to have volunteers to spruce up bulletin boards or repair damaged books.

- Take a collection from parents and staff to buy your school librarian a gift certificate at a bookstore. Make a stipulation that the certificate is for personal books—not books for the school library.

- Encourage your children to say a special "Thank you" to the school librarian.

- Start a program in which children donate a book to the school library on their birthday.

- Secretly take a few pictures of the school librarian. Display the pictures on a special "Thank you, Mrs. Jackson!" bulletin board the whole school sees.

Celebrate with Crafts

Purchase a large piece of colored poster board. Fold it in half to form the cover of a "book." Cut butcher paper to form 4 to 6 "pages" inside the cover. Have an adult use a pointed Phillips screwdriver to poke 5 or 6 holes in the crease of the book. Weave a ribbon in and out of the holes to hold the pages together. Take your giant book to different classrooms so children and teachers can write words of thanks to the school librarian. Let kindergarten students decorate the cover.

Celebrate with Food

Find an artistic parent to bake a sheet cake and decorate it to look like the cover of your librarian's favorite book. It's not often you decorate a cake to look like *War and Peace!*

More ideas: www.iasl-slo.org/dayinthelife5.html

Jellybean Day

Ronald Reagan kept a jar of jellybeans on his desk at all times. Celebrate today by sampling a variety of jellybean flavors.

Celebrate with Fun

- Set out different-flavored jellybeans. Blindfold people to see if they can guess the flavors by taste alone. It's sometimes hard to distinguish between sour apple and grapefruit.
- Come up with your own flavor of jellybean. Draw an advertisement showing the color and describing the flavor. Who wouldn't want to eat a popcorn-flavored mango jellybean?
- Some brands of jellybeans include charts to create specific flavors. If you want root-beer-float flavor, you need 2 vanilla, 2 root beer, and 1 soda jellybean in your mouth. As you chew, the flavors blend to create a new taste sensation. See what flavor you create by mixing 2 blueberry, 1 watermelon, and 1 chocolate jellybean. Chocolate fruit pie?
- Try your skill at sleight of hand. Set 3 cups upside down on a table. Show everyone that you are hiding 1 jellybean under a cup. Move quickly to slide the cups back and forth, in and out to confuse the spectators. Can they keep track of which cup hides the jellybean?

Celebrate with Crafts

Make jellybean jars for gifts. Paint several baby food jar lids a solid color. Let paint dry. Glue jellybeans on the lids with craft glue. Make a distinct pattern or glue the candy randomly. Cover with a coat of decoupage to preserve the jellybeans. Fill the jars with more jellybeans, put the lids on, and hand out to friends.

Spread some jellybeans on the table. After everyone has eaten a few, pass out toothpicks. Let everyone make colorful sculptures using jellybeans and toothpicks. Some of the sculptures might even look like models of DNA.

Celebrate with Food

Ever consider making jellybean bread? Mix up a batch of your favorite white bread dough. (Use a bread machine if you like.) During the last few minutes of kneading, add 1 cup jellybeans. Bake as usual. You'll enjoy multiflavored bread.

Create some custom-made jellybeans. Cut several flavors of jellybeans in half. Press half a strawberry jellybean with half a grape jellybean. They'll stick together to give you a totally new taste sensation.

Earth Day

In 1970 the first Earth Day celebration was named "Give Earth a Chance." The day stressed the importance of improving the quality of our air, water, and living environment. Do what you can to make Earth a better place today.

Celebrate with Fun

- An important part of Earth Day is learning about recycling. Set up an Earth Day carnival using recycled items. Try these ideas for game booths: (1) Stack empty cans and knock down with a ball. (2) Cut 3 semicircles from a box bottom and give the holes point values of 5, 10, and 20. Set the box on the ground upside down. Roll a ball into the semicircles and try to collect the most points. (3) Place 2 Ping-Pong balls on the floor. Let players blow through empty cardboard tubes to push the balls across the finish line. (4) Stuff old socks with newspapers. Tie and use for beanbags at a beanbag-toss booth. (5) Use empty pop bottles for a recyclable bowling game. Children knock down the bottles with a ball.

- Walk through the neighborhood and pick up litter. Encourage neighbors to pick up any trash too. You can soon have a litter-free neighborhood.

- Purchase a new plant to add some natural beauty to your house.

- Encourage family members to turn off the water when brushing their teeth. Try to take shorter showers to save water.

- Show children how food is packaged with excess packaging. Try purchasing items in bulk rather than individually.

Celebrate with Crafts

Make a giant dinosaur out of cardboard boxes of various sizes. Shape your dinosaur by stacking boxes in various ways. When you have a design you like, glue the boxes in place. Cut some boxes apart to form smaller body parts. Paint your masterpiece in realistic or whimsical colors. Donate it to a preschool or kindergarten.

Celebrate with Food

Since Earth Day is about recycling and saving Earth's resources, clean out the refrigerator and eat leftovers!

Purchase food that contains a minimum of packaging. Bring your own plastic bag to hold the broccoli and other vegetables you buy.

More ideas: www.earthdayweb.org and www.planetpals.com

Spring Cleaning Day

APRIL 24 (or pick any day in April)

Is your house a bit dusty and cluttered? Now that spring is here, spend the day cleaning up inside and out so that you'll have more time afterward to plant spring flowers.

Celebrate with Fun

- Give your children a new Slinky today. Tell them everyone is going to "Spring into Action" and help with spring cleaning.

- Assign children job-related titles. Instead of saying, "Jeff, please put the laundry away," tell Jeff he is the official Laundry Lieutenant in charge of getting clothes neatly put away. Then you have the Auto Valet who vacuums and washes the car and the Dynamite Duster who removes dust bunnies. Have children think of other titles for their jobs.

- At school, when the teacher announces, "Cleanup time!" the class automatically begins putting away books and supplies. Develop a code word or song to let children know it's time to get the house in order. Threaten to sing the cleanup song if they don't start picking up toys. Or use the standard cleanup song: "Clean up, clean up, everybody everywhere. Clean up, clean up, everybody do your share."

- Select 1 task per person to be done in every room, whether a thorough dusting or vacuuming that includes the corners.

- Post a special job chart listing ways children can earn money for extra cleaning duties: Vacuum couch cushions—50 cents; sweep garage—1 dollar; clean Rufus's doghouse—75 cents; rake leaves—75 cents.

- Older children can use a hair dryer to blow off dust on your silk plants.

Celebrate with Crafts

Collect all the craft items in the house. Do your children really need 18 bottles of glue? Reduce, Recycle, or Reuse! Pour half-empty bottles of glue in 1 larger container. Throw out brushes with hard bristles. Donate duplicate markers and scissors.

Celebrate with Food

Since the house feels cleaner, plan a meal to help the family feel "cleaner" inside. Serve a meal with fresh fruit and vegetables. Let children help cut up fruit for a fruit salad. Stir-fry vegetables and serve with brown rice. For a surprise, serve an unusual juice like apricot nectar or strawberry kiwi.

Penguin Day

Penguin Day actually began at the Naval Weapons Center in Ridgecrest, California. Continue the tradition by honoring penguins today.

Celebrate with Fun

- Dress up in black and white today. White shirts, black pants, and a red bow tie to add that festive touch.
- Play penguin waddle. Find a foam ball to hold between your knees. Have relay races to see who can reach the finish line by waddling the fastest.
- Tell a few penguin jokes: Why do penguins sit on marshmallows? (So they don't fall into the hot chocolate.)
- Why are penguins popular on the Internet? (Because they have web feet.)
- Emperor penguin "fathers" take charge of their eggs. They keep the eggs warm for 2 months by balancing on the eggs. See if you have any penguin balancers at your house. Tightly roll up a pillow and bind it with rubber bands. Ask family members to balance on their pretend eggs. Can anyone balance for 2 minutes?
- Penguins are the only migratory birds that don't fly. Instead, they swim. Take the family swimming at the local pool.
- With a little imagination, bowling pins look like wobbling penguins. If you can't go swimming, go bowling and knock over a few wooden penguins.

Celebrate with Crafts

It's easy to make a penguin finger puppet out of an empty upside-down film canister. Use white correction fluid to draw a white chest on the penguin canister. Glue on 2 small wiggle eyes and put 2 fingers inside the canister.

Trace around your bare foot and take a good look at the shape. The heel is the head of a penguin's profile! Add a beak and 1 eye. Down by your toe area, draw 2 penguin feet to complete your penguin.

Celebrate with Food

Set out a penguin black-and-white smorgasbord today. Naturally, you'll serve Oreo cookies with milk. Then set out bowls of mashed potatoes, black-eyed peas, chocolate pudding, black licorice, rice, and just for good measure, some white and some dark chocolate.

National Bird Day

Today's special day is in honor of James Audubon, born on April 26, 1785. He is known for his amazingly realistic watercolors of birds.

Celebrate with Fun

- You've probably marveled at the intricacies of a bird's nest. See if your children can make a nest from small twigs and grasses you've collected. Here's the catch! They can only use 1 hand as their "beak" to construct their nest.

- Laugh yourself silly with these bird jokes. What do you give a sick bird? (Tweetment) Where does a 500-lb. canary sit? (Anywhere she wants) Why do hummingbirds hum? (Because they forgot the words)

- Find out your official state bird. See if you can spot it around your house.

- Consider joining the Audubon Society. They have over 560,000 members and manage 150,000 acres of critical habitat. The organization also offers Audubon activities for children. 212-979-3000.

- Look up amazing facts about birds. What is the fastest-running bird? (Ostrich) What is the fastest flying bird? (Peregrine falcon) What do you call someone who studies birds? (Ornithologist) Which bird lays the largest egg? (Ostrich)

- Get a copy of a bird identification book, preferably one by John Audubon. Watch for birds in your area and compare them with the pictures in the book. Look at size, speed of flight, shape, and feeding patterns to identify the birds.

Celebrate with Crafts

Instead of making a craft for yourself, make a treat for the birds. Mix 1 cup suet (available from your store's meat department) with 1½ cups cornmeal and ½ cup chopped dried fruits. Spread greasy mixture inside and around several pinecones. Hang them from trees so birds have a nutritious meal.

Celebrate with Food

Mix up a batch of edible bird nests. Line each section of a muffin tin with waxed paper. This gives shape to your nests. Melt 1 cup chocolate or peanut butter chips in the microwave. Heat for 60 seconds, stir, then heat for 20 more seconds if chocolate hasn't yet melted. Mix chocolate with 1½ cups puffed cereal. Spread around bottom and edges of muffin tin sections. Refrigerate for 1 hour. Remove from wax paper and add 2 or 3 small candy eggs to each nest.

More ideas: www.audubon.org

135

Tell a Story Day

It might be hard for your children to comprehend that storytelling was a popular pastime before television. Revive this classic form of entertainment.

Celebrate with Fun

- Take turns reading a favorite children's storybook with different accents or as different characters. *Little Red Riding Hood* takes on new meaning when told by someone pretending to be Barney the Dinosaur. Pretend you are doing a dramatic reading of *Joseph and the Amazing Technicolor Dreamcoat* on the radio with thousands of people listening.

- Collect assorted items like a sock, teacup, baseball, and toothbrush in a bag. Select someone to start telling a made-up story. After a few sentences, the person reaches into the bag and pulls out an item. Now he or she has to incorporate that item into the plot. After a few minutes, select another person to continue the story with another item from the bag.

- Have a "Tall Tales" contest. Ask a question like "Why does Grandma always mix buttermilk in her mashed potatoes?" or "How do the Empire State Building windows get washed?" Take turns telling the most outlandish stories possible. Perhaps a company has thousands of trained flies with tiny rags on their feet. The flies polish the windows of the building!

- Invite an elderly neighbor or relative to tell stories about their childhood.

- If Grandma lives too far away to visit, call ahead so she can prepare a story. Have children call her and listen to her story on the phone.

- Bring out a Bible story book. Read the story directly from the Bible, then read a children's book embellishing the same story.

Celebrate with Crafts

Forget store-bought or e-books—construct simple books using notebook paper for pages and construction paper for the covers. Give everyone time to write a story and draw pictures in their books. Younger children can dictate their story to an adult. When the award-winning stories are done, read them to each other. Be sure to show the audience the pictures!

Celebrate with Food

Pick a story or chapter from a book to read out loud. Add to the atmosphere by serving food related to the story. If reading *Little House on the Prairie*, serve cornbread. Perhaps you'll read *Goldilocks and the Three Bears* at breakfast. Serve porridge, of course! How about reading *If You Give a Mouse a Cookie* while eating fresh-baked cookies?

International Walk Day

Exercise your body while spending time with your family. Use this day as a starting point for a regular low-cost exercise program.

Celebrate with Fun

- Celebrate today in the obvious way—take a walk. Take a family walk before breakfast. Okay, if you're not that dedicated, take a walk after dinner. Take time to notice bugs on the ground or spring flowers blooming.

- Decide how far you'll go and estimate how long it will take. Tomorrow walk the same distance, but pick up the pace to cover the length faster.

- Give young children a shape cut from paper. On your walk, help them find items matching their shape. Look for round tires or square windows.

- Try a prayer walk. As you walk your neighborhood, pray for people as you pass their homes. If you pass a grocery store, thank God for fresh fruit. Thank him for healthy bodies able to walk. Notice the beauty of nature and acknowledge God's creation.

- If attempting longer hikes, make sure children have comfortable shoes. Nothing puts a damper on the hiking spirit like blisters on little feet.

- If you're feeling unmotivated, think about your dog needing exercise too! Set a goal of taking him for a daily walk. Tell him your plan so you'll feel guilty if you stay home when he wants to bound through the park!

- On longer hikes, try some delayed gratification with younger children. Tell them, "Let's hike to that fallen tree. Then we'll open the candy bar." "Just get over the hill, and then Dad will sing a solo of 'The Bear Went over the Mountain.'" Reaching smaller goals helps children gain the sense of accomplishment that comes with achieving a major goal. When all else fails, sing the never-ending "99 Bottles of Pop on the Wall" . . .

Celebrate with Crafts

All serious hikers need a professional walking stick. Make one for each family member. Collect sturdy sticks and cut waist high to fit each person. Sand until smooth and paint a solid color. Add painted designs or patterns. You might turn your walking stick into a giant snake. Seal with varnish.

Celebrate with Food

Mix together some hiker's gorp to munch during your strenuous walk around the block—1 cup each raisins, peanuts, chocolate chips, dried cereal, sunflower seeds, or other easy-to-eat foods. Store in resealable plastic bags for easy munching.

MAY

National Bike Month
National Book Month
National Strawberry Month
National Egg Month
National Physical Fitness and Sports Month

Weeks to Celebrate

1st Week • National Kids Fitness Week
1st Full Week • Be Kind to Animals Week
1st Week • Safe Kids Week
1st Full Week • National Pet Week
Last Week • National Backyard Games Week

Days to Celebrate

Tuesday of First Full Week • National Teacher Day
1st Thursday • National Day of Prayer
2nd Sunday • Mother's Day
2nd Thursday • Read-In Day
3rd Friday • National Bike to Work Day
Last Monday • Memorial Day
Last Tues/Wed • National Geographic Bee Finals

1 May Day
1 Mother Goose Day
5 Cinco De Mayo
12 Limerick Day
15 National Self-Esteem Day
17 Anniversary of "Sue's" Exhibition
19 Boys and Girls Clubs of America Founded
23 Barney the Purple Dinosaur's Birthday
25 Arthur's Anniversary
27 Adhesive Tape Patented
28 Sierra Club Founded
29 Senior Citizens Day

National Bike Month

As the weather improves, tune up your bikes and start riding again. The exercise and companionship is an easy way to enjoy family fun.

Celebrate with Fun

- Go to a bike store and check out some high-speed, high-cost bikes just for fun. See the bikes professionals use that cost thousands of dollars. Then go home and ride your Schwinn.

- Read a magazine article or book about Lance Armstrong's incredible comeback from cancer. Discuss with your children how he overcame a tragedy by bike riding.

- How many parts of a bike can you name? Find a picture identifying the various components of a bike and see how many your family can name.

- Call local bike shops to see if they'll give a "Family Bike Tune-up" discount if you bring all the bikes in for a tune-up and safety inspection.

- Show your children how you had fun in the good old days before Nintendo and the Internet. Use clothespins to attach playing cards to the spokes of their bike wheels. As children ride their bikes, the cards make a clicking sound once considered very "cool."

- Set up a bike rodeo with different events for your children and their friends. Who can ride from start to finish line the slowest—without putting their feet down? Place paper cups upside down in a random pattern. Place Ping-Pong balls on the cups. Who can weave in and out without disturbing the balls? Draw a wavy chalk line. Who can ride directly on the line? Sponsor a bike-decorating contest. Who can be the most creative using streamers and balloons?

Celebrate with Crafts

Cut out magazine pictures of animals and glue them on individual pieces of paper. Randomly pass out the pictures so family members can design a bike to fit the animal's body. How do you make a bike a snake can ride? What form of bike does a kangaroo need? Let your imagination go beyond 2 wheels and a handlebar.

Celebrate with Food

Bake a round layer cake. This forms the base for your bike wheel. Frost with a light-colored frosting. Place a vanilla wafer or other round cookie in the center. Cut pieces of red or black licorice to form the spokes of the wheel, radiating out from the center of the cookie.

More ideas: www.bikeleague.org; www.bikemonth.com

National Book Month

Books transform people's lives. A story, poem, or bit of advice can have a major impact on someone. Spend this month celebrating the magic of books.

Celebrate with Fun

- Just for fun, estimate how many books you have in the house. Go through and count. Were you close?

- Have everyone do a mini–book report. Select your all-time favorite and share the plot with your family. Why is it special to you? When did you first read it? If you are theatrical, dress up as a character from the book.

- Collect all the books you can bear to sell. Check under children's beds for long-lost books they've outgrown. Take the books to a used bookstore to sell. Some stores give you immediate credit. Let family members select new books to take home. Take the family to a bookstore and look at the thousands of new books. Find some children's books with pop-ups, scratch-and-sniff pages, or other unusual features. Buy one to celebrate this special month.

- Help children see the Bible as the most important book in their lives. Purchase a book on family devotions and use it! This month read sections of the Bible and have creative family devotions. Use props or do some role playing to help children see the Bible as a blueprint for how we should live our lives.

Celebrate with Crafts

Make homemade bookmarks. Cut construction paper or light cardboard into 2″ x 7″ strips. Punch 5 or 6 holes in the top and tie a 6-inch strip of ribbon or yarn to each hole, making a fringed top. Decorate the bookmark with rubber stamps. Use markers to color in and around the stamped pictures. Use the bookmarks as you read, read, read!

Make personal bookmarks with photographs of your dog, family, and friends. Glue the photos to bookmark strips as above and take to a print shop for inexpensive lamination.

Celebrate with Food

Pretend you're in a "Book Reviewers Club." Everyone reads a new book and prepares a short written review, then rates the book on a scale of 1–5 (with 5 being an all-time favorite). Younger children can draw pictures about the book. Eating at a restaurant while sharing your reviews and ratings makes reviewing books an extra-special event.

More ideas: www.nationalbook.org

National Strawberry Month

Ahhh, the joy of biting into a sweet strawberry and feeling the juice dribble down your chin. As summer begins, enjoy the delicious taste of strawberries all month.

Celebrate with Fun

- Set out several strawberries in various sizes. Do a taste test. Are larger strawberries as sweet as smaller ones?

- Squeeze a few strawberries in a small bowl. Use the red juice as paint. Dip a paintbrush in the strawberry juice and paint a picture.

- Here's a picking tip from the professionals: Try to keep the green "cap" attached. Wash strawberries, then remove the cap. If the green cap is removed first, water gets inside the strawberry and dilutes the sweet taste. Pick strawberries together as a family.

- Find a sunny spot in which to grow your own strawberries. Some late-bearing plants can be planted in May to produce berries up until late September.

Celebrate with Crafts

Use a green plastic strawberry basket to make a hot air balloon. Blow up a large red balloon and tie the end. Attach 4 ribbons, about 12 inches each, to the tied end of the balloon. Tie the loose ribbon ends to each corner of the plastic strawberry basket. You now have a strawberry hot air balloon.

Make some long-lasting strawberries. Paint walnuts with red paint. Do you notice how the shape and "bumps" on a walnut look like a strawberry? Use green paint to color the wider end of the walnut, which looks like the stem. Take a fine-tipped black marker and make tiny dots for strawberry seeds. If you want, cut out small leaves from green felt to glue on top of your very sturdy strawberry. Set your strawberries out on a decorative plate for summer-long freshness.

Celebrate with Food

- Naturally you'll want to make strawberry shortcake for dessert. Use different items as a base for the shortcake, like doughnuts, angel food cake, pound cake, Twinkies, ice cream, or granola. Top with sliced strawberries.

- Make a strawberry milkshake: Mix 1 cup milk, ½ cup ice cream, and ½ cup strawberries in a blender on medium speed until thick and smooth.

More ideas: www.heb.com/mealtime/celeb-strawberries.jsp

National Egg Month

This entire month is dedicated to eggs. Whether you eat them or decorate them, find some way to celebrate eggs!

Celebrate with Fun

- Try the standard picnic activity—an egg toss. Stand 4 feet from a partner and toss a raw egg back and forth. (For obvious reasons, do this outside!) After 1 toss, take 1 step backward. Toss again, taking another step backward every time a catch is made. Keep going until a person or the sidewalk is covered with a runny egg.

- Try the relay race in which participants run holding a spoon containing a raw egg. Can any team make it to the finish line without the egg falling off?

- Know how to tell a raw egg from a hard-boiled egg? Spin the egg on a flat surface. If it wobbles, it's raw. A boiled egg will spin fairly smoothly.

- Why dye eggs only at Easter? Keep hard-boiled colored eggs in the fridge for a handy snack. Simply mix one cup very hot water with 1 tsp. vinegar and a few drops food coloring. Let eggs sit in dye for several minutes.

- Instead of cracking eggs on the countertop for scrambled eggs, get kids involved by letting them blow the slimy eggs out of a hole in the shell. Using a pushpin or large paper clip, gently poke 2 holes in each end of the egg. Hold over a bowl and blow hard! Kids love watching eggs plop into the bowl. (For safety reasons, wash hands thoroughly afterward.)

Celebrate with Crafts

Decorate a terra-cotta flowerpot with crushed eggshells. Hard-boil several eggs and dye various colors. Peel eggs for your egg salad sandwich and set each color shell in a bowl. Break shell into tiny pieces and glue on the flowerpot for a mosaic effect. Make distinct designs with the separate colors or mix pieces in a random pattern. When eggshells are dry, plant a flower in the pot.

Celebrate with Food

Make deviled eggs the easy way. After hard-boiling 6 eggs, let cool and then peel. Cut eggs in half and gently spoon out yolks. Mix yolks with ½ cup mayonnaise and ½ tsp. salt in a plastic resealable bag. "Smoosh" the bag to mix well. Cut a small slit in the corner of the bag and neatly squeeze the mixture out of the bag into the hollow egg whites.

More ideas: www.aeb.org/recipes/natl-egg

143

National Physical Fitness and Sports Month

Summer's approaching! Get ready for outdoor fun by becoming more physically active. Use this month to encourage family fitness.

Celebrate with Fun

- Tell your children about your years in high school PE classes. Pretend to be a "tough" PE teacher and lead everyone in jumping jacks and the ever-popular squat thrusts.

- Call a local gym to see if they offer free introductory programs. Many facilities let you participate in an activity on a trial basis. You might be able to take the family to an exercise class or use their pool.

- Make a rule that for this month, "commercials mean movement." Anytime a commercial appears, everyone has to jump up and begin jogging in place or running up and down the hall. No one sits down until the actual program begins.

- Invite children to a game of miniature golf by giving them a golf ball with a note saying, "Be ready at 3 for a crazy game of miniature golf." Afterward have cookies with "tee."

- Plan a family sports workshop. Each person leads in a specific sport. Jeff might teach the family to dribble a soccer ball. Maybe Mom demonstrates her synchronized swimming talents. Four-year-old Sammy can show how to chase a ball that he throws in the park.

- Take the family to a professional sports game. The excitement of a large stadium, popcorn vendors, and cheerleaders gives children a new excitement about sports. Also attend a high school baseball or soccer game. Children benefit from seeing youth involved in sports programs.

Celebrate with Crafts

Try making some tennis ball puppets. Have an adult cut a 2-inch slit in an old tennis ball. This becomes the puppet's mouth. Glue on buttons or wiggle eyes plus yarn for hair. Hold the puppet and gently squeeze the side, making the mouth move. Take turns having puppets direct the rest of the family in exercises.

Celebrate with Food

Bake cupcakes and frost with regular frosting. Give children tubes of gel frosting to decorate their cupcakes to look like a soccer ball, baseball, or basketball.

National Kids Fitness Week

Children are naturally active, so here's your chance to celebrate physical fitness with them. Encourage them to wear comfortable clothing this week. Set an example by wearing your jogging suit and sweatbands even if you are just reading the newspaper.

Celebrate with Fun

- Feat of Fitness: Set up charts and list who jumps the highest, does a cartwheel, or hula-hoops the longest. Make as many categories as necessary so every child excels in at least one event.

- Place 3 tape or chalk lines on the ground 20 feet apart. Label 1, 2, and 3. Everyone stands on line number 1. Yell "Line number 3!" Everyone runs to line 3. Then quickly yell out another number. Children exercise as they run between the lines. No one is "out" if they run to the wrong line. Play until they lose interest.

- If you have young (or uninhibited) children, try this: Have children do the actions that go along with this song sung to the tune of "The Farmer in the Dell": "We are jumping all around, We are jumping all around, In the air and on the ground, We are jumping all around. We are walking all around, We are walking all around, Waving our hands very fast, We are walking all around. We are crawling all around, We are crawling all around, Crawling backward very fast, We are crawling all around."

Celebrate with Crafts

Professional athletes use sweatbands on their wrists, so why not your family? Find old tube socks with holes in the feet. Cut ribbed top sections into 3-inch strips. Stretch strips around a large can so they're taut. Use fabric puff paint to decorate them. Let paint dry. Wear bands during your next workout.

Celebrate with Food

For healthy hearts, discuss good nutrition. Place various fruits, whole-grain breads, and vegetables in individual plastic bags. Children pick strips of paper from a hat that ask them to do an activity. One might say, "Touch your toes 5 times," another, "Run in place 10 seconds." After completing the task, they choose their snack bags.

Pack snacks in paper bags and take a fitness walk to a nearby park to eat. If no park is nearby, walk around the block several times in a zigzag pattern and eat snacks in an outside area away from your house.

Be Kind to Animals Week

You probably love and adore your family pet. Spend a week helping animals who may not have as comfortable a life as your little Pugsy.

Celebrate with Fun

- Take a family portrait with all your pets and hang it in the family room as a reminder of how special pets are.
- Make a flyer announcing "Be Kind to Animals Week." Have children brainstorm ways to show kindness, like 1) Make sure your pet always has fresh water. 2) Exercise your pet. 3) Report neglected or mistreated animals. 4) Keep seeds in the bird feeder year-round. 5) Make sure dogs and cats are spayed or neutered. (This may require an explanation for younger children!) Distribute flyers around the neighborhood, at the library, and at school.
- Visit a local animal shelter so children see what happens to neglected animals. See if the shelter needs help or needs newspapers to line cages or old towels for grooming. (Ask a local hotel to donate worn-out towels.) One family collected old tennis balls from the country club so dogs could play.
- Don't have a family pet? Visit a pet store to decide if a puppy, goldfish, or iguana might be the perfect pet to fit your family's lifestyle.
- Does your local zoo have an "Adopt an Animal" program? For a small monthly fee, you can adopt a gorilla or giraffe. No, you can't bring it home with you! Your donation goes toward its care. You'll receive an adoption certificate and picture of your cuddly 1,200-pound rhinoceros.

Celebrate with Crafts

Purchase a solid-colored collar. Decorate it using puff paint. Write your pet's name, surrounded by hearts and polka dots. Decorate a matching leash for a complete new "outfit."

Make a placemat to keep the floor around your pet's food bowl clean. Cut lightweight cardboard to the size you need. Glue pictures of your pet and family members on it and have it laminated for durability.

More ideas: www.americanhumane.org

Celebrate with Food

Conduct a pet food drive. Many communities offer pet food banks for low-income pet owners. With adult supervision, take a wagon (or a wheelbarrow!) and go door-to-door to people you know own pets. Ask them to make a donation. After your wagon is full, take the food to the pet food bank or a local shelter.

Safe Kids Week

Keeping children safe is a full-time occupation for parents. Somehow they manage to get themselves into situations in which they could get hurt. Here's a week to make a conscious effort to teach children basic survival skills.

Celebrate with Fun

- If your child's clothes catch on fire, it's important they know how to "Stop, Drop, and Roll." Tape a few pieces of red or yellow paper to your child's clothing. When you yell, "Your clothes are on fire!" he should drop to the ground and roll several times until the paper falls off.

- Here's where the fun starts. Teach your dog to "Stop, Drop, and Roll." Train your dog to come when called. As you say "Stop," your dog should stop walking until you say "Drop." Rover lies down and waits for your command to "Roll over." See, you've just trained a dog to help you celebrate Safe Kids Week.

- Plan a mock fire drill. First, discuss with your family where everyone needs to meet in case of a fire. Select an easy-to-reach location away from the house. Remind children not to go back for a favorite toy or the family pet. Practice yelling "Fire!" and then meet at the designated location. Make sure younger children realize this is a pretend drill. Let them know the chance of a fire in the house is very slim.

- Let children help test the smoke detectors. Push the test button (while covering your ears). If it squeals loudly, rest assured the smoke detector is working. If no squeal, replace the batteries!

- Teach young children how to call 911 in case of an emergency. Write the numbers next to each phone in the house.

Celebrate with Crafts

Purchase a piece of colored poster board. Give family members 4″ x 6″ index cards, colored if possible. Each person uses the cards to write a safety rule like "Always wear a bike helmet" or "Don't forget to buckle up." Glue cards on poster board. Display and review often.

Celebrate with Food

Discussing all these safety issues calls for some snack foods. Collect 3 or 4 bike helmets and line them with aluminum foil. Serve popcorn in the helmets. Discuss your safety poster while munching on popcorn.

More ideas: Safe Kids Campaign 202-939-4993; www.safekids.org/state_display.cfm

National Pet Week

Some are cute, some slobber, and some simply swim around. No matter what they do, we love our pets!

Celebrate with Fun

- Whether you have a dog, cat, or hamster, celebrate with a family group hug around your pet. (It might be difficult if your pet is a guppy!)
- Design some unusual pet equipment. How about making a frog trampoline? Try designing a new type of birdcage. Use your imagination.
- Make sure your pets have identification on their collars. (Unless you have a pet tadpole.) Check too whether the fit is right. Sometimes puppies grow so fast you don't notice their collars are getting too tight.
- Teach your pet a new trick. Find a book on training a dog or cat and follow the directions. Maybe you'll get your cat to actually come when you call her.
- Call the local pet shop and ask if pets are permitted in the store. Many pet shops now encourage owners to wander the store with their leashed pets. Take your pet on a "field trip" to the store. Check out the new pet treats or grooming supplies.
- Ask the local 4-H organization about their animal-related programs. Your children might enjoy learning about rabbits or setting up an aquarium. Some 4-H groups even have clubs made up of kids with pet tarantulas!
- Assign children to groom your dog or cat on a regular basis. This helps the animal feel better and cuts down on pet hair on furniture. After brushing your pet, remove the pet hair from the brush and release in the yard. Birds use the hair to line their nests.

Celebrate with Crafts

Make a diorama about your ideal pet. Do kids want a horse? A pet whale? In a box, set up a "scene" depicting your pet's habitat. Horse lovers can make a fence out of craft sticks to corral their steed.

Celebrate with Food

Looking for a treat for your cat? How about making a special sardine soufflé? Pour 2 cans of sardines in a bowl, including the juice. Use a fork to smash the fish into tiny pieces. Add ⅔ cup cooked rice and ¼ cup chopped parsley. Mix well and form into small balls. Serve to your delighted cat. Yum-yum!

National Backyard Games Week

Enjoy the beginning of spring by getting outside and playing games. Invite the neighbors over for even more fun.

Celebrate with Fun

- Begin with an old-fashioned game of Hide and Seek. You might be surprised to know some kids have never played this classic game!

- Divide into groups of 3. Two children hold hands to make a safe "cage." The third child is a diver who stands inside the cage. The diver wants to avoid any sharks swimming around. Another child is "It" and calls out, "Switch cages!" All the divers scurry to get inside another cage. The sharks (more children) can tag any diver outside a cage. Switch roles after a while so everyone has a chance to be a shark, diver, or cage.

- Another all-time favorite involves the classic "Clothes Relay." Divide into teams of 4 or 5. The teams line up 20 feet from the finish line. On "Go!" the first player on each team runs to the finish line and puts on several items of loose clothing. They race back to tag their partners and remove the extra clothes. The game continues until everyone has had a chance to run wearing baggy clothes.

- Borrow several Twister games and tape the plastic sheets together. Play Twister with a large group on the combined Twister "dot" sheet.

Celebrate with Crafts

Your group will be so excited playing games, it would be hard to get them to settle down and do a craft project. Play another game instead!

Celebrate with Food

After all the running, cool down with root beer floats. If you don't like root beer, make some refreshing lemon-lime soda. Mix 2 Tbs. lemon juice, 1 Tbs. lime juice, 1 can apple juice concentrate, 1 cup soda water, and 3 cups ice cubes. Stir well.

For a great backyard snack to go with your floats, bake enough cupcakes so everyone gets one. Provide different colors of frosting along with tiny candies and sprinkles. After all the cupcakes are decorated, display them for the entire group—then eat.

More ideas: www.patchproducts.com

149

National Teacher Day

Use this day to honor the dedicated teachers in your life. Find ways to show your appreciation for the hard work they do in educating children.

Celebrate with Fun

- Be traditional and have children give their teachers a shiny red apple. Then be untraditional and give each teacher a fresh apple pie.

- Teachers often use their own money buying extras for the classroom. Collect money from parents and buy a gift certificate to an educational supply store. Give another gift certificate stating that the next time it rains 2 days in a row, you (or other parents) will come in during recess and play games or lead activities while kids are cooped up inside.

- Make your kids' teachers feel extra special today. Arrange a grand entrance as they arrive at school. Coordinate parents to be in the parking lot with cameras. Act like paparazzi and yell, "Mr. Johnson, can we get your picture please?" Have red carpet placed in front of the classroom doors. Ask kids to swarm their teachers and beg for autographs. This is one morning the teachers won't forget!

- Have your children make a "Top Ten" list about why their teacher is the best. Type it on fancy parchment paper and display it where other parents and staff can see the list.

- Give a personal, handwritten note to your child's teacher. List specific ways your child has benefited from being in the teacher's class.

Celebrate with Crafts

Instead of having your child make a cute but misshapen pencil holder for her teacher, do something practical. (After all, teachers see children's artwork on a daily basis.) Purchase some art supplies for the classroom that aren't normally provided like watercolor crayons, special origami paper, or clay that hardens into pencil erasers.

Celebrate with Food

Make customized chocolate for your favorite teacher. Buy candy bars with a smooth surface (Hershey bars or 3 Musketeers). Unwrap candy. Heat 1 cup white chocolate or peanut butter chips in microwave 60–90 seconds, checking frequently. Pour melted chips into a plastic sandwich bag. Snip off a corner and use the bag to let children "write" their teacher's name on the candy bars. Write other slogans like "The Best!" and "Great Teacher!" Wrap in clear plastic wrap.

More ideas: www.nea.org/teacherday

National Day of Prayer

In 1952 the National Day of Prayer was signed into law by President Truman. Shirley Dobson has been chairperson of the event since 1991. Over 40,000 activities are held nationwide to celebrate this day.

Celebrate with Fun

- Ask your pastor for the names of missionaries your church supports. Display a map of the world and locate where each missionary is assigned. Pray for the missionaries and the people in their countries.

- Find a copy of *The Prayer of Jabez for Kids*. Read it together and discuss the implications.

- Find pictures of family, friends, and people you haven't seen in years. Set aside a few pictures as a reminder to pray for these people.

- Call or e-mail your pastor and ask, "How can we pray for you today?" Also pray for prayer requests members have called in to your church.

- Pray for your children's teachers today. These dedicated men and women are with your children 6–8 hours every day. Even if they are not Christians, let them know you are praying for them.

- Try an "ABC's of Thankfulness" game. Discuss how we should thank God for our blessings. Begin with the letter A and say, "I'm thankful that God gave us Apples." The next person says, "I'm glad God gave us Bathtubs." Keep going until you end by thanking God for Zebras.

- Purchase a number of blank postcards at the post office. Send notes to family and friends to tell them you prayed for them today. Ask younger children to decorate the postcards.

Celebrate with Crafts

Make bookmarks for your Bible with an inexpensive sheet of plastic canvas available at craft stores. Cut plastic in a cross shape about 8" high by 4" wide. Help children thread embroidery floss through a wide-eyed needle. Let them experiment "sewing" in and out of the canvas and create borders or tiny Xs. When design is complete, tie a knot in the end of the floss. These sturdy bookmarks last forever!

Celebrate with Food

As you eat today, stop and pray throughout the meal. Ask God's blessing on the food before you eat. Midway through the meal, thank God for what you've eaten. When your meal is completed, thank God once again for the food you enjoy.

More ideas: www.nationaldayofprayer.org

151

Mother's Day

SUNDAY IN MAY

A dutiful daughter, Anna Jarvis, asked her church to hold a special service on the anniversary of her mother's death in 1907. Since then, Mother's Day has become a holiday on which mothers are honored—and then have to clean their kitchens!

Celebrate with Fun

- Most mothers value the gift of time to themselves. As a special gift, arrange for the family to go away. Yes, go away and let Mom have 2 or 3 hours at home, alone, in a quiet house. She'll be forever grateful!

- Check the local community-events section of your newspaper for a special Mother's Day activity. Many communities offer free concerts or programs for families to come together and celebrate being with Mom.

- Make coupons to give to Mom ranging from "Good for 1 backrub" to "Good for Jennifer to vacuum the living room." Decorate the coupons and put in a colorful envelope.

- Collect various photographs of Mom. Glue them on cardboard and add humorous sayings.

- Give your mom a subscription to a magazine related to her interests. Along with the subscription, tell her the family will give her 30 minutes of quiet time to read the magazine whenever it arrives in the mail.

- Get family members to write a poem about Mom. She won't care about perfect iambic pentameter. Mom will be thrilled to hear her first grader read, "Mom is fun, she plays in the sun. She can run."

Celebrate with Crafts

Purchase a solid-colored apron at a craft store. They come in bib versions or regular tie-around-the-waist styles. Wash it to remove any protective sizing. Pour fabric paint on a paper plate. Let your children press hands in the paint, then press firmly on the apron, creating handprints. Repeat several times so apron is covered with cute little handprints. Let dry, then present to Mom. Use permanent markers to write children's names and ages under each handprint.

Celebrate with Food

Yes, we could describe all sorts of fancy recipes for your Mother's Day celebration—gourmet pancakes, delectable cakes, and even fancy crepes. What Mom would probably enjoy most is going out to eat. That way the food is edible, and she won't have to scrape dried pancake batter off the floor later.

Read-In Day

This nationwide celebration encourages children to read all day long. Many schools have children bring pillows to use while sitting on the floor for reading time. Continue having fun by reading together as a family.

Celebrate with Fun

- Since children probably spent the day reading, provide some physical activity too. Run around your house 3 times. Race kids to the end of the driveway. Bring out the jump ropes and do a marathon jumping session.

- Select a new picture book for your children. Ask their first impressions from looking at the cover. Have them make up a story based on the book's title and cover. After reading the actual book, discuss which story they enjoyed more — their version or the author's. Read another new story to your children. Halfway through, ask them to guess what happens next. Compare their endings to the actual ending in the book.

- Remember the days of oral book reports? Ask each family member to give a short verbal account of their favorite book. Dressing up in costume is optional, although it's fun to see Dad wearing a train conductor's outfit while describing *The Little Engine That Could.*

- Find a book describing new games to play. Follow directions for family fun. Does it tell how to play balloon dodgeball? Line children up along a garage or the side of the house. The person who is "It" throws small water-filled balloons at the rest of the group, who dodge the balloons.

Celebrate with Crafts

Read about making a new craft project. Set out craft books and let children do the same. Here's an idea to get you started: Carve a design in a bar of glycerin soap (like Neutrogena). Use toothpicks or plastic knives to etch a design at least ¼ inch into the soap. Use a paintbrush to lightly paint the "raised" portions of the soap. Press soap on paper to create a very clean stamp.

Celebrate with Food

Some people collect cookbooks simply to read the recipes! Bring out several cookbooks. Ask children which is more appealing, cookbooks with or without pictures. Assign family members to find specific recipes such as appetizers, salads, main courses, and desserts. If you're feeling really ambitious, make the actual meal together.

More ideas: Read-in Foundation www.readin.org

National Bike to Work Day

Each year, about 2 million people participate in riding their bikes to work. Expand on this idea by riding bikes to school or just for fun.

Celebrate with Fun

- If feasible, ride bikes to school with your children. Yes, you'll need to get up earlier, but your children will arrive at school with rosy cheeks. (Of course, you'll be pedaling 2 extra trips to get yourself home and then back to pick children up again!)
- If schedules don't permit biking to work or school, try to incorporate a bike ride after dinner. The whole family benefits from being together as well as getting much-needed exercise.
- Invite neighborhood kids over for a bike carnival. Organize a bike parade around the block. Ride 2 or 3 times around to make it a l-o-o-o-n-n-g parade. Afterward, have a few bike rodeo events (see the ones described on the "National Bike Month" page earlier in May).
- Visit a local bike shop and let family members pick out new bike accessories like a bell or those supercool streamers that flow from the handlebars.
- Double-check that each family member's bike helmet fits properly. Replace any helmets that are too small or have been damaged.
- Don't have bikes for everyone? How about trying in-line skating or skate boarding? Wear protective safety gear and get rolling!
- Planning a long trip? Fill your water bottle ⅓ full and place in freezer overnight. The next day, add water to the ice for an icy cold drink.

Celebrate with Crafts

One benefit of bike riding is seeing things you'd normally miss riding in a car. Make a 3-dimensional picture of the flowers you see when bike riding. Cut several Styrofoam cups to ⅓ their original height. Set on cookie sheets, bottom side down. Place in 250-degree oven for 1½–2 minutes. The cups will melt down to look like a flower with curved petals. Glue "flowers" on paper. Use markers to add petals and stems.

Celebrate with Food

Serve a number of bike-related foods today. For wheels, serve round crackers. Pretzel sticks represent the spokes on wheels. Fig newton bars or candy bars represent handlebars. Pull apart string cheese to form a bicycle chain. Don't forget to take a "brake" for your favorite snack!

More ideas: www.bikeleague.org or 202-822-1333

Memorial Day

Memorial Day originally began to honor soldiers who died in the Civil War. Today, Memorial Day recognizes the men and women who died in any of our wars.

Celebrate with Fun

- Call or visit relatives who have lost a loved one in war. Ask a few sensitive questions to give children an awareness that people who serve our country have family, hopes, and dreams just like all of us.
- Discuss the words on the Tomb of the Unknown Soldier: "Here rests in honored glory, an American soldier known but to God."
- Ask children to share memories of past birthdays, holidays, or events at school. What memories do they have about people who have played an important role in their lives?
- Attend a Memorial Day ceremony if your community sponsors such an event.
- Death is never an easy topic to discuss. As you talk about the meaning of Memorial Day, incorporate your Christian beliefs about death.
- Ask children what it means to be patriotic. Take turns giving short speeches on "Why I'm proud to be an American."
- Wear red, white, and blue today. Buy red socks for family members or blue-and-white T-shirts to show your patriotism.

Celebrate with Crafts

Along with displaying an American flag today, make a handprint flag. Lay out white construction paper 11″ x 18″. Use a pencil to outline where the flag's stars would go in the upper left-hand corner. Let children dip their finger in blue paint to make 50 stars. Use red and white paper to trace around your child's hand. Cut out at least 8 handprints of each color. Make rows of alternating white and red stripes by gluing the paper hands in horizontal rows. The heel of each hand touches the fingertips of the next hand to make red and white stripes.

Celebrate with Food

Make a healthy, patriotic snack today. Line a cookie sheet with aluminum foil. Find a small square or rectangle container to go in the upper left-hand corner of the cookie sheet. Fill with blueberries or blackberries. These represent the flag's stars. To make stripes, simply alternate rows of cherry tomatoes with rows of cauliflower flowerets. Set a bowl of dip on the side.

National Geographic Bee Finals

Do your children know the difference between Albania and Albany? If so, get them involved in the *National Geographic* Geography Bee. Children compete for scholarships and prizes up to $50,000.

Celebrate with Fun

- Have a geographic game show to test your family's knowledge. Sit the contestant in a "hot seat" while the "host" asks questions. The "studio audience" can clap and cheer correct answers. Here are some sample questions: Which state is farthest north: North Carolina, South Dakota, or New Jersey? (South Dakota) East of your time zone, is it later or earlier in the day? (later) Which is not grown in the United States and must be imported: apples, grapes, or bananas? (bananas) In what city can you stand on the steps of the Lincoln Memorial? (Washington, D.C.) Which of the New England states is farthest north? (Maine)

- Ask family members questions about local geographic locations: What's the name of your favorite swimming lake? What river flows through our city? What's the closest mountain range to our home?

- Check out a foreign language tape from the library. Spend some time learning words from another culture.

- Does your church support a foreign missionary? Find out where they live. What are some geographic features of their country?

- Hang up a large map of the world. As friends come to visit, ask them to put a small pushpin in the states or countries they've visited. Ask them to share what the geography was like in Egypt or by the Grand Canyon.

Celebrate with Crafts

What would a Geography Bee be without a question about volcanoes? Make a giant erupting volcano—outside! Pack loose dirt into a mound resembling a mountain. On the top, press down an empty tuna-fish can so it is "buried" on the volcano. Here's the fun part: Put ½ cup baking soda in the can. Add ¼ cup vinegar (with a few drops red food coloring added to make the end result look like hot lava) and watch the volcano erupt with a foam solution. Repeat as often as you want. Cleanup is simple since you just have to remove the can.

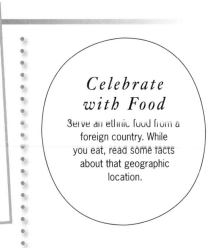

Celebrate with Food

Serve an ethnic food from a foreign country. While you eat, read some facts about that geographic location.

More ideas: www.nationalgeographic.com

May Day

Celebrate the beginning of this month with activities designed to take advantage of the warmer days.

Celebrate with Fun

- Continue the age-old tradition of leaving a May basket on someone's front door. Fill the basket with a springtime treat. Quietly walk to someone's front door, hang the basket, ring the doorbell—and run! Hide in a bush so the recipient can't see who delivered the May Day surprise.

- After playing outside, your children are probably a bit dirty. Make bath time fun with springtime bathtub paints. Mix 1 tsp. cornstarch and ½ cup white liquid hand soap. Pour a small amount into 2 or 3 plastic bowls. Add a few drops food coloring to each bowl. Let kids dip paintbrushes in the soapy paints and draw designs on the bathtub or their bodies.

- Make your own modified Maypole. Find a flagpole or other tall object. Have an adult attach 8–10 crepe paper streamers as high as safely possible. Make sure streamers almost touch the ground. Play lively music as children hold on to a streamer and walk around the Maypole. For sturdier streamers, use bright surveyor tape. This durable tape is found in a variety of colors in hardware stores.

- Since it's May Day, gather some friends and play the old-fashioned game Mother-May-I. You'll probably have to teach some children the rules!

- How many times can children say "may" today? Try using extraformal manners by saying, "May I be excused?" or "May I have more cookies?"

Celebrate with Crafts

Naturally, you need to make a May Day basket today. Purchase large round paper doilies. Place 2 or 3 doilies on top of each other for extra strength. Form the doilies into a cone shape and staple or glue the ends together. Attach a colorful ribbon on top so you can hang the basket from a doorknob. For extra embellishment, add glitter or sparkly stickers to the doily. Fill with flowers or candies.

Celebrate with Food

It's May and the birds are busy looking for worms. Bake a bunch of cupcakes frosted with dirt (actually chocolate frosting). Add a few gummy worms to look as if they are crawling out of the dirt.

More ideas: www.umkc.edu/imc/mayday.htm

Mother Goose Day

Have some fun with these familiar rhymes your children have probably memorized. Find a copy of *The Christian Mother Goose* for a different perspective on the traditional stories.

Celebrate with Fun

- Write the name of several well-known Mother Goose rhymes. Have children act a rhyme out in pantomime for the family. Let children select another to act out complete with costumes and dialogue.
- Find a hill so children can practice being Jack and Jill. Make sure "Jack" wears a crown!
- Set a candle in a candleholder on the floor. Add a piece of red tissue paper for the flame. As you recite "Jack be nimble, Jack be quick, Jack jump over the candlestick," watch your children jump over their own candlestick. Measure who jumps the highest. Add several candlesticks in a row so they can continue jumping from one to another.
- Toss your pillows and couch cushions in a pile on the floor. Let your children take turns acting out the dramatic scene in which Humpty Dumpty "had a great fall." As they fall on the cushions, "all the Kings' horses and all the Kings' men" can try to put poor Humpty back together again.
- Older children might feel silly participating in Mother Goose activities, so keep them busy with this instead: Since Humpty was an egg that cracked, challenge them to develop the most innovative way to crack an egg. They each receive 1 practice egg and 1 egg to use for their demonstration. Can they ride over the egg with their bike? How about squeezing an egg between 2 people?

Celebrate with Crafts

Since Mother Goose is a goose, try painting with geese feathers. Actually, any feathers will do. Dip the end of a feather lightly in paint and stroke across paper. What kind of design does it make? Use different parts of the feather to create a variety of strokes.

Celebrate with Food

Little Miss Muffet sat on a tuffet. (What is a *tuffet*?) Instead of just sitting on a tuffet, make some Little Miss Muffet cookies. Roll out sugar cookie dough ½-inch thick and cut into circles. Place on cookie sheet and add "spider" touches—gently place 8 small pretzel sticks on the cookie for spider legs. Top with 2 raisins for eyes. Bake according to your recipe.

Cinco De Mayo

Since Cinco De Mayo means "Fifth of May," you'll know what day we celebrate this holiday. Every year, Mexicans celebrate the 1862 Battle of Puebla, in which the Mexican troops, outnumbered 3 to 1, defeated Napoleon's French army.

Celebrate with Fun

- Puppet shows are traditional during Cinco De Mayo. Ask children to put on a puppet show with puppets from their toy box or simply with socks over their hands.

- Try your own version of the Mexican Hat Dance. If you can't find a recording of the music, simply "sing" the song as children dance around a large hat placed on the floor.

Celebrate with Food

Make a batch of traditional Cinco De Mayo cookies. Beat ½ cup butter and 4 Tbs. confectioner's sugar. Add 1 tsp. vanilla, 1 cup sifted flour, and 1 cup ground pecans. Mix well, then roll into small balls. Place on greased cookie sheet. Bake at 300 degrees 30–40 minutes. Remove from cookie sheet. Roll in powdered sugar. Makes 12–15 cookies.

Celebrate Cinco De Mayo at your favorite Mexican restaurant. Or stay home and serve a traditional meal of enchiladas, frijoles (beans), and tamales.

Purchase or make several varieties of salsa. Compare favorites. Some salsa recipes use fresh peaches or other fruit.

Celebrate with Crafts

Celebrate with a piñata. Blow up a large, sturdy balloon. Tie end shut and wrap it in strips of paper dipped in papier-mâché paste. To make paste, mix 1 cup flour with 3 cups water. Stir well; add 1 cup glue. Dip newspaper strips in paste and smooth onto balloon, overlapping so balloon is covered. Let dry, then add another layer paste. When dry, paint in bright colors. Cut a small opening in the balloon's narrow end. Fill balloon with candy and small trinkets. Tape opening shut. Get ready for wild fun as kids try to hit the piñata to get their treats.

Mexicans enjoy making paper banners called "papel picardo" on holidays. The paper is traditionally cut with hammers and chisels. Try an easier way by using scissors to cut tissue paper. Fold a tissue paper sheet accordion style. Cut small slits and shapes in the paper. Unfold the sheet and set it aside. Cut several more sheets in various colors, then tape together to form a colorful banner.

Limerick Day

"There once was a girl named . . ." That's the beginning to most limericks. Have fun reading and writing limericks today as you celebrate the birthday of limerick writer extraordinaire Edward Lear.

Celebrate with Fun

- It's Limerick Day, so write some silly rhymes. Here's the "proper" limerick formula: Lines 1, 2, and 5 rhyme and lines 3 and 4 rhyme. The limerick can begin any way, but traditionally starts with "There was a young boy from . . ." or "There was a dog named . . ."

- Help children get the feeling for limericks by letting them fill in the blanks:

  There was a young _____ from _____

  Who never wanted to _____

  So she tried to _____

  And then became _____

  That was the _____ of _____.

- Find some poems by Edward Lear. Read his wide variety of limericks to your children. He's most known for his *Book of Nonsense* written in 1846. He also wrote *The Owl and the Pussycat*.

- Set up a "Limerick Wall" to display your children's poems.

Celebrate with Crafts

Show your children Edward Lear's sketches. He had a very simplistic drawing style and used simple black pencils. Ask children to draw pictures in Lear's style to go along with their limericks. Select the best poem and drawing from each child to put in a frame.

Make sand beads to wear while you write limericks. Mix 1 cup sand with ¼ cup glue. Form into various-shaped beads. Poke a toothpick in the centers to form a hole. Let dry in the sun before stringing the beads for a necklace.

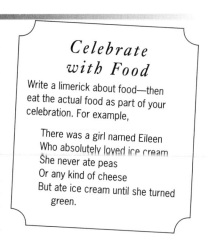

Celebrate with Food

Write a limerick about food—then eat the actual food as part of your celebration. For example,

There was a girl named Eileen
Who absolutely loved ice cream
She never ate peas
Or any kind of cheese
But ate ice cream until she turned green.

More ideas: www.umkc.edu/imc/limerick.htm

National Self-Esteem Day

Children with positive self-esteem have confidence to make responsible decisions. Today show your children you think they are competent and special.

Celebrate with Fun

- Think back to your high school days and come up with a "cheer" to wake up your children. How about this all-time favorite?

2, 4, 6, 8

Who do we appreciate?

Go-o-o-o Alison!

(Wearing a short cheerleader's skirt is optional.)

- Take your child aside and with a twinkle in your eye, tell her you have a new job as a newspaper reporter. (To add to the effect, wear a baseball cap with a sign reading "Press" on the brim. Carry an official-looking notebook.) Explain that you are writing a feature story about your child and need to know as much as possible. Ask questions like: What would be your ideal pet? Describe a time you helped a shy child at school. Where would you like to go on vacation? What 5 words describe you?
- After the interview, type up an "article" about your child. Tape it inside the newspaper. Casually say there's an interesting article on page 6. Have your child read the feature article to your family.
- Give your children confidence in public speaking skills. Collect a bag of unrelated items: a dirty sock, 1 stick of gum, a rubber spatula, and so on. Take turns reaching in the bag, selecting an item, and then "selling" it to the rest of the family. Pretend you are one of the fast-talking salespeople at the fair and describe all the wonderful uses for a toy car with only 3 wheels. You'll have plenty of laughs while developing creativity and confidence.

Celebrate with Crafts

Instead of making a craft project from scratch, let the professionals take over. Let your children look around a craft store and select a project. Take it home and work on it together. Most major craft stores carry a line of craft kits called Glory Mountain. You'll find in one kit all the necessary supplies to make 12 projects.

Celebrate with Food

Make a batch of your favorite rolled cookie dough. Use a gingerbread cookie cutter to bake cookies in the shape of children. Let kids use frosting to decorate each cookie to look like themselves.

Anniversary of "Sue's" Exhibition

On this day in 2000, Sue, the largest and most complete *Tyrannosaurus rex* ever discovered, went on display in Chicago. Celebrate with dinosaur activities of your own.

Celebrate with Fun

- Use chalk and have children trace Sue's length on the driveway or sidewalk. She is 41 feet long and would have weighed 7 tons!

- Scholastic published a book called *A Dinosaur Named Sue* by Fay Robinson. Check it out at the library and read it as a family.

- *Tyrannosaurus rex* had an extremely long neck, making it difficult to drink water on the ground. Show children what it's like to drink with a long neck. Have them get on their hands and knees and try to drink from a bowl of water without bending their elbows.

- Since dinosaurs are big, play a "big" game of modified basketball. Have 1 person hold a hula hoop horizontal to the ground. Use a large beach ball to dribble, and try to shoot baskets through the hula hoop.

- Play a game of "Dancing Dinosaurs." Children pair up, standing with their elbows linked together, back-to-back. When someone calls out "Dancing Dinosaurs," everyone runs around to find a new partner, linking elbows with the new person.

- Dinosaurs walked through various terrains. Ask children to get on hands and knees to pretend they are dinosaurs. As they "walk" around the living room, say, "Pretend you are a dinosaur walking in mud," or "How would a dinosaur walk in a gigantic bowl of Jell-O?" or "Show me what a dinosaur looks like walking on ice." Children adapt their movements according to their "environment."

Celebrate with Crafts

Serve chicken or turkey soup for dinner—that's what you need to get some bones. After boiling the bones, spread them on a cookie sheet. Let dry thoroughly. Give children the assorted bones and ask them to make their own dinosaur skeleton. They can glue the bones onto cardboard. Make up scientific-sounding names for their skeletons.

Celebrate with Food

Serve a dinosaur sandwich for lunch or dinner. Order a 3-foot (or 6-foot if you are really hungry) sandwich from a deli. Some delis will bake you the 6-foot roll so you can make your own dinosaur-length sandwich at home.

More ideas: www.fmnh.org/sue

Boys and Girls Clubs of America Founded

MAY 19

Boys and Girls Clubs provide safe, educational, and fun activities for children in their neighborhoods. Pretend you have your own community center right in your own home.

Celebrate with Fun

- Boys and Girls Clubs have enthusiastic staff. Today have the adults in your house act like camp counselors. This means perky personalities and fun, fun, fun! Forget about being a responsible parent. When children come home from school, greet them with a cheerful "Ashley! It's so good to see you! Join us for Bingo! You can win a giant candy bar!" (Notice the exclamation points—you'll be talking with a very excited voice.)

- Games are a big part of Boys and Girls Club activities. Surprise your family—play games before homework. Have children pretend they are robots and move with sharp angular motions. Call out various speeds: "Robots, move slow." "Robots, move extra-fast."

- Have some neighborhood kids come over and play "Mingle, Mingle." Children walk around randomly, arms in the air, fingers wiggling as everyone says, "Mingle, Mingle, Mingle." The person who is "It" calls out a number: "3!" The kids immediately try to crouch down in groups of 3. Repeat several times, using different numbers.

Celebrate with Crafts

Get wild—let kids try homemade finger paint. Mix 1 cup liquid laundry starch, 1 cup cold water, and 3 cups soap flakes. Spread on a hard surface so kids can make pictures using thick paint and their fingers.

Boys and Girls Club staff aren't afraid of messes. Follow their example and place a large solid-colored paper or cardboard outside. Pour several Tbs. paint on the paper in different spots. Give children a flyswatter so they can "swat" the globs of paint. You'll see some truly abstract paintings!

Celebrate with Food

Make an ice-cream cake for dessert. Soften 3 quarts ice cream, any flavor. Line a medium-sized bowl with plastic wrap. Spread a layer of ice cream in the bowl. Crush a package of Oreo cookies. Spread 1 cup crushed cookie crumbs on the ice cream. Add another layer of ice cream, more cookie crumbs, and a last layer of ice cream. Freeze several hours. Place bowl upside-down and remove cake by pulling on the plastic wrap. As the rounded cake slides out, remove the plastic wrap and enjoy.

More ideas: www.bgca.org; for ice-cream recipes, www.razzledazzlerecipes.com/icecream

Barney the Purple Dinosaur's Birthday

Everyone's favorite dinosaur celebrates his birthday in an unusual way—he has a party on the 23rd of each month. That's 12 birthdays a year!

Celebrate with Fun

- Dress up in purple and watch at least 15 minutes of Barney on TV. Get your teenagers involved in singing, "I love you, you love me . . ."
- Play traditional preschool games with your family. Remember Simon Says? Play it saying, "Barney says." Select someone to give directions like "Barney says jump up and down" or "Barney says touch your toes." If the command is "Turn around" (not "Barney says"), children keep doing what they were doing. Give directions fast to "catch" older children.
- Barney loves bubbles! Make homemade bubbles by mixing ½ cup dishwashing liquid, 2 Tbs. corn syrup, and 1 cup water. Let sit overnight. Bend chenille stems into circles for bubble wands. Tape 4 straws together and dip in solution. Blow to create many tiny bubbles.
- If it's sunny, play Shadow Tag outside. The person who is "It" tries to tag another person by stepping on his or her shadow.
- Get a partner and stare at each other for 30–60 seconds. Turn back-to-back as 1 person changes 3 things about themselves. Unbutton a button, put your watch on the opposite hand, or untie your shoe. See if your partner can guess what you changed.
- See who can do the best imitation of Barney telling children to be kind to each other. Stuff pillows in your shirt for a roly-poly belly just like Barney. Gently bump into each other while saying in a very polite way, "Excuse me." We all know how Barney stresses good manners.

Celebrate with Crafts

Give everyone 2 paper plates to decorate with purple markers. Spread glue on 1 entire plate. Before pressing the 2 plates together, insert a wooden paint stirrer for a handle. Press together and let dry. Blow up several purple balloons. Use your paper plate rackets to bat the balloons back and forth.

More ideas: www.pbskids.org/barney

Celebrate with Food

Make crunchy banana cookies—without an oven. Place 3–4 graham crackers in a plastic resealable bag. Let children crush crackers into fine crumbs with a rolling pin. Slice a banana into small circles and drop into the bag of crumbs. Shake gently. Pull the bananas out and eat your crunchy cookies.

Arthur's Anniversary

Celebrate the anniversary of the first publication about everyone's favorite aardvark—Arthur. The series of 75 books has sold over 30 million copies.

Celebrate with Fun

- Bring out the Arthur books to read. If older children think Arthur books are too babyish, ask them to read one to a younger child.
- Turn on PBS and watch the Emmy award-winning *Arthur* TV show. Discuss the "predicaments" in which Arthur finds himself.
- Just what kind of an animal is an aardvark? Use the dictionary or other books with photographs and descriptions of aardvarks. Did you know that aardvarks use their claws to dig into termite nests and then eat the termites? They have sticky tongues to help them catch bugs. The name aardvark means "earth pig."
- One of Arthur's hobbies is reading. Have a read-aloud time for your kids to take turns reading Arthur stories while being videotaped. Replay the video in 6 months to see how children's reading skills have improved.
- In the book *Arthur's Family Vacation*, Arthur sends postcards back to his friends. Pretend you're on vacation. Buy postcards from your own hometown and send them to distant friends and relatives. They'll be surprised to get a postcard from you.
- Arthur loves playing in his tree house. If you don't feel like building a 2-story tree house, at least make a tree house fort. Drape a large sheet over a tree branch, spread out the ends, and enjoy your instant tree house.

Celebrate with Crafts

Since aardvarks have very sticky tongues, make a sticky picture with contact paper. Give each child a 9" x 12" piece of clear contact paper. Place shapes cut out of construction paper on the sticky contact paper to make a picture. When picture is complete, place another sheet of contact paper on top. Hang in a window.

Celebrate with Food

In the book *Arthur's Crunch Cereal Contest*, Arthur decides to write a jingle about his favorite cereal. Have children choose their favorite cereal and do the same thing. As they eat, ask them to write down a short, catchy song to market their cereal. Sing the jingles to each other.

More ideas: www.pbskids.org/arthur

Adhesive Tape Patented

In 1930 Richard Drew developed the adhesive tape most of us use regularly. Later, 3M manufactured the tape under the brand name Scotch Tape.

Celebrate with Fun

- Use tape to examine your fingerprints. Scribble a postage-sized square on paper with black pencil. Make sure the marks are dark. Firmly press a finger on the pencil marking. Place a strip of scotch tape on your fingertip. Remove tape and place it on white paper. You'll have a clear image of your fingerprint.

- Hold your 4 fingers together and wrap Scotch Tape around them sticky side out. Use hand as an inexpensive lint remover. "Tap" on black pants and the couch where the dog lays. You'll be amazed at the hair and lint that collects on the tape!

- Have a teenager in the family? Scotch tape can be used as a blackhead remover! Press a piece of tape over your nose. Rub the tape firmly on your skin—then zip! Pull the tape off, removing dead skin and blackheads! (How's that for a practical idea?)

- Write a note telling your family where dessert is hidden. Rip the note into 10 or 15 pieces. Have the family use tape to put the note together and find the treat.

- Put strips of tape over someone's mouth. Ask them to talk. Can you understand what they say? (Caution: not recommended for anyone with a beard, mustache, or goatee!)

- Get crazy and give each other inexpensive face-lifts. Use tape to pull your sagging skin back to your ears or lift your nose. Take pictures of your strange family!

- Make 10-inch "tape doughnuts" to put on the end of your fingers. See who can pick up the most items.

Celebrate with Crafts

Give each family member cardboard, Scotch Tape, and duct tape to build a boatlike "floating vehicle" that will hold a small stuffed animal. Place your waterproof contraptions in the bathtub and time how long each stays above water. Does your animal stay dry?

Celebrate with Food

Serve a variety of "sticky" foods today. Try fruit leather, peanut butter, marshmallow cream, taffy, apples in caramel dip, cotton candy, and honey. (Not all at one meal though!)

Sierra Club Founded

Have you ever visited a national park? The Sierra Club, founded in 1892, promotes conservation of our natural environments. Get outside and enjoy fresh air, grass, and the spring breeze.

Celebrate with Fun

- Take a hike, even if it's around the local elementary school. If you live by longer trails, enjoy a more extensive outdoor experience.
- Many national parks have a "Passport" book describing parks around the nation. Purchase one so children can get the official stamp in the Passport whenever they visit a national park.
- On a long hike, take a few safety precautions: (1) Dress in layers. It's easier to take off a sweatshirt than to find an extra sweater. (2) Carry a first aid kit at all times. Fill it with extra Band-Aids since that's what you'll use most. (3) Let someone know where you are going and when to expect you home.
- When young children hike, keep their interest by singing songs or setting minigoals. Tell them, "Let's hike to that big tree across the path, and then we'll eat our raisins." Vary the way you hike too. Try hopping on 1 foot. Skipping is fun also! If the path is smooth, walk backward.
- Try a coin-flip walk if you are in a park with intersecting trails. This also works in a suburban neighborhood. Begin walking. At the first intersection or fork in the trail, flip a coin. If the coin is "heads," you turn left. If the coin falls on "tails," you walk to the right. The coin determines your direction.

Celebrate with Crafts

This long-term craft project will soon get family and friends involved. As you walk, look for twigs in the shape of letters. Sure, you'll quickly find I or Y, but just try to find a B! Check exposed roots for best luck at finding obscure letters. As you find your natural letters, mount them on a board (of course, you can't bring the tree roots home). Soon you'll get a call from Grandpa saying, "I found an S! "

Celebrate with Food

Ever open your backpack on the trail and find a smashed sandwich with potato chip crumbs? Whatever you pack on your hike, enclose it in a plastic container. Freeze a juice pack to cool your food. By the time you're thirsty, the juice will be ice cold and super refreshing!

More ideas: www.sierraclub.org

Senior Citizens Day

They are called senior citizens, the elderly, mature adults, and prime-timers. Whatever you call them, celebrate today with someone who is wise with the experience of many years of living.

Celebrate with Fun

- Invite your favorite seniors for a family meal. They'll enjoy being around the noisy, hectic activities of a typical family. (And they'll probably be glad to go home to peace and quiet afterward!)

- Not all seniors sit on their porch in rocking chairs. Find some older adults who are still active in their church or community. Introduce them to your children as positive role models. A few gray hairs doesn't mean it's time to put away the jogging shoes. Find a book or a magazine article about seniors who accomplished things during their later years. Read about Grandma Moses, who began painting in her late seventies, or Art Linkletter, who is still actively speaking and writing at 90. Thousands of seniors participate in the Senior Olympics. The oldest person to carry the Olympic torch for the 2002 Olympics was 102!

- See if the library has recordings of old-time radio programs. Turn off the TV and listen to *Little Orphan Annie* and *The Lone Ranger*. Ask a senior to explain what life was like without TV and the Internet.

- Send a card or call all the seniors in your life and wish them "Happy Senior Citizens Day!" They'll be pleased to hear from you.

Celebrate with Crafts

Call a local senior activity center and ask if your children can meet some of their crafters. You might meet a gentleman who carves whistles from pieces of wood or a smiling grandmother who quilts intricate patterns. It's good for children to see seniors still actively pursuing their hobbies.

Celebrate with Food

Many seniors grew up during the Depression. Have one tell your children about food-rationing cards that regulated the sugar and eggs families received. Bake a Depression cake—with no eggs, butter, or milk! In a saucepan mix 2 cups packed brown sugar, 2 cups hot water, 2 Tbs. bacon grease (or shortening), and 2 cups raisins. Boil 5–6 minutes. Let cool. In a bowl mix 3 cups flour, 1 tsp. salt, 1 tsp. baking soda, and 1 tsp. cinnamon. Pour raisin mixture into dry ingredients. Mix well. Pour into 2 greased loaf pans. Bake 45 minutes at 325 degrees.

JUNE

National Dairy Month
National Candy Month
Fresh Fruit and Vegetable Month

Weeks to Celebrate

2nd Full Week • Great Outdoors Week
2nd Full Week • National Clay Week
4th Week • National Camping Week

Days to Celebrate

1st Saturday • National Trails Day
3rd Sunday • Father's Day

1   Superman's Birthday
5   Gingerbread Day
7   National Crayon Day
9   Donald Duck's Birthday
14 Flag Day
19 Butterfly Day
21 First Day of Summer
23 National Pink Day
24 Eat Cereal Day
25 Eric Carle's Birthday
27 "Happy Birthday" Written
27 Paul Bunyon Day

National Dairy Month

Milk, cheese, eggs, ice cream, and yogurt are dairy foods we enjoy on a daily basis. Instead of just eating these dairy products, try celebrating them.

Celebrate with Fun

- Give your family white T-shirts. Draw black or brown "cow spots" on the shirts with markers so you resemble cows.

- Many dairy farms are open to the public this month, so take your children to see that milk comes from cows, not the grocery store's dairy section. They might even get to milk a cow or collect eggs from the hen house.

- Did you know the average cow produces 90 glasses of milk a day? Set out all the glasses in your house to demonstrate. If you don't have 90 glasses, set out 10 and have children imagine 9 times as many.

- Make some "dairy squirt guns." Purchase surgical latex gloves. Help children fill gloves with water and hold tightly at the tops. Use a safety pin to poke a hole or two in the tip of 1 finger. You've just made a squirt gun that looks like a cow's udder. Go outside and squirt each other.

- Have you ever seen a fainting goat? These animals actually faint and fall over if spooked by a loud noise. Take turns pretending to be goats casually chewing grass. The person who is "It" yells or makes a loud noise, causing the "goats" to faint.

Celebrate with Crafts

Read the book It Looked Like Spilt Milk, in which children make up stories about cloud formations. Create your own spilt milk pictures. Fold pieces of blue construction paper in half. On 1 half, drop 2–3 "splotches" of white paint. Fold paper over with paint on the inside and rub the outside to spread the paint. Open the page. What does your spilt milk drawing look like? Come up with a story to go with the design.

Celebrate with Food

Mix up a delicious milkshake. Put ½ cup sliced strawberries, ½ cup cold milk, and 2 scoops vanilla ice cream in a blender. Blend on medium speed for 30–45 seconds. Serve with a few sliced strawberries on top.

Instead of a milkshake, make a dairy-based smoothie. Use the blender to mix ¼ cup milk, ½ cup dry powdered milk, 1 sliced banana, and ½ tsp. vanilla. Drop in 4–6 crushed ice cubes and blend well. Smooth, cool, and frothy!

National Candy Month

The entire month of June is devoted to celebrating candy. Set aside a few days to go all out with sweet fun.

Celebrate with Fun

- Throw caution to the wind and serve candy for breakfast! (Not an entire candy bar—just a small piece.)
- Have a candy-tasting party. Blindfold people and have them taste assorted candies. See who can guess the difference between a Heath bar, Big Chew, and Clark bar.
- Bring out the pencils and play "Guess That Candy Bar!" Ask people to write the names of the actual candy bars that fit these descriptions: Bumpy street (Rocky Road); Charlie Brown's admirer (Peppermint Patty); happy nut (Almond Joy); sweet infants (Sugar Babies); ex-New York Yankee (Baby Ruth); the day a worker likes best (Pay Day); a trio of buddies (3 Musketeers); funny laugh (Snickers); famous New York street (5th Avenue); I can't remember the name (Whatchamacallit); Superman's real name (Clark bar); small hills (Mounds); bovine flops (Milk Duds); little feline—big feline (Kit Kat); our galaxy (Milky Way); Supernova (Starbursts).
- Have fun playing "Lifesavers Relay." Everyone has a toothpick in their mouth with a Lifesaver on it. Carefully try to transfer the Lifesaver from your toothpick to a partner's toothpick.

Celebrate with Crafts

Use candy bar wrappers to decorate a box for storing special items. Glue wrappers in a random pattern on the box. Cover with a coat of decoupage to form a shiny covering for your box.

Celebrate with Food

Caution: This activity is not for people with squeamish stomachs (10-year-old boys adore it though). Make Kitty Litter Cake! Bake and frost a sheet cake. Pour 1 cup Grape-Nuts into a resealable plastic bag. Crush with a rolling pin. Pour the crushed cereal over the cake to resemble kitty litter. Here's the fun part: Put 10–12 Tootsie Rolls in the microwave for 12–15 seconds. Unwrap and "pinch" the softened ends of each Tootsie Roll so it looks like, well, like what you'd find in a kitty litter box. Serve the cake by scooping up pieces with a *new* kitty litter scooper!

More ideas: www.candyusa.org

Fresh Fruit and Vegetable Month

JUNE

Celebrate this month by taking advantage of all the fresh fruit and vegetables available right now. You may find children choosing fresh pineapple over cookies. (Well, it is possible!)

Celebrate with Fun

- Play "Fruit Basket Upset." Sit in chairs in a circle, with 1 chair fewer than the number of players. Randomly assign children to be bananas, apples, or oranges. The leader calls out different fruits: "Oranges!" means all the oranges jump up and find another chair. The person without a chair waits for the next round. When the leader calls out "Fruit Basket Upset!" everyone changes seats.

- Visit a farmer's market or U-pick farm. Ask the sellers at the market how they grow their produce. Let children purchase an unusual fruit or vegetable and sample an organically grown apple. Does it taste different than a commercially grown apple from the store?

- Go to a U-pick strawberry farm and show children the work involved in getting fresh fruits and vegetables to the store. At first children eagerly pick and eat, but soon they'll tire and want to go home. Push children to pick for another 30 minutes. It's hot, monotonous work. Explain how migrant children pick fruit for hours on end the entire summer.

- Growing pumpkins or zucchini? Cut pieces of contact paper (not clear) in the shape of hearts. Stick the hearts on your developing squash. After several weeks, remove the sticky hearts. You'll have heart imprints on the skin where the sun didn't hit it.

Celebrate with Crafts

You've probably played with Mr. Potato Head. Try making a Mr. or Mrs. Potato Head using real potatoes. Cut up small pieces of carrot, green peppers, or zucchini. Use toothpicks to attach assorted vegetables to a baking potato. Strips of peeled apple skin make lovely ringlets. Add a bowtie by cutting a piece of jicama in the shape of 2 triangles, points touching. After admiring your artwork, remove toothpicks and stick the potato in the microwave for dinner.

Celebrate with Food

Serve a meal of stir-fried vegetables with a side dish of fresh fruit salad. Let children participate in chopping all the fruits and vegetables. Younger children can use plastic knives to cut bananas and soft vegetables.

Great Outdoors Week

Smell the fresh air! Feel the grass under your bare feet! Enjoy the sun as you eat a picnic in the park! This is a week to enjoy being outdoors.

Celebrate with Fun

- Send the family on an outdoor nature scavenger hunt. Set a time limit and make up a list of items to find like a twig shaped like an S, a heart-shaped rock, a flower petal, 3 small pinecones, and the biggest leaf.
- Go camping at a local park. Borrow a tent if necessary. Children enjoy sleeping under the stars, and food tastes better cooked over a campfire.
- To really experience the great outdoors, borrow or rent an RV for a minivacation this week. Enjoy soft beds and indoor plumbing while in a state or national park. Take advantage of programs provided by park naturalists. More information on RVs: www.gorving.com
- Look for 4-leaf clovers on your lawn.
- Play "Sponge Splat." Put several sponges in a bucket of water. One family member stands against the side of the house while others take turns tossing wet sponges at the "victim." Sponges must be thrown below the shoulders. The goal is to make the target person flinch.

Celebrate with Crafts

If you're going to be at the beach, you'll need a beach towel. Lay out a solid-colored towel on a sidewalk or other hard surface. Pour some fabric paint in a disposable pie plate. Help children place 1 bare foot in the paint. Then have them step on the towel to make a footprint. Make several footprints with different colors of paint. Let paint dry before taking to the beach.

Celebrate with Food

You might see animal tracks while hiking in the woods. Make some bear track cookies. Mix ¾ cup peanut butter with ¼ cup brown sugar, 1 tsp. vanilla, 1 can condensed milk, and 2 cups all-purpose baking mix. Shape into "footprints" that look like bear tracks. Break small pretzel sticks in half. Poke pretzels into the footprint to look like claws. Bake at 350 degrees for 8–10 minutes.

More ideas: www.funoutdoors.com

National Clay Week

Whether making an elaborate pot or playing with a preschooler, using clay allows opportunities for creativity. Try these recipes for hours of fun.

Celebrate with Fun

- Get ready for a day of making bowls and vases. Prepare an area where clay can be used all day. Cover a large table with a plastic cloth or old shower curtain. Set out assorted clay-shaping tools like plastic knives, a garlic press, a rolling pin, and other tools to embellish your clay projects.

Celebrate with Crafts

To celebrate National Clay Week, here are several popular clay recipes. Make one or try them all!

Preschool clay: This recipe gets its name because even a 4-year-old can make it. Mix 2 cups flour and ⅜ cup salt in a bowl. Stir in ¾ cup hot water until smooth. Knead on a floured working area. Keep kneading until clay is smooth and pliable. Divide into smaller batches and knead in various colors of food coloring. Stores well for several weeks in the refrigerator.

Ever popular play clay: Mix 1 cup flour, ½ cup salt, 1 cup water, 1 tsp. vegetable oil, food coloring, and ½ tsp. cream of tartar in a saucepan. Stir over medium heat until mixture suddenly "clumps" together. Transfer clay to a floured surface. When clay cools, let children knead until smooth. Store in covered container in the refrigerator. For dazzling clay, stir in 1 tsp. glitter.

Older children enjoy making clay dough from ordinary bread. This clay is good for making small items such as jewelry or doll dishes. Cut the crust off 2 pieces of white bread. Tear bread into small pieces. Mix with 1 Tbs. glue until smooth yet sticky. If mixture is too dry, add a drop more glue. Keep kneading until all "stickiness" is gone. Shape your item with the clay. Let dry at least 3 days before painting.

Celebrate with Food

When you get tired playing with clay, try eating some! Here's an edible recipe so that kids can actually play with their food. Mix together 1 cup peanut butter, ½ cup honey, and 2 cups powdered sugar. Knead until soft and pliable and begin making your shapes. (It's a good idea to wash hands first.) Eat and enjoy!

National Camping Week

Forget about staying at a fancy 5-star hotel. Grab the family and enjoy the great outdoors while camping under the stars.

Celebrate with Fun

- If you are new to camping, take a trial run in the backyard. Set up your tent, inflate the air mattress, and put on the bug repellent. Figure out how the new tent is assembled in your backyard before attempting it in a spot miles from civilization. Younger children feel more comfortable knowing they are close to home . . . and indoor plumbing.

- If you've watched *Survivor*, you've seen teams struggle to start a fire without matches. Challenge your family to get a fire going using Boy Scout ingenuity—but no matches.

- If you've never camped before, ask camping-savvy friends if you can tag along on their next outing. You'll pick up tips to make future camping trips a positive experience. One good tip is to provide all children with a safety whistle to blow only if they are lost or in danger.

- Cut off about 12 inches of pantyhose from the toe. Drop in a bar of soap and tie directly above the soap. Make a loop with the remaining pantyhose to slip over the water faucet at your campsite. Now you have a constant supply of soap for easy cleanup.

- Find a book of campfire songs. Sit around the campfire (as smoke gets in your eyes) and sing some rousing songs like "Kum Ba Ya" and "On Top of Old Smokey."

Celebrate with Crafts

While camping, give each child a resealable plastic bag to collect small acorns, stones, and twigs. After the camping gear is stowed away at home, give each child a flowerpot. Spread tile grout over the outside of the flowerpot. Let children gently press their camping treasures into the grout. Let dry for a permanent reminder of your trip.

Celebrate with Food

It wouldn't be camping unless you roasted hot dogs! Add a twist to traditional hot dogs by making pigs in the blanket. Use refrigerated biscuit dough as the "blankets." Give children a hunk of dough and tell them to roll it out like a fat snake. Wrap the doughy snake around the hot dog. Roast as usual with a stick over a campfire, until biscuit dough is golden brown.

National Trails Day

Put your children's energy to good use. Celebrate National Trails Day by taking the family on a hike. Even if you go just a mile or two, you might discover hiking is an activity all ages can enjoy.

Celebrate with Fun

- Get the family excited about the hike. Offer to buy milkshakes for everyone completing the hike without complaining. Ask children to find the most unusual rock or the "crookedest" tree. Make up names for plants you can't identify. Greet other hikers with a cheery "Hello."
- Teach children the importance of "Hug a Tree" if they get lost. Rescuers find people who stay in one location more easily.
- If you take the family dog along, make sure he has water. Many pet stores carry collapsible dog bowls that easily fit in a pocket or backpack.
- Take a litterbag along to pick up trash careless hikers leave behind. Set a good example by making sure all your trash is carried back out. Leave the trail cleaner than before.
- The National Park Service has many programs encouraging the public to help clear trails, paint signs, and the like. See if your family can participate in an organized activity connected with trails and hiking.
- Start a "Hiking Rock" collection. Every time your family takes a hike, find a unique rock (preferably a small one!) to commemorate the trip. Display so children can say, "I remember we got that rock the time Dad fell in the creek!"
- If you have a truly reluctant hiker, let them listen to music on their headphones during the hike back to the car.

Celebrate with Crafts

As the family hikes, look for unusual twigs or sticks. Find a stick with "personality." Make sure everyone has a twig to take home. Use your twigs for sculptures. Can you paint yours to look like a snake? How about gluing on some leaves and creating a twig person?

Celebrate with Food

Give children control over packing their own backpacks. Let them choose string cheese, fruit leather, or oranges. Freeze juice packs the night before. After being in the backpack for several hours, the juice will still be icy cold. Be sure to add a sweet treat to give that extra boost of energy.

More ideas: www.americanhiking.com

176

Father's Day

In 1910, Spokane, Washington, was the site of the first Father's Day celebration. Since then, millions of fathers enjoy the day by getting new ties and pajamas. This year, do something different for Dad.

Celebrate with Fun

- Tell Dad one of his gifts today is that the family will let him watch at least half of a baseball game on TV without interruption. (If you really feel generous—the entire game!)

- Interview Dad to get a better idea about who he is. Ask questions about his childhood, his dreams, and his embarrassing moments.

- Using the computer or just your artistic talent, design an award certificate for Dad like "Greatest Guy to Build Things" or "Outstanding Dad Who Can Still Do a Cartwheel." Put the award in a frame so your dad can hang it with pride.

- Give your dad a gift basket full of his favorite snacks and a certificate for a trial membership at the health club he's been talking about joining.

- Start a new tradition—ask Dad what he'd like to do on this special day. Carry out his "wish" every year. This could be the year you start the tradition of joining Dad in bed in the morning to eat chips and wrestle.

- Take a picture of family members holding a sign saying, "We love you!" Put in a frame and send to Dad's office the Friday before Father's Day.

- Plan a "this is what you are really like" skit for Dad. Act out and exaggerate his mannerisms. Do a spoof of his favorite sayings and activities. Have family members dress up like his second-grade teacher or his first girlfriend.

Celebrate with Crafts

Since Dad is "King for the Day," make him a royal crown. Cut a strip of lightweight cardboard 3" x 25". Decorate it to look like a crown. Cover with aluminum foil or paint with gold paint. Add lots of glitter, shiny sequins, and fake jewels. Measure the strip to fit around Dad's head. Staple ends together and crown your favorite king.

Celebrate with Food

Purchase long loaves of French bread or ask your baker to bake you 3-foot-long submarine sandwich loaves. Your dad is your hero, isn't he? Let him make a king-sized hero sandwich. Set out a variety of cold cuts and cheeses. Let Dad be first in line to make his hero sandwich.

Superman's Birthday

JUNE 1

In 1938 the first issue of *Superman* comic books was published. Since then, the popular superhero has inspired many boys to wear tights on Halloween.

Celebrate with Fun

- Is your family brave enough (at least the guys) to have a "tights parade"? If Superman can be seen with tights in front of hundreds of people, can you? If you're modest, wear a pair of shorts over your tights.
- Superman is faster than a speeding bullet and leaps over tall buildings with a single bound. You don't need your children jumping over buildings. Instead, try a few other Superman feats of agility. See if your children can:

  1. Run from one end of the yard to the other in 30 seconds.
  2. Measure who can jump the farthest.
  3. Jump up high enough to slam-dunk a basketball.
  4. Lift up the "phone booth" in which Clark Kent changes clothes (okay, it's just a box).
  5. Hear you as you whisper, "Go clean your room." (Superman has superhearing.)

- Clark Kent was a newspaper reporter. Have children write a newspaper account of a crime and describe how Superman saved the day.
- Why are people fascinated with superheroes? Ask your children about Spiderman, Batman, and Superman. Are they positive role models? Can people be heroes in ordinary ways, without flying or leaping from buildings? Who are some heroes from the Bible?

Celebrate with Crafts

Transform a large refrigerator box into a phone booth. If Clark Kent changes clothes in a phone booth, why can't your children? Paint the box a solid color. Cut a door that opens and closes. Use a contrasting paint to add details. Time children to see who can run into the phone booth, change into a different outfit, and run out again the fastest.

Celebrate with Food

The only thing Superman fears is Kryptonite. This green substance makes Superman weak and unable to exhibit his superhuman strength. See if your superheroes can survive your own form of Kryptonite. Serve lime Jell-O cut in cubes. Ask children to perform feats of strength, then have them eat the green Jell-O. Can they still jump high and leap wide?

Gingerbread Day

The aroma of freshly baked gingerbread makes everyone ready for a glass of milk and a cookie. Today, enjoy this tasty snack and some fun activities.

Celebrate with Fun

- Get some exercise outside chasing human "Gingerpeople." As your children yell, "You can't catch me—I'm the Gingerbread Man!" try to tag them. Take turns trying to catch each other.
- Purchase a small piece of fresh ginger. Use a knife to scrape the ginger and release the distinct smell.
- After reading *The Gingerbread Man*, make up your own ending. Where was he running? What would happen if he ran into your neighborhood?
- In *The Gingerbread Man*, the trusting cookie rides across a river on the fox's back. Have children pretend they are the fox. Place a small stuffed animal on their back. See if they can flip the stuffed animal off their back and catch it with their mouth.

Celebrate with Crafts

Use brown paper bags to make a chain of decorated Gingerbread men or women. Trace around a gingerbread cookie cutter on the bags 10 or 12 times. Cut out people and color their eyes and mouths. Glue on thin white rickrack to resemble white frosting. Staple or glue gingerbread hands together to form a chain.

Celebrate with Food

Naturally you'll bake some gingerbread cookies on this special day. Cream together ⅔ cup shortening, ½ cup packed brown sugar, 1 tsp. cinnamon, ¼ tsp. ground cloves, 2 tsp. ground ginger, and a pinch salt. Mix in 1 egg, then mix in ¾ cup molasses. In a separate bowl sift 3 cups flour, ½ tsp. baking powder, and 1 tsp. baking soda. Stir into the creamed mixture until well blended. Chill 1 hour. Preheat oven to 375 degrees. Roll out ¼ dough at a time on a lightly floured board to ⅛-inch thickness. Cut with cookie cutters and transfer to a greased (or nonstick) cookie sheet. Repeat with remaining dough. Decorate with raisins as you like. Bake 8–10 minutes.

Make your favorite French toast recipe, adding 1 tsp. powdered ginger for a distinctive new taste.

179

National Crayon Day

Your children will find it hard to believe that back in 1903, a box of Crayola crayons had only 8 colors: red, yellow, orange, blue, violet, green, brown, and black. The box also cost a whopping 5 cents!

Celebrate with Fun

- How often do you hear, "I need a new box of crayons"? Collect the crayons from drawers and toy boxes. Sort out all the broken crayon stubs to use for the following craft projects.

Celebrate with Food

Who has time to eat when there's so much to do with all those crayons?

Celebrate with Crafts

Dump some of your broken crayon pieces into a tub of cold water. Let soak 10–12 hours. Drain them and remove the paper. Now make giant muffin crayons. Line muffin pan sections with aluminum foil. Drop in ½-inch peeled crayon stubs till each section is half full. Put in oven 6–8 minutes at 300 degrees. Have an adult watch to see when they begin melting. Carefully take the muffin pan out and cool for 1 hour. Remove foil and start drawing with your big chunk crayons!

Almost every preschooler has made crayon mosaics using crayon shavings. Have younger children get shavings from their crayon sharpener. Let kids sprinkle shavings on a piece of waxed paper in a random pattern. Cover with another sheet of waxed paper. Have an adult iron over the sheets with low heat. As soon as the shavings start to melt, remove the iron. The shavings and

waxed paper bond together. Children can cut designs into shapes if they like.

Set out paper lunch bags. If possible, buy some in colors. Using crayons, decorate the bags like houses. Draw chimneys, curtains, doorknobs, and flower boxes. Stuff bags with newspaper and staple tops shut. Set up a village as a tabletop display of creative architecture.

Purchase fabric crayons that are made to create permanent designs on fabric. Color a picture on paper with the fabric crayons. Place paper upside-down on a shirt, pillowcase, or other fabric. Follow the package directions to iron the design on the fabric. Just remember—the drawing makes a reverse print. If you write anything, all the letters need to be backward.

More ideas: www.crayola.com

Donald Duck's Birthday

Yes, even a duck needs to celebrate his birthday. Have a quacking-fun time with this birthday party.

Celebrate with Fun

- Who has the best Donald Duck voice in your family? Take turns doing Donald Duck impersonations.

- Have a waddle contest. Set up a modified obstacle course so people have to walk around and over different items. Hold a loaf of frozen bread between your knees. (Ducks eat bread, you know.) Time each other to see who can waddle through the course the fastest. If the bread falls, go back and begin again. Don't forget to quack the entire time!

- How long has it been since you've played Duck, Duck, Goose? Grab family and friends to play this popular preschooler game. Sit everyone in a circle and select 1 person as "It." He or she walks around the outside of the circle, lightly tapping people on the head and saying, "Duck, Duck, Duck, Duck, Goose!" The "Goose" jumps up and races "It" back to the open space in the circle.

- Sing the "Rubber Ducky" song. Get the rubber ducky from the bathtub and hide it. The person who finds the yellow fellow gets a day off from doing chores.

Celebrate with Crafts

Make a floating Donald Duck. Wash a clear plastic 2-liter pop bottle. Lay the bottle on its side. The cap represents Donald's nose. Use permanent markers to draw eyes. Glue yellow craft foam "feathers" to the sides. Add ½ cup small pebbles inside bottle for weight and balance. Reseal cap and let Donald float in a tub of water.

Plan a "Design a Wardrobe for Donald" contest. Give everyone a rubber duck. Set out an assortment of fabric scraps, markers, lace, and other assorted items. Have people create outfits for their ducks. Have you ever seen a duck dressed as a biblical character in robes? How about a duck in a bathing suit?

Celebrate with Food

Celebrate today with a birthday cake. Use blue frosting for water and place a plastic duck in the middle of the "lake."

Flag Day

Hooray for the red, white, and blue! Bring out all your flags and display them proudly in honor of Flag Day.

Celebrate with Fun

- Buy red, white, and blue bandannas for the family. Let people express their individuality by wearing them however they want. Who puts one around their neck or through their belt loops? Who uses one as a headband?
- Play John Philip Sousa music throughout the day. Instead of walking to the bathroom, lift your knees and march.
- Stand facing a flag and say the "Pledge of Allegiance" as a family. Afterward, pray for the president and our country.
- Ask your family if they know what the colors represent on the flag. The 13 stripes represent the 13 original colonies. The red stands for bravery, the white for purity, and the blue for justice.
- Create a family flag. Use a large piece of felt as the background. Cut shapes and designs that represent your family's interests from felt scraps. Attach the flag to a dowel and fly in a prominent location.
- Walk around the neighborhood and count the number of flags being displayed. Set an example by flying several flags at your house.
- Since legend tells us Betsy Ross sewed the first American flag, honor her with this game. If you're in a pool, instead of playing "Marco-Polo," play the same game, only yell out "Betsy-Ross!"

Celebrate with Crafts

How about a Flag Day wreath? Use a white paper plate as the base. Cut out a 4-inch hole in the center. Cut red, white, and blue striped ribbon into 4-inch strips. Glue ends of ribbons shut to form "doughnuts." Randomly glue on the ribbon doughnuts to cover the entire paper plate, forming a red, white, and blue wreath.

Make Flag Day napkin holders by cutting cardboard wrapping-paper tubes into 3-inch sections. Paint the sections with red or blue paint. Dip hard end of a small paintbrush into a contrasting paint color. Dab the paint on the cardboard. The paintbrush end forms perfect polka dots. After decorating sections, insert red, white, and blue napkins.

Celebrate with Food

Make some patriotic flagpoles. Melt 1 cup almond bark or white chocolate chips. Dip a pretzel log halfway in the melted chocolate. Roll immediately in red, white, and blue sprinkles. Let cool before eating your flagpole.

More ideas: www.flagday.org

Butterfly Day

It's likely you see some of the more than 700 different species of butterflies around your yard. Find ways to enjoy these beautiful winged creatures on this special day.

Celebrate with Fun

- Plan a butterfly garden. Butterflies are attracted to flowers with clusters of blossoms. Put in some Queen Anne's lace or yarrow. Sunflowers and snapdragons will also bring butterflies around to sip the nectar.

- After your flowers are blooming, provide a "picnic area" resting place for butterflies. Place sand and water in a shallow pan on the ground. Butterflies need moisture and a smooth rock to land on. Have children occasionally pour sugar water over the rock for a butterfly dessert.

- Butterflies love flowers. Make a special 2-tone flower. Fill 2 glass jars with water. Add 4–5 drops different-colored food coloring to each glass. Carefully slice a white carnation stem lengthwise ¾ of the way up toward the flower. Place half the stem in 1 jar and carefully, so the stem doesn't tear, place the other half in the second jar. Let stand overnight. In the morning you will have a 2-tone carnation. People with surgical skills can cut stem in thirds to produce a tricolored flower.

- Have everyone place a plastic bag over each arm, then pretend to be butterflies flitting from flower to flower.

Celebrate with Crafts

Make a colorful butterfly from a sandwich bag. Cut up colored tissue paper into 1-inch square pieces. Place inside a regular sandwich bag. (not the resealable kind). Tape the bag shut. "Scrunch" the bag in the middle to form 2 butterfly wings. Twist a chenille stem around the bag to form the body and antennae for the butterfly.

Celebrate with Food

Serve a butterfly sundae after planting your butterfly garden. Place 2 strips of red or black licorice on a plate. Scoop out 2 spoonfuls of ice cream as the "wings" and place on each side of the licorice. Put chocolate chips on the ice cream for butterfly spots.

Try a fruit-flavored banana butterfly. Slice a banana in half lengthwise. Place on a plate, cut side down. Place apple slices in an overlapping pattern on both sides of the banana body to represent wings. Use a toothpick to hold 2 grapes in place on the banana as eyes.

More ideas: www.butterflies.com

First Day of Summer

JUNE 21

Your friends in Australia are getting out their sweaters while you're enjoying the first day of summer. Celebrate the longest day of the year with fun outdoor activities.

Celebrate with Fun

- Spend some time outside today. Early in the day, have your children stand on the sidewalk. Trace around their shadows. At noon, have them stand in the same place and trace their shadow again. At 5 P.M. repeat again. Point out the different shadow lengths as the sun moves across the sky.

- Softball is a summertime favorite. Put a twist on it by playing "1 Base Softball." Divide your group in half (any number can play). Team A is in the outfield, which is the entire playing area, even next to the batter. Team B is at bat. There's only 1 base about 25 feet from the batter. Any ball is considered fair. The runner hits and races to the 1 base. The next batter hits and races to the base also. Runners can stay on the base as long as they want. Perhaps 5 people on base decide to run home at the same time, making the score 5-0. Since any ball is fair, outfielders can catch any ball and tag the runners out; 3 outs are allowed, just like traditional softball. The game moves quickly since most people can hit the ball even a short distance. Play for 5 innings or until people lose interest.

Celebrate with Crafts

Grass grows quickly this time of year—ask the person who mows your lawn. Grow some grass heads of your own. Decorate plastic or Styrofoam cups like faces, complete with goofy smiles. Poke a couple holes in the cup bottoms. Fill the cups with potting soil. Top with 1 Tbs. grass seeds. Pat seeds down. Cover with a thin layer of dirt. Sit cups in a sunny location and water. In a week your cup faces will be sporting great green hair. Braid the hair or add a few bows to spruce it up.

Celebrate with Food

A low-calorie healthy watermelon pizza tastes wonderful on a hot summer day. Cut a 1-inch-thick round slice all the way through a seedless watermelon. That's your pizza "dough." Top the pizza not with pepperoni, but with sliced strawberries, cherries, or berries. Cut into wedges and enjoy a refreshing summer treat.

184

National Pink Day

From the time a baby girl is born, she's swaddled in pink. Sure, some girls turn into tomboys, but we all still enjoy pink hearts on Valentine's Day and pink bubblegum.

Celebrate with Fun

- Set out several clear bowls or glasses half filled with water. Let children experiment making various shades of pink using red food coloring and eyedroppers. If the dye is too dark, they can add more water.

- Make a "Top Ten" list of things that are pink. Include cotton candy, cherry sherbet, and fuzzy pink slippers.

- Collect pink items to wear today. How about pink hair bows, pink socks, and pink underwear?

- Pigs are pink (in a muddy sort of way). Remove all breakables from a room and play a pig game. Select a farmer. Everyone else is a pig stuck in the mud. The farmer is blindfolded as the pigs hide under tables and behind chairs. The farmer says, "Here, Piggy, Piggy." All the pigs say, "Oink-oink," while the farmer tries to find a pig and identify who it is.

- Buy some pink bubble gum. Have a bubble gum blowing contest. Which family member can blow the biggest pink bubble?

- Write with pink crystals. Mix ¼ cup water, 2 Tbs. Epsom salts, and 2 drops red food coloring. Use a paintbrush to write your name with the solution on a dark piece of paper. Let the paper dry for several hours. The Epsom salts leaves your name in shiny crystals.

Celebrate with Crafts

Mix up pretty pink play dough. In a medium saucepan mix together 1 cup flour, ½ cup salt, 1 cup water, 1 tsp. vegetable oil, ½ tsp. cream of tartar, and 1 package unsweetened cherry Kool-Aid. Cook over medium heat, stirring constantly. The mixture will form a clump. Dump the clay on a floured surface and knead for 2–5 minutes. Use to make pink dinosaurs and pink giraffes. The Kool-Aid gives a pleasant scent as well as the bright pink color.

Celebrate with Food

Mix up a batch of pink lemonade to sip on all day long.

Serve strawberry sorbet or sherbet in pink ice-cream dishes.

Set the table with a pink tablecloth. A dollar store is a great place to buy inexpensive pink plates and cups. If the males in your family complain about too much pink, tell them it's "mauve" instead.

Eat Cereal Day

Cereal isn't just for breakfast anymore. Many people enjoy a bowl of cereal and milk for a snack or even for dinner.

Celebrate with Fun

- Draw a game of Tic-Tac-Toe on paper. Use 2 kinds of cereal to take the place of traditional Xs and Os.
- Wrap boxes of cereal with solid-colored paper. Give your children markers to design their own games and activities for the back of the boxes. They can include crossword puzzles and word searches. When finished, they trade boxes with someone else and complete the activities.
- Give everyone a cereal box. Have them pretend to be doing a TV commercial to "sell" the rest of the family on the merits of their cereal.
- Use a computer or get a photo enlarged so you can glue your child's big picture on a cereal box. Let them be today's "Wheaties Champion."
- Look at the nutritional facts on boxes of cereal. Which cereal has the most sugar? Which provides the highest percentage of vitamins? Encourage children to eat more of the nutritious brand of cereal.
- If you have a stale box of cereal on hand, set the cereal out for the birds.
- Take your children to the store and look at the price per pound for several cereal boxes. Some cereals cost more than steak!

Celebrate with Crafts

Elizabeth Taylor wears million-dollar necklaces. You'll look just as elegant wearing your "Loopy Cereal" necklace. Cut 18-inch pieces of yarn. Tightly wrap 1 end with Scotch Tape to form a "needle." Set out O-shaped cereals. String the first piece of cereal on the yarn and tie a knot at the end so the cereal doesn't slide off. Continue stringing cereal, using the taped needle end to make it easier. When the yarn is full of cereal, tie the ends together and put it around your neck. When you get hungry, just eat your necklace!

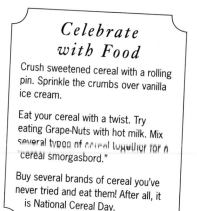

Celebrate with Food

Crush sweetened cereal with a rolling pin. Sprinkle the crumbs over vanilla ice cream.

Eat your cereal with a twist. Try eating Grape-Nuts with hot milk. Mix several types of cereal together for a "cereal smorgasbord."

Buy several brands of cereal you've never tried and eat them! After all, it is National Cereal Day.

Eric Carle's Birthday

Popular children's author Eric Carle is probably well-known to your children. Reread Carle's famous books while celebrating his birthday.

Celebrate with Fun

- The book *The Little Cloud* shows clouds in various shapes. Go outside and watch the clouds. Have children find cloud animals or shapes.
- *Harold and the Purple Crayon* focuses on the color purple. Celebrate by incorporating purple into your life today: Wear purple shirts or socks. Drink purple grape juice. Add a drop of blue and a drop of red food coloring to make purple milk. Serve red cabbage for dinner, which turns a purplish color when cooked. Buy purple paper plates for dinner. Buy a shiny purple eggplant. See if children will eat it.
- Make rainbow-colored ice cubes to go with the bright colors in Eric Carle's books. Fill 3 cups with water. Add a few drops red, yellow, or blue food coloring to each. Pour red water into an ice cube tray till ⅓ full. Freeze 2–3 hours. Pour in yellow-colored water till tray is ⅔ full. After letting yellow water freeze, fill rest of tray with blue water and freeze. Serve your multicolored ice cubes in glasses of clear water.

Celebrate with Crafts

Make a "Very Hungry Caterpillar." Give children 6–8 white paper plates each. Punch 2 holes in each plate directly across from each other. Use paper fasteners to connect the plates, making a wiggly caterpillar. Color the plates with markers or crayons.

Create a cloud picture to go along with *The Little Cloud*. Stretch a few cotton balls so they are flattened. Glue to a piece of blue construction paper. Let dry. Use a thin line of glue to outline each cloud. Sprinkle glitter on paper, then shake over a wastebasket to remove excess glitter.

Eric Carle frequently used tissue paper collages to illustrate his books. Draw a picture with a few basic shapes like a house, fish, or stained-glass window. Cut colored tissue paper into 1-inch squares. Spread glue over your entire picture. Place tissue paper squares inside the lines, overlapping colors to create your own Eric Carle illustration.

Celebrate with Food

Make a "Very Hungry Caterpillar" cake. Buy 4–6 packages "snowball" snack cakes. Place snowballs touching each other in a line on a tray to resemble a caterpillar. Decorate the head of the caterpillar with licorice stick antennae and M&M eyes.

"Happy Birthday" Written

Even if it's not your birthday, you can celebrate the "birthday" of this famous song written in 1924. Some records show it to be the most often sung song in the world.

Celebrate with Fun

- Gather everyone together and sing "Happy Birthday" to someone or something. Could it be the bird's birthday? Try singing "Happy Birthday" to one of the Beanie Babies gathering dust in the toy box.

- Try your hand at writing a whole new song to celebrate birthdays. Divide into groups of 2 or 3 to compose and perform the song. Who knows? You may just start a whole new tradition!

- Amaze your family with some background on the origin of "Happy Birthday." Mildred Hill and her sister, Patty Smith Hill, wrote the song and had it published in 1859 as "Good Morning to All," a classroom greeting song. In 2010 the song will enter public domain when the copyright expires.

- A birthday party wouldn't be complete without presents! Give everyone 5 minutes to find a "white elephant" gift and wrap it. Then exchange gifts. It's always fun to get a broken radio without a volume button.

- Try singing the words to "Happy Birthday" using a different tune. Can you sing the song to the tune of "Row, Row, Row Your Boat"?

- Celebrate by playing Mylar balloon tennis. Use tennis or badminton rackets to bat a Mylar balloon back and forth. The Mylar balloon is sturdy enough to hold up to vigorous games of balloon tennis.

Celebrate with Crafts

Instead of wearing those silly pointed birthday hats, make birthday crowns. Give everyone a strip of paper 24″ x 3″ long. Decorate the strip with bows, sequins, glitter, and ribbons. Wrap it around your head, measure, and staple so it stays on. Wear the crown while singing "Happy Birthday."

Celebrate with Food

How else would you celebrate the birthday of "Happy Birthday"? With a birthday cake, of course! Add a few candles and have everyone make a wish as they blow them out.

Paul Bunyon Day

Enjoy celebrating this holiday in a big way by honoring the legend of a big guy and his big blue ox.

Celebrate with Fun

- Tell a few tall tales today. The story of Paul Bunyon tells us he was so fast he could blow out the candle at night and be in bed before it was dark. Time your children. How long does it take them to turn out the light and hop in bed? Time them again so they can try to beat their record.

- Another legend involves Paul Bunyon's ox. Paul found a baby ox on a bitterly cold day. The ox turned blue because of the extreme cold. Later, Babe the Blue Ox grew so fast that one morning his entire barn was resting on his back. Let children pretend to be Babe while balancing a large pillow on their backs. Have races to see who can cross the finish line without the pillow falling off their backs.

- Contact a local Toastmaster's group and ask when they are having their next "Tall Tales" contest. Toastmasters is a public speaking organization that sponsors competitions in which members try to tell the most outlandish story or tall tale. Attend their contest if possible. You'll enjoy hearing talented storytellers tell their made-up stories.

- Paul Bunyon used his ax to cut down thousands of trees. Have your children make a flexible ax for this activity: Go outside and stand 10 feet from a tree. Pour 1 cup uncooked popcorn in a sock. Tie a knot in the sock, making your flexible hatchet. Take turns holding the sock by the "leg" end and swinging it around before tossing it at the tree.

Celebrate with Crafts

Make something big in honor of Paul Bunyon. Ask an appliance store to save you 1 (or 2!) large refrigerator boxes. Let children use the box to create a fort, a spaceship, or a barn for Babe the ox. Have an adult cut out openings for doors and windows.

Celebrate with Food

Make some giant blue muffins. Mix a batch of biscuit dough using biscuit mix. Roll dough to 1-inch thickness. Use a soup bowl to cut the dough in large circles to make giant biscuits. In a small bowl, beat 1 egg white with several drops of blue food coloring. Use a clean small paintbrush to draw blue pictures using the egg white paint. Bake according to recipe directions. How many gigantic blue biscuits can you eat?

JULY

National Ice-Cream Month
National Hot Dog Month
National Picnic Month
National Recreation and Parks Month

Weeks to Celebrate

3rd Week • National Avoid Boredom Week

Days to Celebrate

1st Sunday • Build a Scarecrow Day
4th Sunday • Parents' Day

3–6 • Tom Sawyer Days (varies but always includes the 4th)
July 3–August 11 • Dog Days of Summer

  2 National Literacy Day
  4 Independence Day
  5 Baby Boomer Day
  5 P. T. Barnum's Birthday
  7 Father/Daughter Take a Walk Together Day
  8 Be a Kid Day
  8 Raffi's Birthday
 10 Teddy Bear Picnic Day
 11 Cheer Up the Lonely Day
 12 Paper Bag Patented
 14 Celebration of Amelia Bedelia
 22 Anniversary of the Pied Piper of Hamlin
 24 Cousin's Day

National Ice-Cream Month

In 1984 Ronald Reagan declared July to be National Ice-Cream Month. It's your American duty to celebrate by eating ice cream during July.

Celebrate with Fun

- Throughout the day you pick to celebrate, whenever someone says "ice cream," everyone needs to give the ice-cream cheer. In loud voices, yell, "I scream, you scream, we all scream for ice cream!"

- Have an ice-cream eating contest. Place equal amounts of ice cream in bowls. See who can eat theirs first—using only their mouth, no spoons!

- The Ice Cream Association has ranked the most popular flavors of ice cream:

  Vanilla—29 percent
  Chocolate—8 percent
  Butter Pecan—5 percent
  Strawberry—5 percent
  Neapolitan—4 percent

- Many ice cream companies now label their ice cream with creative titles like "Moosetracks," "Chubby Hubby," and "Wavy Gravy." Create some unique ice-cream titles of your own. Describe the ingredients in your new best-selling ice cream.

Celebrate with Crafts

Make some miniature ice-cream cones using communion cups. After communion at church, take home the plastic cups for the "cones." Wash first! Place a small dab of glue on a medium-sized fuzzy pom-pom. Place inside the plastic cup as the 1st scoop of ice cream. Top with a smaller red "cherry" pom-pom. Set your tiny ice-cream sundaes on the table while you eat ice cream.

Celebrate with Food

Plan an "ice-cream potluck." Invite family and friends to come sample a wide variety of flavors. Have people bring a pint of their favorite ice cream. Supply ice-cream cones so people can have a triple scoop of butter pecan, cherry chip fudge, and Phish food. (Yes, that's a flavor!)

Make some Rock-and-Roll ice cream with your family. You'll need a 3-lb. coffee can and a 1-lb. can. Into the washed small can, pour ½ cup milk, ½ cup half-and-half, 1 Tbs. sugar, ¼ tsp. vanilla, and a pinch of salt. Seal can well and place inside larger can. Pour 1–2 cups rock salt around smaller can and 2 cups crushed ice. Seal the larger can well. Have children roll the can back and forth down the sidewalk for 15 minutes. Open both cans and enjoy smooth ice cream.

National Hot Dog Month

This all-American food is so popular that over 16 million are sold every year. Celebrate this month by enjoying a variety of activities involving hot dogs.

Celebrate with Fun

- Old-time hot dogs were connected into long links of dogs. Play a game of "Hot Dog Hug." Get 2 teams of 5 or 6 kids together. Line the teams up single file, with each holding on to the person's waist in front of them. The last person in line has a red sock hanging from the waist of their pants. The object of the game is for the first people in each team's line to grab the "tail" of the opposite team.

- If you don't know your dog's birthday, select a day this month to celebrate Rover's birthday. Serve a few cut-up hot dogs along with his dinner. Don't forget to take a picture of him wearing a silly pointed party hat.

- Sacrifice 1 hot dog and bun to play "Hot Dog Catch." Holding a bun open with 2 hands, stand 5 feet away from a partner who is holding a hot dog. Partners take turns tossing and catching the hot dog, using the bun as a catcher's mitt.

- Oscar Mayer often has a nationwide contest looking for children to sing the Oscar Mayer song in an adorable style. Have your own contest to see who can charm the socks off the judges by singing:

> "I wish I were an Oscar Mayer Wiener,
> Oh that is what I'd really like to be
> 'Cuz if I were an Oscar Mayer Wiener,
> Everyone would be in love with me."

Celebrate with Crafts

Here's an edible craft: Use a hot dog in a bun as your canvas. "Decorate" your hot dog using mustard, ketchup, and relish. Write your name or draw yellow mustard flowers. Vote on the most creative hot dog.

Celebrate with Food

For variety, get brave and try a vegetarian hot dog. Sample a few different brands to find one your family enjoys.

Serve personalized hot dogs to your family. Use a squeeze bottle to write your child's name on their hot dog with ketchup or mustard.

Invite friends over for a Tube Steak Barbecue. Don't worry about your budget—tube steaks are actually hot dogs!

More ideas: www.hot-dog.org

193

National Picnic Month

Enjoy the sunny days of summer by having numerous picnics this month. Even ordinary food tastes better when eaten outdoors.

Celebrate with Fun

- Invite friends over for a potluck picnic. Have people bring food that begins with the first letter of their last name. The Clarks will bring cookies while the Petersons bring potato salad.

- If a pond or lake is nearby, teach children how to skip rocks. (Or find a more skilled "skipper" than you to teach your children.) It's fun to watch a flat rock "skip" over the water.

- Plan some traditional picnic games. Find burlap bags to use for sack races. Use old pantyhose legs to make ties for a 3-legged race. Don't forget the ever popular egg toss.

- Don't worry if it rains on your picnic day. Put the gingham tablecloth on the living-room floor and pretend you're outside. Gather all the houseplants to put around the tablecloth. You'll think you are outside because of all the greenery.

- If you've invited friends over for a picnic, play Hide and Seek and add a new twist—have all the adults hide while children scurry around looking for their parents.

- Go on a "36-inch" hike. Set a hula hoop on the ground. Sit around the outside edge and see what animals are found inside the circle. Look for tiny bugs and worms. See if anyone can find a 4-leaf clover.

Celebrate with Crafts

Make twig people from small twigs lying around your picnic area. Set out twist ties to attach the twigs to each other. Long pine needles tied together also make arms and legs. Use the "caps" from acorns to adorn your twig person's head.

While waiting for the hamburgers to cook, decorate place mats with leaf people. Collect different-sized leaves. Have everyone glue 1 leaf to their paper place mat. Use markers to turn your leaf into a person or animal. It's interesting to see how a leaf on 1 place mat becomes the body of a man while another leaf turns into a hat on a kangaroo!

Celebrate with Food

Why do picnic foods always have to be potato salad and hot dogs? Plan an ethnic picnic. Serve foods from other countries. Barbecue meat for Mexican carne asada or skewer minimeatballs for an Italian dish.

National Recreation and Parks Month

Most communities have a local Parks and Recreation department. Get a copy of their activity schedule and check out the programs.

Celebrate with Fun

- Set a goal to participate in one activity sponsored by your Parks and Recreation department. Sign up for a yoga class, take your dog to obedience lessons, or attend a family concert.

- Visit a new park in your community. Ask friends for tips on their favorite parks.

- Plan a few recreation programs of your own. Assign family members one day of the week to plan a family activity. You'll enjoy a week in which David leads a scavenger hunt on Monday, Mom plans a picnic on Tuesday . . .

- Ask if your local Parks and Recreation department needs volunteers. Some departments look for help planting trees or clearing trails. Other times they need volunteers to help with a Special Olympics track meet. These opportunities allow you to give back to your community.

- Build an outdoor fort. Put sheets over the swing set or over the picnic table. Crawl inside and read funny stories together. If you're really ambitious, make a fort using branches and brush. Collecting the natural materials takes more time, yet they create an "authentic" backyard fort.

Celebrate with Crafts

Collect an assortment of flowers and leaves. Place them between the pages of a seldom-used book. Put a weight on the book. After several days, gently remove the flat flowers and use them to decorate note cards or stationery.

On a hot day, let young children "paint" your garage or car. Don't worry! It's safe. Hand children a bucket of water and paintbrushes. Let them paint whatever they want, even the front door. The water darkens the surface and then quickly dries in the sun. They can paint the same area over and over.

Celebrate with Food

Cut up pieces of fruit to make fruit kabobs. Set out an assortment of apples, grapes, bananas, and pineapples. Cut in bite-sized pieces and slide on bamboo skewers. Pack a bunch of fruit kabobs and eat them at your favorite park.

More ideas: www.activeparks.org; www.sondrascrafts.com/book_5.php

National Avoid Boredom Week

How often do you hear "I'm bored!" from your children? Celebrate today by showing children how they can create their own fun so you'll never have to hear moans and groans about boredom again.

Celebrate with Fun

- Make a list with your children of all the things they like doing. Visiting Disneyland weekly may not be possible, but list ordinary activities like visiting the park, making cookies, riding bikes, and playing card games. Post the list on the fridge. The next time a child is bored, silently point to the list and have them select an activity appropriate for that time.

- Most communities offer a wealth of free summer activities. Call the Parks department or check the newspaper. Be adventurous—visit the college arboretum or an antique sailboat exhibit. When children see you finding interesting things to do, they just might be inclined to do the same.

- Assign each child to be "Camp Counselor" for a day. They come up with fun activities, planning ahead to get supplies (and permission). Your Junior Counselors might organize a scavenger hunt, create a craft, or lead a campfire sing-a-long. Many children are surprised to find out it takes some effort to organize people and supplies for games or crafts.

- Give your children an old typewriter or record player. Many garage sales sell them for less than 1 dollar. For safety, cut off any electrical cords. Have children use small tools to disassemble the appliance. Let them unscrew the back of a radio or actually look inside an old computer. Offer a prize if someone can put all the pieces back together again!

Celebrate with Crafts

Make the ever popular summertime craft item, a decorated pencil holder. Give every child an empty soup can (with no sharp edges) and 25–30 wooden craft sticks. Let them decorate the sticks with markers or crayons and glue the sticks onto the cans. To make it easier for little fingers, put a rubber band around the can, then slip the sticks underneath to hold them in place while the glue dries. Use the cans as handy storage containers for pencils or markers.

Celebrate with Food

To avoid boredom, go to a grocery store and let everyone pick out 1 food item they've never tasted before. How about jicama or canned blackberries? Take the items home for a taste-testing adventure.

Build a Scarecrow Day

We normally think of scarecrows only in the fall, surrounded by crisp leaves and pumpkins. Get a head start on the traditional scarecrow season by celebrating today.

Celebrate with Fun

- Dress up like scarecrows. Put on overalls or jeans with flannel shirts. Add straw hats so you look like a scarecrow family. Once you're dressed up, take turns scaring each other. One person hides. Everyone else walks around trying to avoid the scarecrow, who jumps out yelling, "Go away, birds!"

- At the turn of the century in England, young boys were human scarecrows. They lived in crude huts in the fields and used wooden clappers to scare away birds. Select someone as a human scarecrow. Put 3–4 silk flowers at their feet. The rest are "birds" trying to grab the flowers. See who can steal the flowers before the scarecrow yells, "Shoo!"

- Here's a handy trick to stuff a scarecrow: Instead of stuffing a pair of pants with straw or padding, fill pantyhose. The straw stays neatly in the pantyhose. Then stuff the chubby pantyhose inside a pair of pants.

Celebrate with Crafts

Place a broom on the ground to make a clean-cut scarecrow. The straw part forms your scarecrow's face. Use craft foam to give the broom personality with eyes, nose, cheeks, and even dimples. Stuff a shirt and pants with plastic grocery bags. Slide the broomstick through the shirt neck, the pant waist, and 1 leg. Heavy-duty duct tape will hold the shirt collar around the "neck." Stick broom handle firmly into the ground so scarecrow stands proudly upright. Tuck pant legs into old shoes.

Make miniature scarecrows out of chenille stems. Twist stems to form the body with arms and legs. Attach a small Styrofoam ball for the head. Use fabric scraps to add ragged-looking clothes and a hat. Set up a tabletop display of your scarecrow village.

Celebrate with Food

Make edible straw stacks. Microwave 1 package chocolate chips and ½ cup peanut butter for 1 minute. Stir and microwave another 1–2 minutes until melted. Add 4 cups straw. Not really! Add 4 cups chow mein noodles. Stir well. Drop "straw" mounds on waxed paper. Eat straw when cool.

197

Parents' Day

It seems like every day is Kids' Day—why not a day set aside to honor parents? Tell children it's their duty to make this day special for their parents. Lecture them about how lucky they are to have such kind, loving, creative, and funny parents!

Celebrate with Fun

- Ask the kids (if you're brave enough!) to put on a play depicting their mother and father. Sit back and see yourself through the eyes of your children. You may come away with insights into your parenting techniques. You might ask, "Do I really nag that much?"

- Pretend your family is on a game show. Set up questions for kids and adults to answer like: Where did Dad propose to Mom? What is the name of Shannon's ballet teacher? What food makes Steven gag? What sport did Dad play in high school? What did Mom do on her first roller-coaster ride with Dad? What is Shannon's favorite subject in school? How did Dad get the scar on his chin? See if parents can answer questions about their children and vice versa.

- Help children understand parental responsibility. Get a big flip chart–sized paper. Have kids list things parents are responsible for, like paying bills and mowing the lawn. Continue until there are 20–25 items. Children forget parents have to schedule dental checkups, supervise employees at work, coach soccer, volunteer at school, and buy groceries.

Celebrate with Crafts

See how well your children know you. Give each child construction paper and old magazines. On 1 side write "Mom likes," and on the other "Mom dislikes." Kids cut out pictures of situations or items Mom likes or dislikes and glue them on the appropriate sides. Have them do the same with Dad. Afterward, look at the pictures. Did your children capture your true likes and dislikes?

Make a family portrait with every family member drawing someone besides themselves. Frame your work of art.

Celebrate with Food

Remember the scene in the original movie The Parent Trap in which Haley Mills and her twin prepared a romantic meal for their parents? Drop very subtle (and not so subtle) hints that your children should prepare a romantic meal for you and your spouse. If nothing else, settle for the kids watching a video while you and your beloved eat peanut butter sandwiches alone —in peace and quiet!

National Literacy Day

It's a little-known fact that today is set aside by presidential proclamation to encourage people of all ages to read. Bring out the books, magazines, and even cereal boxes!

Celebrate with Fun

- Send written messages on different surfaces to family members. Write "I Love You" on a wide strip of uncooked lasagna! Use a bar of soap to write a message on a mirror. Buy a message board and write down a "thought for the day" for family members.

- Draw your own comic strip, complete with written captions. Tape it to the comic page in your newspaper for your family to find.

- Contact your local literacy department and see if they need volunteers. Your time could help a person break the barrier of illiteracy.

- Stress the importance of reading. Get young children interested by letting them dictate a story to you. Write it down and ask them to draw illustrations. Read their completed book so children see how words and pictures create a story.

- Put a large blackboard in a convenient location. Children love drawing and writing on the board "just like their teacher does." Or buy some blackboard paint and use it on a wall. Children can then write and erase on the wall just like on a regular blackboard!

- If you have prereaders, let them "read" the newspaper with you. Ask them to point out certain letters. Can they find a letter that is the same as the first letter in their name?

- Children quickly learn to read when television is at stake! Set a TV time limit and have children check the newspaper to find the TV schedule. Ask them to circle the shows they want to watch during their TV time.

Celebrate with Crafts

Ask your child to make alphabet flash cards for a younger child. Use 3" x 5" index cards. Have them neatly print a letter from the alphabet on 1 side. On the other side, they draw an item beginning with that letter. Give the completed alphabet cards to a child learning to read.

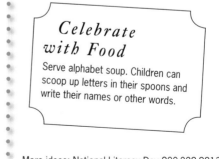

Celebrate with Food

Serve alphabet soup. Children can scoop up letters in their spoons and write their names or other words.

More ideas: National Literacy Day 800-228-8813

Tom Sawyer Days

In Hannibal, Missouri, over 100,000 people attend the Tom Sawyer festival each year. You won't need quite that many people to celebrate at your house.

Celebrate with Fun

- Find an abridged version of *The Adventures of Tom Sawyer* to read as a family so you know why and how to celebrate.

- Have a Tom Sawyer and Becky look-alike contest. This means overalls and straw hats for the boys and frilly cotton sundresses for Becky.

- Borrow a frog from the pond to have a frog-jumping contest. Draw a chalk circle on the sidewalk. Place frog in center and wait. Wait some more until the frog decides to jump. Measure how far your frog leaped. No frogs around? Try a human frog!

- Tom and Huck built a raft to float down the Mississippi River. Let children build a raft for an action figure. Find small branches they can tie together. Let them experiment with different techniques to build a raft that supports their action figure. Float rafts in bathtub or wading pool.

Celebrate with Crafts

Tom Sawyer became famous for getting other people to whitewash his aunt's fence. Make some milk paint. Pour 1 can evaporated milk into several small containers. Add different colors of food coloring to each container of milk. This mixture makes a shiny paint.

In a cave with many passageways, Tom and his friends read the names, dates, and pictures scrawled on the walls. Make a cave drawing by cutting a brown paper bag into a flat section. Color a picture on it, pressing so the crayon makes a dark drawing. Write some names or dates to make it look like something found on a cave wall. Crumple the paper into a tight ball, unwrinkle, then crumple again. Repeat 10–12 times. Flatten the paper. Paint over picture with watercolors. The paint will resist the crayon drawing and soak into the wrinkles. Blot up any excess paint. Hang on the closet wall and pretend you are finding your picture in a dark cave.

Celebrate with Food

Tom and Huck fished in the Mississippi, then ate their catch. Find a place where children can catch fish. Some communities sponsor youth fishing derbies in well-stocked ponds. Check if a "Catch and Clean" program exists in your area. Children catch fish, and a professional cleans the fish so you can cook it at home.

Dog Days of Summer

This 40-day period is traditionally the hottest time of the summer. Find ways to celebrate by keeping cool.

Celebrate with Fun

- This time of year children run through sprinklers. Attach a sprinkler to a tree or swing set so the water sprays down for a whole new way of keeping cool. For extra fun, set up a sprinkler obstacle course. Borrow sprinklers from the neighbors so you have 4 or 5. (Tell neighbors to come join the fun.) Children race from one sprinkler to the next, performing tasks like hula hooping under one, jumping rope under another, doing a cartwheel through one, crawling over another, and trying to keep a newspaper dry while racing through the final sprinkler.
- Sing some "cold" songs like "Frosty the Snowman" or "Walking in a Winter Wonderland."
- Fill a wading pool with cold water. As children play in the pool, dump in several trays of ice cubes. For more ice fun, put a cookie sheet or cake pan in the freezer. Fill to the edge with water. Freeze overnight. Remove the flat "iceberg" to put in your children's wading pool. Let kids float action figures on the ice.

Celebrate with Crafts

Cool down by making some paper snowflakes. Fold a coffee filter in half, then into quarters, then eighths. Cut small shapes and slits in the paper. Unfold your frosty snowflake.

Ever mistakenly left a box of crayons in a car on a hot day? Use that same technique to make crayon paintings. Put different-colored unwrapped crayons in some tuna fish cans and place cans in baking dish half full of water. Bake at 300 degrees 10–15 minutes or until crayons melt. Have an adult remove from the oven. Use old toothbrushes or cotton swabs to dip in melted crayon and paint pictures.

Celebrate with Food

Make frozen pudding cups to cool you down in the heat. Mix up any flavor instant or cooked pudding. If you like, add a few chocolate chips. Pour into small plastic cups. Stick plastic spoons or wooden craft sticks in the centers. Make a small slit in the centers of paper cupcake liners. Slide a liner over each spoon until it touches the cup. The liner will catch drips as children eat their pudding pops. Chill overnight.

Barbecue some hot dogs to celebrate Dog Days of Summer.

Independence Day

The Declaration of Independence was approved on July 4, 1776. Americans celebrate that event with picnics, fireworks, and a swell of patriotism.

Celebrate with Fun

- Organize a spontaneous neighborhood Independence Day parade. Spread the word that it will begin in front of your house at 2 P.M. Participants come dressed in red, white, and blue and ride decorated bikes. Adults pull toddlers in red wagons. When everyone has assembled, parade around the block. More than likely, your participants will be so excited they'll vote to repeat the parade several times.

- Purchase as many American flags as your budget allows from a dollar store. Display them proudly inside and outside the house and in your parade.

- Pass out red, white, and blue chalk and have children decorate the sidewalk and driveway with Fourth of July greetings.

- Sing patriotic songs and try to find the second and third verses to "The Star-Spangled Banner" and "America the Beautiful."

- Many pets are scared of noisy fireworks. Make sure your family pet is in a secure area so it doesn't run away during the blasts of firecrackers.

Celebrate with Crafts

"Blow" some holiday fireworks. Drop a few tsp. slightly runny tempera paint randomly on pieces of construction paper. Each person blows on the paint with a clean drinking straw. The paint splatters out like colorful fireworks. Keep blowing until the whole pieces of paper are covered.

Make some sparkling crystals to celebrate. On July 2 or 3, set out 4–5 charcoal briquettes in a shallow bowl. In a separate bowl, mix 6 Tbs. salt, 6 Tbs. liquid bluing (in the laundry section of grocery stores), 6 Tbs. water, and 1 tsp. ammonia. Add a few drops various colors food coloring on top of the briquettes. Slowly pour the water/ammonia mix over the briquettes. Within 24 hours, small colorful crystals will form.

Celebrate with Food

Make this easy Independence Day cake. Bake a rectangle cake. Frost with white frosting. Place blueberries in top left corner to resemble stars. Cut strawberries in half. Arrange in even rows across rest of cake, leaving lines of white frosting showing to represent the red and white stripes.

Baby Boomer Day

Some people say Baby Boomers are the "Greatest Generation." Turn this day over to celebrate people born between 1946 and 1964. For most of us, this means reliving our teenage years.

Celebrate with Fun

- Find your wire-rimmed sunglasses! Wear your bell-bottoms! (If they fit.) Put on your mood ring. Dress up as if you were back in high school. Baby Boomers were active in protesting and making their opinions heard. After you look like a true hippie, start "campaigning." Let children know why you think they need an earlier bedtime.

- Remember the sit ins of the '60s and '70s? Stage your own sit-in to protest how unappreciated you are. Go on strike—refuse to drive anyone to soccer unless their bedroom is clean. Stage a protest with signs on a stick, letting your family know you're tired of their complaints about your cooking.

- Encourage children to stick up for their beliefs. What cause do they support? Help them make signs and stage a mock protest about their issue. Show them what it's like to speak up when "hecklers" are in the crowd.

- Sprinkle your conversation with "Peace, Man," and "Love is where it's at." Don't forget to add "groovy" to every sentence.

Celebrate with Crafts

Can't find your favorite peace symbol necklace? Make another one. Bend a sparkly chenille stem into a circle. Twist ends shut. Use 2 more chenille stems to form the peace symbol (a modified Y shape). Attach ends to round circle. Use an 18-inch piece of yarn to wear peace symbol around your neck.

Remember the tie-dyed T-shirts you wore when you were fit and trim? Get out an old shirt and have children help you tie-dye your shirt to help you relive your youth.

Find a solid-colored headband or use a strip of cotton. Dip wads of crepe paper in water. Immediately blot wet crepe paper onto headband. Do several colors. The dye transfers from the crepe paper to the fabric, making a tie-dyed headband.

Celebrate with Food

Bake cupcakes and frost as usual. Provide assorted candy to decorate the cupcakes with flower designs. Flower Power Forever!

203

P. T. Barnum's Birthday

We've all heard of the "Greatest Show on Earth," founded by J. A. Bailey and P. T. Barnum. Celebrate with your own homemade circus.

Celebrate with Fun

- Have each family member perform a feat of skill, daring, or just plain silliness. Be sure to reward Dad's attempt to stand on his head with lots of cheering and clapping. Someone could do a magic trick or perform the ever popular routine of throwing a bucket of "water" at the audience (actually a bucket filled with tiny scraps of tissue paper).

- Play "Back-to-Back Balloons." Stand back-to-back with a partner and have someone place a balloon between the partners. They need to squeeze their backs together to keep the balloon in place. Have races to see which pairs can cross the finish line without dropping their balloon.

- P. T. Barnum was known for exhibiting Jumbo, the giant elephant, in America. Play "Elephant Tag." Bend your shoulders over while extending your arms to form a long trunk. Play tag in the usual way, except the person who is "It" tries to tag people with her trunk.

- Place a length of yarn or string on the ground to serve as a tightrope. Watch family members display death-defying feats of daring on the "tightrope."

More ideas: www.barnum-museum.org

Celebrate with Crafts

What would a circus be without clowns? Make face paint to help give you an extra-bright smile. Mix ½ cup solid vegetable shortening and ½ cup cornstarch about 3 minutes, until very smooth. Divide mixture into 2–3 small bowls. Add 1 tsp. powdered paint in different colors to each bowl. Mix well. Use as face paint to make distinctive clown faces. Cleanup is simple using a washcloth, soap, and water.

Make goofy cone hats to wear throughout the day. Cut a quarter circle from a large piece of paper or light cardboard. Bend the curved edge to fit your head and staple or tape shut. Decorate with sequins, buttons, and scrap ribbons.

Celebrate with Food

Unless you have your own cotton candy machine, serve this clown ice-cream treat. Use an ice-cream scoop to form a ball of ice cream on each plate. Use M&M's to form eyes, nose, and mouth. Top with a wafer cone for an edible hat.

Father/Daughter Take a Walk Together Day

This annual celebration helps fathers and daughters spend time together. Along with taking a walk, try some of these other activities.

Celebrate with Fun

- Naturally, you'll want to take a father/daughter walk. You could stroll around the neighborhood, but why not try something different? Drive 2 or 3 miles down the road and take a walk in a slightly different area. Or catch the local bus and get off at a location that looks interesting. After your walk, hop back on the bus for the return trip home.

- Take a trip down memory lane (even if your daughter is only 6). Ask your daughter questions like: What was the best birthday present you ever received? What would be your ideal vacation? What do you enjoy doing when you're with Dad?

- Do something silly and spontaneous with your daughter. This can be hard if you are a serious person, but go ahead, try something crazy. If she's young, let her dress you in a princess costume—complete with makeup! Go order the largest ice-cream sundae available to eat together. Do something to make your daughter say, "Dad—you're great!"

- If your daughter is older and comes home after dark from basketball games or youth group meetings, start a "Welcome Home" tradition. Keep an electrical candle lit in the front window until she's safely home.

- Enjoy the warm summer air. Tonight when it's dark and fireflies are out, sit with your daughter on a cozy blanket and look at the stars together. You might end up answering questions like "Is there really a God?" and "How did the stars get in the sky?"

Celebrate with Crafts

Set out a pile of old magazines. Using scissors and glue, make collages about each other. Dad cuts out pictures depicting his daughter's personality and accomplishments. Your daughter gets a chance to make a pictorial description about you. Discuss the collages afterward to find out what your daughter really thinks about you!

Celebrate with Food

Take your daughter to her favorite restaurant, even if that means eating at Happy Harry's Hamburgers. Let her order whatever she wants. When ordering your meal, tell the server how special your daughter is to you. Naturally your daughter will blush, but she'll also feel special because of your comments.

Be a Kid Day

For the under 12 crowd, every day is Be a Kid Day. Today, no matter what your age, relax, have fun, and be a kid all over again.

Celebrate with Fun

- Ask a favorite kid what he or she enjoys doing. Then join in. Swing at the park, ride a bike through mud puddles, and slurp your soup. You're a kid today, so forget about your usual adult responsibilities.

- Give every family member 25 cents. Go to a store that sells penny (or inexpensive) candy. Relive the joy of deciding between tiny Tootsie Rolls or packs of Bazooka bubble gum. Now that you have your gum, see who can blow the biggest bubble.

- Play Legos or blocks with your children. This is Be a Kid Day, so avoid acting like an adult and saying things like "Be careful, that tower will fall," or "Follow the directions on the Lego box." Simply enjoy playing with your children on their terms. Cheerfully dress your daughter's Barbie doll in 17 different outfits. That's what you'd do if you were a kid, right?

- Find 2 baby bottles. Fill with water and have a baby bottle race to see who can drink the water the fastest.

Celebrate with Crafts

Make bath time fun with a giant bath ball. Crush 4 Alka-Seltzer tablets into a fine powder. Add 4 Tbs. cornstarch and ½ cup baking soda. Have an adult microwave 6 Tbs. coconut oil and ¼ tsp. essential oils 12–15 seconds. Stir into dry mixture. Form mixture into tennis ball–sized balls. Let dry overnight. The next day, drop a bath ball into the tub for fizzing fun!

Make Jell-O play dough. Mix 1 cup flour, ½ cup salt, 1 cup water, 1 Tbs. oil, 2 tsp. cream of tartar, and a 3½ oz. package unsweetened Jell-O in a saucepan. Stir well over medium heat to the consistency of thick pudding. Cool. Knead on a floured surface and use to make kid-friendly sculptures.

Celebrate with Food

Eat dessert first! Have a bowl of the canned chicken noodle soup you ate as a child. Make a sandwich with plain old white bread. Add chocolate syrup to your glass of milk. Ask your children about their favorite meal and make it for the family. You could also all go to McDonald's for Happy Meals!

Raffi's Birthday

He goes by only one name, and children around the country know the words to his popular songs. Celebrate Raffi's birthday with a musical celebration.

Celebrate with Fun

- Hold up your favorite Raffi record, tape, or CD and sing "Happy Birthday." Vote for your favorite Raffi song. Is it "Baby Baluga"? "Brush Your Teeth"? Sing the family favorite together.

- Almost every Raffi concert includes "If You're Happy and You Know It." Make up your own verses. How about "If you're hungry and you know it, wiggle your nose" or "If you're tired and you know it, take a snooze." Act out your words.

- Raffi's songs teach important lessons. "My Mommy Comes Back—She Never Would Forget Me" reassures children their parents always pick them up from school or soccer practice. Discuss some safety rules. Whom should children call if no one comes to pick them up after ballet? Develop a secret family password so if you have to send a friend to pick up a child, your friend can say the password, reassuring your child it's okay to get in the car.

- Tonight when everyone is getting ready for bed, sing Raffi's toothbrushing song: "I brush my teeth, cha cha cha, I brush my teeth, cha cha cha." Repeat, and repeat again!

Celebrate with Crafts

Raffi sings traditional children's songs too. Make your own spiderweb while singing "The Itsy Bitsy Spider." Cut white paper the size of a shoe-box bottom. Place paper inside box. Pour ½ cup black paint in a bowl. Drop in a marble. Use a plastic spoon to coat the marble and scoop it out. Drop it on the paper in the shoe box. Gently shake box back and forth, watching the marble "paint" a spiderweb design on paper. Drop marble in paint again for more webs. Try using several colors of paint for a multicolored web.

Celebrate with Food

One of Raffi's newest songs is "Jane, Jane," written with Jane Goodall in support of her work with chimpanzees. Try a little chimpanzee food—eat fried bananas. Peel several bananas and place in a buttered frying pan over medium heat. Fry 8–10 minutes, turning occasionally and adding 1 Tbs. butter. Remove from pan and eat. The warm bananas take on a new flavor and consistency.

More ideas: www.raffinews.com

207

Teddy Bear Picnic Day

It's not only people who enjoy picnics. Teddy bears want to have fun outside also!

Celebrate with Fun

- Collect all the teddy bears in your house for a picnic. Line them up for a group photo. Put them all in a picnic basket. Cover them with a cloth. Let children reach in and try to guess which teddy bear they are feeling.

- Read the book *Brown Bear, Brown Bear, What do you See?* Help your teddy bears act out the story.

- Play the memory game. The first person says, "I'm going on a picnic and in my basket I have an Apple." The next person repeats Apple and adds an item beginning with B. Continue adding items through the alphabet until someone has a memory lapse.

- Play Elvis's song "Teddy Bear." Put on a show in which the teddy bears lip-sync to the song. Then sing a rousing chorus of "The Bear Went over the Mountain." Let children act out the song with their teddy bears.

- Draw a child-sized teddy bear on a large piece of cardboard. Have children color the fur, add a hat, decorate the vest, etc. Cut a hole where the teddy bear's face would be. Have children poke their faces out of the hole. Take pictures of your adorable teddy bears.

Celebrate with Crafts

Make a picnic basket out of a paper lunch bag. Evenly fold the top of the bag several times, making a rim. Cut 2 strips of paper 2″ x 10″ from another paper bag. Attach the paper strips to form handles on the "basket." Use your basket to carry lightweight picnic supplies.

Create great teddy bear masks with paper plates and yarn. Draw a bear's face on a paper plate. Cut eyeholes so children can see. Punch holes about 1 inch apart around the entire plate. Tie pieces of brown or gold yarn in each hole for a shaggy fur look. Have children hold their masks in front of their faces.

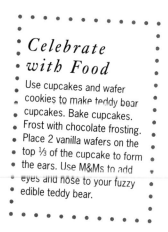

Celebrate with Food

Use cupcakes and wafer cookies to make teddy bear cupcakes. Bake cupcakes. Frost with chocolate frosting. Place 2 vanilla wafers on the top ⅓ of the cupcake to form the ears. Use M&Ms to add eyes and nose to your fuzzy edible teddy bear.

Cheer Up the Lonely Day

It's summer, school's out, and, as the song goes, "Living is easy." Take time out from the enjoyable days of summer to cheer up someone who might be feeling a bit lonely.

Celebrate with Fun

- Brainstorm with your family about people who might need a pick-me-up. Did your elderly neighbor just return from the hospital? Is a relative going through a hard time? Know a young mother overwhelmed with 2 toddlers? Call your church to find out who needs extra encouragement.

- Put together a "You are special" gift basket. Include some treats, an inspirational book, and a small potted plant, all topped with a bright bow. Deliver it to a person who needs encouragement. Stay for a visit as you deliver the basket.

- Bring your well-trained family pet to visit a nursing home. Some centers allow mellow cats or dogs to visit with the residents, many of whom gave up beloved pets when they came to the nursing home. Or ask the nursing home if you can bring an impromptu kids' choir. Gather neighborhood children and put on a concert. Don't worry about singing in tune. The kids' natural enthusiasm and spontaneity will make up for their lack of professionalism.

- Contact your local Meals on Wheels program. They might refer you to a shut-in who would welcome a visit. Let your children take along stuffed animals or favorite toys to share.

- Role-play situations with your children on how to be a friend. Can they make a new child in Sunday school feel comfortable? What should they do when kids pick on another child? By role-playing, your children gain valuable empathetic skills and learn about other people's feelings.

Celebrate with Crafts

You never know when someone will need to be cheered up. Make greeting cards to keep on hand. Give children paper and stickers and show them how to write greetings like "We thought about you today" or "You are special." When needed, send a homemade card to someone.

Celebrate with Food

Invite someone over who hasn't been with a family lately. It doesn't matter that you aren't serving prime rib with champagne. A lonely person will enjoy simply observing the hustle and bustle of an ordinary family eating spaghetti. Make extra servings for your guest to take home.

Paper Bag Patented

Paper bags do more than hold your lunch. Celebrate using paper bags in more ways than you ever thought was possible.

Celebrate with Fun

- Crumple the tops of paper lunch bags together and blow up the bags. Try popping them with your hands to see who makes the loudest bang.
- Put an item inside a bag. Shake it. Can your family guess the item by sound alone? Try to guess the item by feeling it from outside the bag.
- Give everyone a paper bag containing 1 ordinary item like a spoon or tape roll. Each person looks at their item and thinks of unusual ways to use it. Write ideas on the outside of the bag. After 10 minutes, read lists out loud. Display bags to remind family members of their creativity. Who knew a ruler could be used to flip a tomato into the salad bowl across the kitchen?
- Ever heard of the unknown comic? He would appear on television shows wearing a paper bag over his head. Perform your own version of paper bag humor. Cut eye and mouth holes in a large bag and take turns appearing as the unknown comic. Put the bag over your head and perform a song or tell jokes. Even the worst knock-knock joke is funny when Dad tells it inside a paper bag.
- Choose a partner for paper bag skits. Each team gets a bag containing 3 unrelated, identical items (maybe a pencil, dirty sock, and orange). After 5 minutes practice, each team performs a skit incorporating the items. You'll be surprised at the difference in each skit, even though the props were identical.

Celebrate with Crafts

Paper bag luminaries add a festive glow around your house while celebrating Paper Bag Day. Cut small designs in the sides of lunch bags. Add 2 cups sand or dirt to each bag. Place a votive candle in the center of the sand. Place the luminaries on your porch or driveway. Light candles to create your party atmosphere.

Celebrate with Food

Set out lunch bags filled with assorted foods. One bag might contain apples, another cheese slices, and another pretzels. Seal the bags and bring them to the living room. Plan an indoor picnic at which people have to guess the contents of the bag before eating. Then mix and match the items to create a paper bag dinner.

Celebration of Amelia Bedelia

(Peggy Parish's Birthday)

Who hasn't laughed at the innocent blunders of Amelia Bedelia? When she is told to "draw the drapes," Amelia produces a lovely drawing. She has good intentions, but often gets mixed up. Spend time today being silly and, of course, reading some Amelia Bedelia books.

Celebrate with Fun

- At the library, check out as many Amelia Bedelia books as possible. Since the books are short, read them throughout the day.

- Have 1 family member dress up like Amelia. Find a flouncy dress with an apron. Make an old-fashioned maid's hat to add to the look.

- Try some of Amelia Bedelia's activities—her way. She is told to measure 2 cups of rice. Have children use a tape measure to measure 2 cups of rice stacked on top of each other. Amelia is also instructed to put the light out, so she hangs lightbulbs from the clothesline. Is it actually possible to hang lightbulbs on a clothesline? Amelia's employer tells her to put colored balls on the Christmas tree. Amelia dutifully purchases an assortment of tennis, soccer, and footballs. She has a difficult time getting the balls to stick on the tree. Collect the balls around your house and try propping them in an outdoor tree.

- Have a family discussion about communication. Have you ever told your children to do something, but they totally misunderstood what you wanted? What are some ways to improve family communication?

Celebrate with Crafts

When Amelia Bedelia is told to dress the chicken, she's supposed to prepare and stuff the chicken for dinner. Instead, Amelia dresses the chicken in clothes! Sketch out a picture of a chicken. Ask everyone to use markers and "dress" their chicken. How about a chicken in a cowgirl outfit? Ever see a chicken in a tuxedo or a tutu? Get silly with your sketches.

Celebrate with Food

These candy flowers look like something Amelia Bedelia would serve for dessert. Make Jell-O in small paper cups. Chill until firm. Glue small construction paper "petals" around a flat sucker. (Keep plastic sucker wrapper on.) Stick your candy flower in the Jell-O to make an edible dessert.

211

Anniversary of the
Pied Piper of Hamlin

Celebrate with Fun

- Refresh your memory by reading the story of the Pied Piper again. Most libraries have several versions of the story. Read more than one and decide which version you like best.
- Select a musical family member to play an instrument or whistle. Let them lead you in a parade through the house—or if you are really brave, through the neighborhood. Follow wherever they lead.
- The children in the story of the Pied Piper followed him completely out of town. You don't have to leave town, but play Follow the Leader. Take turns so everyone has a chance to be the leader.
- Sit down and write your own family version of the story. What problem could happen in your community? How could the problem be solved? What type of music can you incorporate into the story?
- Ahead of time, cut out 150–200 pieces of yellow paper in the shape of cheese wedges. Hide them throughout the house. Have a contest with the "rats" in your family to see who can find the most pieces of cheese.
- Spend a few minutes in a serious discussion with your children about the importance of not going with strangers. What would your son do if a stranger asked him to help find a lost puppy?

Celebrate with Crafts

The Pied Piper used music to lead the rats out of town. Make your own music! Set out empty tin cans, bottles, cardboard tubes, and other odds and ends. See how creative everyone can be making their own musical instruments. March around the house and see if people follow each other.

Celebrate with Food

Since rats like cheese, you have 2 options: (1) Serve a delicious cheesecake for dessert. (2) Cut up cheese and dig out your old fondue pot. Have a snack of cheese fondue with bread cubes.

Cousin's Day

O ften a special kinship exists among cousins. Have a great time sharing activities with your relatives.

Celebrate with Fun

- Set up a family chain letter to keep in touch with cousins. Simply write a letter describing what is happening in your life. Send it to a cousin, with directions to add to the letter and send it on to another relative. The "last" cousin mails the letter back to you. As editor of the *Cousin's Gazette*, make photocopies of all the entries and send to each cousin. You could do this by e-mail, yet there's still something special about receiving handwritten messages.

- Call your cousins simply to say "Happy Cousin's Day!"

- Compile the e-mail addresses of all your cousins. Send everyone a free e-mail greeting announcing Cousin's Day along with e-mail addresses. Hopefully you'll all be able to communicate throughout the year.

- Invite cousins to come over for a "Get to Know You" party. Write up a set of trivia questions about everyone. See how well cousins know answers to questions like "Who played 'Ode to Joy' at their last piano recital?"

Celebrate with Crafts

Make a family tree so everyone can see how they are related. Sketch a tree on a large poster board. Cut out numerous construction paper leaves and write the names of relatives on the leaves. Attach leaves to the tree in the proper chronological order.

Use large paper bags to make matching cousin costumes. Open a large brown grocery bag. Cut a circle in the bottom for your head. Cut 2 arm holes in the sides about 3 inches from the bottom. Skinny family members can slip their costumes over their heads. If you carry a few extra pounds, simply cut a slit up the front of the bag to the neck hole. This creates an instant paper bag vest. Decorate your inexpensive costumes with feathers, markers, and trims.

Celebrate with Food

If cousins live nearby, plan a casual potluck. Ask everyone to bring a dish that starts with the first letter of their name. That way you'll enjoy Suzie's sandwiches and Ted's terrific tamales.

AUGUST

National Inventor's Month
American Artist Appreciation Month
National Watermelon Month

Weeks to Celebrate

1st Full Week • National Clown Week
2nd Week • National Apple Week
2nd Full Week • Don't Wait—Celebrate! Week
3rd Week • Weird Contest Week

Days to Celebrate

1st Sunday • Sisters Day
1st Sunday • National Family Day
1st Saturday • National Mustard Day
Last Tuesday • Touch a Heart Tuesday

 2   Friendship Day
 3   Parks Day
10   National Garage Sale Day
11   Play in the Sand Day
13   International Left-Handers Day
15   Wizard of Oz Day
15   National Relaxation Day
17   National Thrift Shop Day
22   Be an Angel Day
27   *Guinness Book of World Records* First Published
29   Mary Poppins's Birthday
30   National Toasted Marshmallow Day

National Inventor's Month

What would your life be like without the invention of the microwave? Without the toilet? This month invent something of your own. Maybe your family will apply for a patent!

Celebrate with Fun

- In *Beauty and the Beast*, Belle's dad was an inventor creating all sorts of innovative devices. Have everyone make simple sketches of their own invention. Sketch with blue pencils for a blueprint effect.

- The Japanese word *chindogu* means "completely worthless invention." Divide your family into groups of 2 or 3. Give each group a bag of 5–7 unrelated items like a deflated soccer ball, plastic mug, toy car, or even an empty shampoo bottle. The groups have half an hour to develop a completely worthless invention using their objects. (Tape or string can be used to attach items together.) Have a special ceremony at which each group displays their worthless invention. Be prepared for some real uselessness! You can also see some unique inventions on Wacky Patent of the Month: www.colitz.com/site/wacky.htm

- Switch the focus from useless to worthwhile. Find a microscope and see how ordinary items appear when magnified. Astound your family by informing them that Anton van Leeuwenhoek invented the microscope in the 1670s. His primitive microscope magnified items to 270 times their size.

Celebrate with Crafts

Find a picture of a Rube Goldberg invention. Goldberg is known for his whimsical contraptions. His bell-ringing machine involved many steps. First a bowling ball falls on a cat's tail. The cat jumps on a chair. The chair falls on a lamp. The lamp knocks the bell off the nightstand. The bell rings! Make your own Rube Goldberg invention to ring a bell. Glue, tape, staple, or tie items so that they cause a chain reaction to ring the bell. Leave the contraption on display to show visitors how inventive you are.

Celebrate with Food

The Earl of Sandwich invented the sandwich in 1762. He wanted an easy meal to eat while gambling in pubs, so he ordered meat slabs placed between 2 pieces of bread. Invent your own sandwich. Put out various foods and experiment in making a peanut butter, banana, raisin, and chopped celery sandwich. Invent a clever name for your scrumptious sandwich.

American Artist Appreciation Month

Michelangelo, van Gogh, and Picasso are world famous. But what about American artists? This month acquaint your family with the many talented American artists.

Celebrate with Crafts

Georgia O'Keefe was known for painting bold, colorful flowers. Have children paint white coffee filters with watercolors. Let dry. Cut scallops so filters look like flowers. Glue your Georgia O'Keefe flowers to construction paper to make 3-dimensional pictures. Add petals and stems with a green marker.

Find a copy of the famous *Girl in Red Dress with Cat and Dog* by Ammi Phillips. Phillips was one of the few artists during the early 1800s to support himself completely by painting. Have your child put on a red outfit to recreate the painting. If you don't have a cat or dog, substitute stuffed animals. Have other family members paint or sketch the scene. Compare your different artistic styles.

Jackson Pollock is sometimes known as Jack the Dripper because he spread his canvas on the floor and dripped on paint. Lay an old sheet outside on the grass. Let children dip a brush and "flick" on the paint.

Roy Lichtenstein's unusual art style was noticed in the early '60s. He used comic strip techniques to paint with dots and bold stripes on large canvases. His paintings often included words like "POW" or "KNOCK KNOCK." Glue pieces of paper together or buy poster board. Encourage children to paint BIG pictures with bold lines and 1 or 2 cartoon-type words.

Celebrate with Fun

- Visit a museum that displays American artists' works. Find a painting of people and have your children recreate the scene by posing in the same positions as the people.

- Children sometimes quickly lose interest in art museums. Select an "item" for them to observe in each painting, perhaps shoes, eyebrows, or flowers.

Celebrate with Food

Make an edible greeting card. Spread chocolate pudding on a graham cracker. Cover with another cracker. Now spread vanilla pudding on the top cracker and cover with 1 more graham cracker. Place in freezer 1 hour. Use gel frosting to write "Get Well Soon" or "I Love You" on your tasty card.

National Watermelon Month

These large, heavy, and flavored fruits are a tasty treat on a hot summer day. Did you know Thomas Jefferson grew his own watermelons? Don't worry about calories. Watermelons are 98 percent water.

Celebrate with Fun

- Wrap a watermelon in foil. Find a place to bury it in the backyard or at a park. Tell your children they'll need to find a giant buried dinosaur egg. Make up clues that take children from one location to another until they finally find their gigantic dinosaur egg.

- Play Tag with "base" being a watermelon on the ground. Children race around trying to tag each other. The only safe place to avoid being tagged is to be touching the watermelon.

- Make frozen watermelon popsicles. Cut chunks of watermelon to fit in an ice cube tray. Stick a wooden craft stick in the watermelon and freeze.

- Purchase a regular watermelon and a seedless variety. Compare taste and texture. Which does your family enjoy more?

- Participate in a traditional seed-spitting contest. Collect watermelon seeds and have participants compete in different events that might include the farthest spit, most unusual spit, and best spit by someone dressed in a costume.

Celebrate with Crafts

After eating your watermelon, collect and dry the seeds. Use them along with dried lima beans, unpopped popcorn, and dried split peas to make a seed/bean collage. Glue the dried items on a sturdy piece of cardboard.

Celebrate with Food

Eating watermelon is a tasty treat, but watermelon also makes a great vehicle for creative carving. Set out 2 watermelons and divide your family in half. (If you have a large family, you might need more watermelons.) Teams try carving the watermelons into an exotic flower or bowl. Many books or magazines have pictures of carved watermelons to serve as inspiration to your family.

More ideas: www.watermelon.org

National Clown Week

Make your family laugh this week by acting silly. Remember, "Everyone loves a clown!"

Celebrate with Fun

- Put on an outlandish costume so your children are greeted by a clown at breakfast. Wear a fluorescent-colored wig with your huge red lipstick-decorated mouth.
- At least once this week, try the famous "toss a bucket of water on someone" clown trick. At the appropriate time, preferably when you're dressed as a clown, threaten to toss the bucket on a family member. Carry out your threat—only with the bucket full of confetti!
- Professional clowns actually "register" their face designs. Each clown has a very distinct way to decorate his or her face. Use face paints on your children's faces. Let them "register" their pattern on paper first, then duplicate the design on their skin. Are all the faces different?
- Clowns frequently perform while balancing items on their heads. Set up a tabletop balancing center. Place a ruler on top of a sealed liter bottle of pop. Collect small items to place on each side of the ruler, trying to maintain an equal balance. Keep going until everything topples!

Celebrate with Crafts

Bend an 8½" x 11" piece of construction paper to form a cone with 1 end smaller than the other. Tape ends to hold cone together as a "clown megaphone" so your children can be louder than ever! Have them decorate the megaphone with stickers and glitter paint, then yell, "Ladies and Gentlemen—welcome to the greatest show on earth!"

Celebrate with Food

You need popcorn and peanuts at the circus. In a resealable plastic bag, mix 3 cups popped popcorn, ½ cup shelled peanuts, ½ cup raisins, and ½ cup chocolate chips. Seal bag and shake, shake, shake!

Make a supersimple clown cake. Find a clown picture or draw one if you feel artistic. Draw the clown holding up 1 arm as if holding balloons. Bake your favorite cupcakes and frost in several colors. Place the clown picture on the table, with the cupcakes serving as "balloons" above his outstretched arm. Attach pieces of yarn from the cupcakes to the clown's hand. You've just assembled a circus clown cake using only cupcakes!

More ideas: www.nationalclownweek.com; clownresourcedirectory.com

National Apple Week

From a shiny red apple in your lunch to a delicious apple crisp, this versatile fruit is always a great treat.

Celebrate with Fun

- How long since you've bobbed for apples? Fill a sink or tub with warm water. Toss in a few apples. Take turns trying to grab an apple using only your mouth.
- Make a simple apple fondue. Slice apples and dip them in a variety of easy sauces. Try honey, yogurt, cinnamon sugar, and melted caramels.
- We all know apples grow on trees. Play this game in which apples can be found all around the great outdoors. Get a group together to cut out at least 100 paper apples. After they're cut, 1 person hides the apples under bushes, in trees, and on the ground. Race to collect the most paper apples. This game can easily be played over and over again.
- Tie an 18-inch string to an apple stem. Have someone hold the other end of the string. Get a volunteer to try to take a bite of the apple as it swings in the air. No hands allowed!
- Teach your children the old-fashioned game of "Stem Twist." Show them how to slowly twist their apple stem while reciting the alphabet. Pay close attention to when the stem breaks off. That letter is the first letter of the person's name you'll marry!

Celebrate with Crafts

Everyone will love wearing their flying apple butterfly shirt. Slip a magazine into a solid-colored T-shirt. (This prevents paint from soaking through.) Spread out 2 Tbs. paint on a paper plate. Cut an apple in half from the stem to the bottom. Dip the apple into the paint. Press firmly on your shirt. Lift the apple to reveal a butterfly shape. When paint dries, use different-colored paint to draw the body and antennae on top of the butterfly. Let dry before wearing.

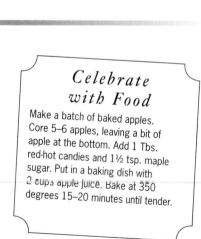

Celebrate with Food

Make a batch of baked apples. Core 5–6 apples, leaving a bit of apple at the bottom. Add 1 Tbs. red-hot candies and 1½ tsp. maple sugar. Put in a baking dish with 2 cups apple juice. Bake at 350 degrees 15–20 minutes until tender.

More ideas: usapple.org/industry/applemonth

Don't Wait—Celebrate! Week

All too often as hardworking adults, we forget to have fun with our family and friends. This holiday reminds us to add an atmosphere of celebration to an ordinary day.

Celebrate with Fun

- Get silly and celebrate throughout the day. Have balloons and streamers around the breakfast table. Decorate your children's lunch bags with happy face stickers and mushy sayings. Use cookie cutters to cut your daughter's toast in creative shapes. Make a big "Celebrate!" sign for the front door so people coming home know there will be more fun inside. Play some games before doing homework.

- Play family Hide and Seek. Kids love finding their parents contorting their bodies to fit behind the clothes hamper. For an advanced version of Hide and Seek, secretly "prepare" a clever hiding place. Rearrange clothes in the closet or empty a large box ahead of time.

- Fold napkins into fancy designs. Don't worry about taking lessons in origami; just fold the napkin in accordion pleats and tie with a big bow. Or "scrunch" a paper napkin in half to form wings. Tie on a plastic spoon and you have a butterfly napkin holder.

- Buy a package of those annoying birthday paper blowers. Throughout the day yell, "Don't Wait—Celebrate!" as you blow and the paper streamer unfurls in someone's face.

Celebrate with Crafts

Balloons are always festive, so plan a balloon decorating party. Set out various sizes and shapes of balloons. Use permanent markers to write "Don't Wait—Celebrate!" on them. Glue on plastic wiggle eyes and ribbon to make "Celebration Balloon People." Before you blow up a balloon, add some unpopped popcorn—then when you blow it up and tie it, you'll have a noisemaker!

Celebrate with Food

Let kids play with their food today. Place a spoonful of peanut butter on everyone's plate, along with a few goldfish crackers. Now "Go Fish!" Dip 1 end of a pretzel stick in peanut butter. Then try to catch a goldfish cracker with the peanut butter "hook."

Serve some "octopus dogs." Cut the bottom half of a hot dog into 4–5 lengthwise strips. Microwave 30–45 seconds. Have an adult remove the hot dog to reveal an octopus with curled legs.

More ideas: www.pattysachs.com; www.partyplansplus.com

Weird Contest Week

Ocean City, New Jersey, celebrates this entire week by holding a variety of weird contests. Pick a day for crazy activities in your house, or hold one crazy contest each day this week.

Celebrate with Fun

- Have each family member come up with the rules and supplies for a weird contest to try this week.

- Just so your family doesn't think you are totally weird, tell them about the real World Extreme Ironing Championship. Eighty contestants from ten countries were judged on the degree of difficulty achieved while ironing. Some ironed while bouncing on a trampoline or hanging upside down from a tree. One ironed while balancing on a surfboard in the river. Ask family members to demonstrate unique ways of ironing. Don't worry about actually plugging in the iron. Just be creative with a cool iron, and be sure to take a few pictures.

- Invite friends and neighbors over for weird contests. These could include:

  Balancing blobs of Jell-O on your head while going through an obstacle course

  Making up a rap song about your favorite pet

  Making unusual sounds using only your body

  Sculpting with aluminum foil

- Every year, David Letterman features the winner of the "Smelliest Sneaker Contest." Yes, there actually is such a contest in which judges have the "honor" of smelling and judging feet. Who would be the winner in your family?

Celebrate with Crafts

Give family members sheets of newspaper and masking tape. Ask them to design a costume or a clothing item to wear using newspaper. The Sunday comics make delightful hats or neckties.

Celebrate with Food

Try a "Create a Shape Contest" with toast. Give everyone a piece of lightly toasted bread. Assign a shape such as a heart or triangle. Create that shape by using only your teeth. The best shape is declared the winner. For an advanced contest, try forming a star or even a Volkswagen!

Sisters Day

Many sisters share a strong bond of love and affection. Don't have a sister? Then celebrate the spirit of sisterhood with a female friend.

Celebrate with Fun

- Plan a fun activity with your sister. She'll probably be amazed to know there is a holiday called "Sisters Day." Begin with a cheery phone call wishing your sister a Happy Sisters Day. (Of course, if you share a bedroom with your sister, simply yell to her from across the room.)

- How about inviting a few other sisters over for a wild sisters sleepover? Make "Sisters Only" signs. Play a game in which sisters have to feed each other Jell-O. Share what makes the sister relationship so much fun.

- Do a secret good deed for your sister. Can you imagine what she'll think when she looks in her drawers and finds her clothes neatly arranged? Could you do some of her chores for her?

- Get your creative juices flowing and write a poem for your sister. Get mushy and tell your sister just how special she really is to you. Remember, poems don't have to rhyme. You don't need to find a word that rhymes with "Samantha." Use free-form verse instead.

- Share your favorite book with your sister. You might have a great discussion comparing *The Very Hungry Caterpillar* with *Tales of a 4th Grade Nothing*.

- Even though it's Sisters Day, spend some time apart writing each other letters. Write about your sister's positive traits. Describe how you enjoy being with her as she sings Broadway musicals. Sign and date the letters and store them to exchange next year on Sisters Day.

Celebrate with Crafts

Make matching sister sweatshirts to wear on your next outing. Purchase solid-colored sweatshirts. Slip a magazine inside so paint doesn't soak through. Using fabric paint, draw 2 CD-sized circles on the front of the shirts. Paint the circles with flesh-colored paint. They are your faces. When dry, draw self-portraits on the faces. Trade shirts and draw another self-portrait. Wear on your next trip to the mall.

Celebrate with Food

What's your sister's favorite food? Make her favorite batch of cookies or buy her the pizza she adores. If your sister lives too far away for you to mail her a hot-fudge sundae, send a gift certificate instead.

National Family Day

Have you ever heard children complain, "Our family just has too much fun"? Of course not! Begin the month of August with a day of family fun.

Celebrate with Fun

- Wake up the family in an untraditional way. Try playing loud polka music or banging some pots and pans. If your family is open to new experiences, dress in an outlandish costume and wake everyone up as you sing and do the cancan by their bed.

- Make mealtime fun today. Place small novelty gifts by everyone's place at breakfast. Those plastic Groucho Marx glasses with fake mustaches are a great way to make eating cold cereal a fun experience. (Available from the Oriental Trading Company: www.orientaltrading.com)

- Family fun can involve short, easy-to-do activities. Have someone hold a stretched wire hanger horizontally to the floor. Other family members play Balloon Basketball and toss small balloons into the "hoop." Since you have coat hangers and balloons handy, play Balloon Volleyball. Stretch wire coat hangers into diamond shapes. Stretch a pantyhose leg over the hangers to form "paddles." (Bend the hook end so no one gets poked.) Tie a string across a room or the garage as a net. Use your inexpensive pantyhose paddles to bat the balloons back and forth over the string.

- Play tourist in your own community. Attend free concerts, have lunch at the park, and take part in summer festivals—all close to home.

Celebrate with Crafts

Design a "Family Fun Mural." Obtain a large sheet of newsprint or colored butcher paper 8 or 10 inches long. Lay it on the floor and let family members make sketches of fun activities they'd like to do this month. Tape the mural in the hallway. Try to fit in as many of the activities as possible. Cross off each sketch after the family has completed the fun event.

Celebrate with Food

Give everyone a few dollars to help purchase dinner. If within walking distance, stroll to the closest store. Everyone has 10 minutes to buy food items for dinner. (If common sense prevails, tell everyone they need to buy at least 1 fruit or vegetable.) Try to keep purchases a secret. When you arrive home, spread out the food and eat the most unusual meal ever!

National Mustard Day

Mustard is more than a yellow streak across your hot dog. This popular condiment even has its own mustard museum in Mount Horeb, Wisconsin.

Celebrate with Fun

- Purchase a few gourmet mustards. Some mustards actually have raspberry flavoring. Experiment with different flavors of mustard on your sandwich or hot dog. You may develop a taste for extra-spicy mustard!

- Write a poem called "An Ode to Mustard." Begin with "We love the taste of mustard, and even eat it on our custard . . ."

- Save plastic mustard bottles. Fill with water and use as squirt guns on unsuspecting friends. Squirt water messages on the sidewalk.

- Hold contests with several inexpensive squirt bottles of mustard (naturally, all these activities are done outside):

  See who can squirt their mustard the farthest.

  Stack 3 empty yogurt containers on top of each other. Squirt the mustard to try to knock down the containers.

  Watch children write their names with mustard.

- Matthew 17:20 says, "If you have faith as small as a mustard seed, you can say to this mountain, 'Move from here to there' and it will move." Discuss faith with your children. Purchase mustard seeds from your grocery store's bulk food department.

Celebrate with Crafts

Use a yellow mustard squeeze bottle as a rocket ship. Glue on craft foam fins and rocket boosters. Cover pennies with aluminum foil. Attach to the rocket ship to look like important, expensive space equipment.

Make a mustard-yellow collage. Use yellow paper as the background. Look around the house for yellow items to use. A yellow pom-pom could be the sun. Use yellow buttons as centers for yellow flowers. Yellow crayons can add embellishments along with yellow pieces of material. Don't forget to hang your picture with yellow thumbtacks!

Celebrate with Food

Some mustard lovers put mustard on pretzels, licorice, and even ice cream! Instead of trying to eat a mustard-covered cupcake, decorate a hot dog. Make your hot dog look like a bumblebee. Put yellow stripes across the bee's "body." Add 2 toothpicks to the head for antennae. Use tiny mustard dots for the eyes. Don't worry about getting stung by this bee!

More ideas: www.mustardmuseum.com or 608-437-3986

225

Touch a Heart Tuesday

Do something special for the ones you love. Sometimes we get so busy with day-to-day chores, we forget to show people we care.

Celebrate with Fun

- Wake each family member with a special kiss and an "I love you." Much better than an impersonal alarm clock!

- Plan an afternoon teatime with your children or friends. Set the table with fine china (or colorful paper plates). Serve open-faced sandwiches and cookies. Even boys will come if you decorate round cookies like baseballs. Share how special your family and friends are to you.

- Do a secret good deed for friends or family members. It can be as simple as placing a candy bar on their pillow or as extravagant as sending roses to their office.

- Contact someone you haven't seen in a long time. Can your children call a relative? How about sending an electronic greeting card to someone? Better yet, write a personal letter telling why they are special to you.

Celebrate with Crafts

Here's a messy but meaningful craft: Grab a family member's old outgrown shoe. Cover a worktable with plastic cloth or newspaper. Mix up ½ cup flour, 1 cup water, and ¼ cup glue to make papier-mâché. Work together dipping strips of newspaper in the glue mixture. Wrap the wet paper onto the old shoe. Cover the shoe except for the sole and "foot opening." Let dry. When the newspaper is hard, paint it with tempera paint. Place a baby food jar full of water inside the shoe. Add a few flowers. You've just made a unique family shoe vase.

Celebrate with Food

The aroma of fresh-baked bread makes the whole house feel full of love. Use your favorite bread recipe (or buy frozen rolls) to make flowerpot bread. Wash 2 or 3 new clay flowerpots. Rub the inside of the pots with oil. Bake the empty flower pots in the oven for 1 hour at 350 degrees. Have an adult remove the pots. Place a piece of aluminum foil in the bottom of each pot. Put bread dough in each flower pot. Let dough rise in a warm place for 1 hour. Punch down dough, then let rise another 30 minutes. Place dough-filled flowerpots in the oven for 25–30 minutes at 450 degrees. Be an angel and give a flowerpot to someone who needs cheering up.

Friendship Day

Anyone who has attended camp has sung, "Make new friends, and keep the old, one is silver, and the other's gold." That's what Friendship Day is all about.

Celebrate with Fun

- Throw a party for all your friends. Invite people for a casual get-together simply to celebrate your friendships. If you don't want to clean house, invite everyone to meet you at a local park for conversation, food, and a few games.

- Send e-mail greeting cards to people you can't see personally. They'll be surprised to find out there even is a Friendship Day.

- Write a letter to a friend you haven't seen in years. Enclose a picture of yourself. Reminisce about the good times you had when you saw each other frequently.

- Make a new friend today. Start a conversation with someone in line at the grocery store. Encourage your children to talk to a child they normally don't sit with on the bus. One of you might just meet a kindred spirit.

- Tell everyone you meet, "Happy Friendship Day!"

Celebrate with Crafts

Make friendship frames for your best buddies. Collect puzzle pieces from your 1,000-piece puzzle with the missing pieces. Spread glue on 4–5 pieces. Drop glue-covered puzzle pieces into a plastic bag filled with ¼ cup glitter. Close top of bag and shake. Gently remove the sparkly pieces and glue them on a cardboard frame. Repeat the process until you have all the glitter pieces you want. Give the glittery frame to your best friend.

Celebrate with Food

Make taffy with a friend. In a saucepan, mix 1¼ cups sugar, ¼ tsp. salt, ½ Tbs. cornstarch, ½ cup corn syrup, 1 Tbs. butter, and ¾ cup water. Boil until 250 degrees on a candy thermometer (adults only). Remove from heat. Stir in ½ package unsweetened drink mix. Pour mixture on a greased baking sheet. Let cool. Get your friend to butter his hands and start stretching the taffy between you. Stretch until smooth. Then cut into bite-sized pieces.

For another fun treat, mix together 3 cups popped popcorn and 1 box circus animal cookies. Try to find the wild animals hiding in the popcorn.

Parks Day

Enjoy the warm days of summer by visiting a park. Even the most populated communities have a few parks for people to enjoy.

Celebrate with Fun

- Set aside a few hours to visit parks in your area. Explore the hiking trails you never knew existed. Ask the Parks department if they need help clearing a trail or picking up trash. Your family will benefit from a feeling of accomplishment at improving their community.

- Play "Stick-It." Get on a swing and start pumping. The object is to jump off the swing, land on both feet, and "stick-it" without falling over. See who can jump out the farthest. Make sure to have an adult nearby to monitor the safety factor.

- According to the American Recreation Coalition, these are the top 10 recreational activities done by adults with children at home in 2001. How many of these can you do at a park?

  1. bicycling on the road
  2. horseback riding
  3. RV-ing
  4. campground camping
  5. swimming
  6. motorcycling/ snowmobiling
  7. motorboating
  8. fishing
  9. hiking
  10. downhill skiing

More ideas: www.funoutdoors.com

Celebrate with Crafts

If you go to a park early in the morning, you might find spiderwebs. Make your own by giving everyone a sheet of plastic wrap. Squeeze glitter glue in a spiderweb shape. When the glue dries, the spiderweb pulls off the plastic wrap. Take your webs home and hang from the ceiling.

Celebrate with Food

Even though people like to sleep in during the summer, wake up your sleepyheads for an early morning breakfast in the park. Pack your gingham tablecloth along with juice, muffins, bagels, and granola bars. To make oranges juicier, have your children roll the oranges down the slide several times. Enjoy exercise, fresh air, and breakfast all before 8 a.m.

National Garage Sale Day

Depending on where you live, garage sales might be called tag sales or yard sales. By any name, they are a great way to reduce clutter in your home.

Celebrate with Fun

- Get the family to agree to sell some of their items and hold a National Garage Sale Day event. You need some things to put in your driveway when the crowds come!
- Encourage neighbors to participate. A neighborhood garage sale draws more buyers. Think about it—if you were going to spend the morning garage sale browsing, which ad would appeal more to you? "Family garage sale with lots of clothes, toys, and furniture" or "15 families in one neighborhood selling clothes, toys, and furniture"? The more families participating, the larger the crowd of people coming to buy.
- You can never have too many garage sale signs. Have teenagers make signs of various sizes. Post along roads and even alleys. (Don't forget to remove signs after the sale.)
- Set out items so they are easy to view. Label boxes well: "Boys' Toddler Pants" and "Girls' Hair Accessories."
- Let children sell their items at their own table. It's good experience in salesmanship and making change.
- Have a large amount of change available. You don't want to lose a sale because you can't make change for a $20. A word of caution: Keep close tabs on your change box. Unfortunately, some people's money boxes have been stolen in the middle of the selling chaos.

Celebrate with Crafts

Offer crafty people a chance to sell their homemade items. Make large signs so buyers know they'll need to pay more for these specially handcrafted items than for your 10-cent garage sale items.

Celebrate with Food

Have fresh hot coffee available for a reasonable fee. Early morning buyers are apt to linger longer while sipping coffee, plus you'll make a few extra dollars!

Play in the Sand Day

Remember the fun you had playing in the sand as a child? The warm sand was perfect for digging holes and building sand castles. Even if you don't live by the beach, you can have fun playing with sand.

Celebrate with Fun

- If you live near the ocean or a lake with sand, grab the sunscreen and hit the beach. Surprise your children by packing a picnic breakfast to enjoy while starting the day playing in the sand.

- Set out a plastic bucket or a small wading pool. Dump in a bag of playground sand. Children will spend hours digging in the sand and pretending they are at the beach—even if you live in the middle of Kansas.

- At the beach, set up a game of beach bowling. Fill 10 empty pop bottles ⅓ full of water to keep them from tipping over in the sand. Place the bottles "bowling pin" style in 4 rows. Use a beach ball to try to knock down the bottles.

- Squeeze a little math into your day of sand play. Stand close to the water and write a math problem in the sand with a stick. Your children try to write the answer before a wave washes away the problem.

- Pretend the waves are hot lava. Stand close to where the waves break and see who can get closest to the water's edge before getting buried in the "lava."

Celebrate with Crafts

Use sandpaper to make several craft projects. Using an old pair of scissors, cut different shapes out of sandpaper. Place the shapes on a flat surface. Cover with paper and rub gently with a crayon. The raised sandpaper shapes create colorful imprints on paper.

Use a sandpaper background for sand painting. Use a black marker or crayon to draw a simple design like a kite or butterfly on fine grit sandpaper. Spread glue on certain areas of the picture. Sprinkle colored craft sand on the glue. Let dry, shake off excess, and repeat using different-colored sand on different parts of the picture.

Celebrate with Food

It's Play in the Sand Day, so eat a "sandwich." Buy children some pixie sticks, which contain candy "sand." Make sure they wash their hands before pouring the fine-powdered candy sand in their hands.

International Left-Handers Day

Know any lefties? In Ireland, left-handed people were thought to be friends of leprechauns. Today, studies show left-handers excel at tennis, swimming, and basketball.

Celebrate with Fun

- Use this day to honor any left-handers in your family. They get to choose the evening meal and what TV shows to watch, and they don't have to make their beds.

- Experience what a left-hander experiences on a daily basis. Any lefty can tell you how difficult it is to use right-handed scissors! First thing in the morning, have everyone switch to using their nondominant hand. Everyone writes their name and a sentence such as "I have been right-handed all my life." If right-handed, go through the day using your left hand. If left-handed, switch to being right-handed. Notice how awkward it is. At the end of the day, write the same sentence again. Is it easier after practicing with your nondominant hand all day?

- Tell your family that left-handers make great creative thinkers. Four out of five original designers of the Macintosh computer were left-handed.

- What would it be like to go through the day without hands? Try using your feet to do what hands normally do. Write your name with your toes or try to dial the phone. Can you get food to your mouth using your feet?

- Use both left and right hands to play a hand-clap game. One person claps out a pattern: clap-clap-pause-clap-pause-clap-clap-clap. The rest of the group tries to imitate the pattern.

Celebrate with Crafts

Make "handy-creations" by tracing around your hand on paper. Cut out your paper hand. Glue it to another paper as the basis for a picture. What can you make out of the hand? Turn the hand into a turkey, with the fingers as feathers. Watch creativity flow as everyone draws a different item using their paper hand.

Celebrate with Food

Set the table with the silverware on the opposite side of the plates. Ask everyone to eat with their left or nondominant hand. Try to get the peas to your mouth, and be careful picking up your glass of milk!

More ideas: www.left-handersday.com; Lefthanders International, Box 8249, Topeka, KS 66608 (913) 234-2177. (Their magazine features great ideas on how left-handers can adapt to a right-handed world.)

Wizard of Oz Day

In 1939 *The Wizard of Oz* premiered at Grumman's Chinese Theater. Since then, this movie has become a classic. Did you know Shirley Temple was originally cast to play the role of Dorothy?

Celebrate with Fun

- Cut out several yellow paper rectangles. Lay them on the floor about 12 inches apart, starting at your children's beds. Have children follow the bricks all through the house to the breakfast table.

- In one *Wizard of Oz* scene, the apple trees come "alive" and pelt apples at Dorothy and her friends. Find a tree-filled park. Have 1 person hide behind a tree and try to pelt the rest of the group with foam balls as they run by the trees.

- Sing a rousing chorus of "If I Were King of the Forest." Discuss what each of you would do if "King of the House." What changes would you make? How would you enforce new policies?

- Wake your children with your best interpretation of Glenda the Good Witch. Set a plastic tiara on your head. Gracefully waltz into your son's room. In your sweetest Glenda voice say, "Good morning, my sweet Sam. It's time to get your precious body out of bed."

Celebrate with Crafts

Create your own Emerald City. No need to buy exotic jewels—use cardboard wrapping tubes and boxes. Children glue tubes on the boxes to make castle turrets. Spray paint or use tempera paint to color your castle emerald green

Make a ruby slipper: Trace around each person's foot on cardboard. On 1 side, complete this sentence: "There's no place like home because . . ." On the other side, use a black marker to make your foot shape look like a shoe. Cover with glue and sprinkle lavishly with red glitter. Hang the shiny shoes around the house and read why home is a special place to be.

Celebrate with Food

Make a yellow brick road cake to carry out your *Wizard of Oz* theme. Bake a sheet cake. Frost bright yellow. Spread an aluminum foil "road" across your table. Cut individual serving pieces of cake and place end to end on the foil for bricks on the road. Let family members use black gel frosting to outline their "brick" and add dots and dashes to give the brick a textured look. Sing "Follow the Yellow Brick Road" while eating your cake.

National Relaxation Day

We're all rushed trying to keep up with the demands of everyday life. Use this day to let a few commitments slide as you sit back and relax.

Celebrate with Fun

- Try driving home from the places you normally go by a different route. You'll notice a new florist shop or a house with a great color of paint. Take a walk with your children and stroll down a street you usually pass by in the car.

- Plan a "no-cooking" day. Let family members make their own meals and clean up after themselves! You'll relax knowing there's no major meal preparation. Besides, your children will survive by eating peanut butter and jelly sandwiches all day.

- Get a book of jokes and riddles to read together. All you have to do is laugh.

- Turn off the TV and read or work on a puzzle together. The quiet atmosphere is relaxing once you get used to the lack of constant background noise!

- Go to a park and let children run and play while you lounge on a blanket and pretend you're on the Riviera. Show your children pictures of Cleopatra. See if they will serve you grapes while you relax.

- Hire a local high school student to come over and entertain your children for an hour or two while you relax.

Celebrate with Crafts

This is not the day to attempt a gold-plated, life-sized papier-mâché sculpture of your best friend. Instead, simply bring out a new coloring book. You'll find it very therapeutic and calming to mindlessly color within the lines.

Make sure to have some modeling clay on hand today. Give everyone a piece and watch creative juices flow. Enjoy being together while sculpting animals and people.

Celebrate with Food

How about making some good old-fashioned root beer floats? Pour root beer over vanilla ice cream. Slurp with a straw. Someone will say, "Why don't we make these more often?" Sit outside and slowly enjoy your frosty treat.

233

National Thrift Shop Day

Some people have never set foot in a thrift shop, while others find incredible bargains in these secondhand stores. See what fun you can have discovering some treasures.

Celebrate with Fun

- Ask friends about their favorite thrift shop. Stop by and find a distinctive dinner plate to designate as the "you are special" plate. When your son gets an A on his spelling test or your spouse needs a pick-me-up, serve them dinner on the special plate.

- Take the family to a thrift store. Give everyone 2 dollars to spend on the most unique item they can find. Come home and share the bizarre items you discovered.

- Usually thrift shops get their items from donations. Have a family "get rid of clutter" evening. Go through closets, drawers, and the garage to find good-quality items to donate. You'll have more space, and the thrift shop benefits too. Don't forget a receipt for your taxes.

- Thrift shops are a great place to update your children's dress-up box or put together a dress-up kit for a young friend. You'll find elegant ball gowns and sparkly purses that will provide hours of creative fun.

- Ask your children to humor you as you take a trip down memory lane. Walk the aisles of a thrift store and point out fashions you used to wear and the metal lunch box you proudly carried to school. Point out a typewriter. Explain how correction tape was used for typing mistakes.

- Purchase a gift certificate at a local thrift store and donate it to a homeless shelter. Your small contribution could help a mother buy shoes or a warm coat for her child.

Celebrate with Crafts

Thrift shops are a collection of mismatched items, so make a mismatched collage. Collect a sturdy piece of cardboard and assorted items (purchased at a thrift shop?) like small toys, buttons, plastic spoons, and items from your junk drawer. Glue the items on the cardboard in a free-form modern art collage.

Celebrate with Food

Purchase a unique teapot. Let everyone select 1 tea cup that appeals to them. Don't worry that everything doesn't match. This china is for your eclectic tea parties. Use the cups every time you have a tea party to show you don't need expensive china to have fun.

Be an Angel Day

Most of us think of angels as the cute winged creatures we find modeled in gift shops. The phrase "Be an Angel" describes someone who is helpful to others. Celebrate today by being an angel in your own way.

Celebrate with Fun

- Be an angel by giving a birthday party with a twist. Discuss your child's next birthday celebration. They'll probably want a cake, balloons, and lots of presents. Plan a Peter Pan Party. Many hospitals are encouraging children to help sick hospitalized children. Your child sends out party invitations that include an envelope asking for a monetary donation instead of a birthday gift. Your child takes the donations to the hospital, has a tour, and chooses how the money will be spent. Contact www.peter panchildrensfund.org.

- Angels in Action is a contest acknowledging children who help others. Each year it honors children who make efforts to be "angels" by volunteering. Contact www.gp.com/consumerproducts/angelsinaction to see how your child can apply for this award.

- Angels can fly, so why not your stuffed animals? Have everyone select a small stuffed animal and design a parachute to help it "fly." Help younger children attach a parachute bandanna or plastic bag. Have an adult drop the parachute animals from an elevated location. See which animals "fly" and which crash to the ground.

- Make a list together of positive things family members can do to be an angel, things like looking for Mom's glasses when she misplaces them, taking out the trash without being asked, and not hogging the remote control. Try to do 2 or more items on your list every week.

Celebrate with Crafts

Gift shop angels are often made of delicate porcelain with tissue-thin wings. Make some kid-friendly angels using pasta. Use smaller-sized rigatoni noodles as the base for the body. Glue on a bow tie pasta to form your angel's wings. A large button or lima bean is the angel's head. Hang your angel from the ceiling with string or dental floss so it can watch over the family's activities.

Celebrate with Food

Purchase an angel food cake. (Unless you want to go through the hassle of beating egg whites while trying to make a homemade cake.) Serve slices of angel food cake topped with fresh berries and whipped cream.

Guinness Book of World Records
First Published

In 1955 the *Guinness Book of World Records* was first published. Since that time, over 70 million copies have been sold around the world. Read about the amazing feats people accomplish in order to be included in the book.

Celebrate with Fun

- Get a copy of the book and find interesting records. What feats of physical strength has someone accomplished? Are animals included in the book? Find a record held by a child.

- Stewart Newport is the "Keeper of the Records" for the book. He helps determine which records are included. Has anyone in your family done something outstanding? Check the guidelines for being included. Maybe you'll be listed in next year's edition!

- Set up some silly "stunts" for family members to try. Attempt to break the world record in: Stacking up saltine crackers. Balancing on 1 foot while singing "Row, Row, Row Your Boat." Walking a distance with a balloon clinging to your head. Making the most consecutive free throws tossing a stuffed animal through the basketball hoop.

- Give everyone 15 minutes to demonstrate their ability to "Break a World Record." (Even if no record in their event exists.) Stress that all stunts must be safe. No one may demonstrate the ability to eat a peach with the pit! Have fun watching your highly talented family show off.

- Adapt some of the book's records to your family. One record includes the most nationalities in a sauna—29 men from 29 countries crammed into a sauna in Sweden for 10 minutes. Set a record for "the most people fully clothed to stand in the Johnson family bathtub for 2 minutes."

Celebrate with Crafts

Set the world record for the fastest artist. Announce an item to draw like "a baby licking a lollipop." Everyone sketches as quickly as possible while still producing a recognizable object. Afterward, try to guess what the scribbles represent.

Celebrate with Food

Many Guinness records involve food. No sense wasting food by trying to eat 58 hot dogs in 12½ minutes. Race through your neighborhood and try to set a world record in "collecting the most cans of food to be donated to a food bank in 20 minutes." Collect the cans in a wagon as you run from house to house.

More ideas: www.guinnessworldrecords.com

Mary Poppins's Birthday

In 1964 the movie *Mary Poppins* hit the big screen. Children around the country wished they could trade in their "ordinary" babysitters for Mary Poppins.

Celebrate with Fun

- First and foremost, rent the *Mary Poppins* video. Ask children their favorite parts of the movie. Act out those scenes.

- In one scene the children and Mary Poppins laugh, and laugh, and laugh until they end up floating toward the ceiling. Play your own version of this laughing game. One person tries to get everyone to laugh. Everyone struggles to keep a straight face as Dad pretends to be a ballerina.

- Look through the garage to find the kite you used last spring. Go outside to fly it in a safe area while singing Mary Poppins's "Let's Go Fly a Kite!"

- Is there a carousel nearby? Take a spin. Who knows? Perhaps the carousel horses will magically turn real and take you on a ride through the countryside, just like in the movie.

- Try speaking to each other in proper English accents. Instead of abruptly yelling, "I have to go to the bathroom!" quietly announce with an accent, "Excuse me. I need to visit the loo." You'll sound so refined.

- Can anyone spell "Supercalifragilisticexpialidocious" in your family? Can anyone say it backward like Mary Poppins?

- Remember how Mary Poppins snaps her fingers and the children's bedrooms are instantly cleaned? Take your children to their rooms and snap your fingers. Time them to see how long it takes to get toys picked up.

Celebrate with Crafts

Mary Poppins often used her umbrella. Hers was a very sensible black, but you can liven up your umbrellas with puff paint. Design a border around the edge and along the "ribs" of an open solid-colored umbrella. Add butterflies, rainbows, or any other design you like. Let paint dry thoroughly before closing the umbrella.

Celebrate with Food

In England, children have their teatime daily. Set out your best china, a nice tablecloth, and some pretty flowers for an afternoon tea. It's traditional to serve open-faced cucumber sandwiches and tea. Add a few cookies to complete the fare. Don't forget to use your best manners and extend your pinkie while drinking the cup of tea!

National Toasted Marshmallow Day

Who doesn't enjoy the feeling of sticky fingers that comes from roasting marshmallows?

Celebrate with Fun

- Under adult supervision, build a small bonfire and toast marshmallows. No room for a blazing fire? Roast marshmallows over the barbecue.

- Find a partner. One person opens their mouth, and the other tries to toss a miniature marshmallow inside.

- Try a tossed marshmallow throw (similar to an egg toss). Throw a marshmallow back and forth with a partner, taking a backward step after each toss. You can even play this game indoors!

- Have a marshmallow-stacking contest. See who can stack the most marshmallows on top of each other.

- Everyone uses toasted marshmallows to make s'mores. Get creative and invent a new recipe that uses toasted marshmallows.

- Play a game of Chubby Bunny. Put 3 large marshmallows in your mouth and say, "Chubby Bunny." Add another marshmallow and repeat "Chubby Bunny." Continue until you start laughing and can't get any more marshmallows inside. Who can fit in the most?

Celebrate with Crafts

Even though it's summer, make some marshmallow snow people. Dampen the bottom of a large marshmallow. Stick it on top of another marshmallow for the snowman's body. Use your fingers to "smush" another marshmallow into a smaller ball for the head. Use pretzel sticks for the arms.

Celebrate with Food

You thought you'd simply be roasting marshmallows outside today? Oh no! Celebrate by making indoor miniature s'mores. Break graham crackers into 1-inch squares. Melt ½ cup chocolate chips in the microwave. Spread the melted chocolate on the tiny graham squares. Give everyone a toothpick and several miniature marshmallows. Under adult supervision, "roast" your minimarshmallows over votive candles. When the marshmallow is golden, place between 2 graham cracker squares and enjoy. Go ahead and eat 10 or more!

SEPTEMBER

American Newspaper Month
Better Breakfast Month
National School Success Month
Children's Good Manners Month

Weeks to Celebrate

Week after Labor Day • Play Days
2nd Week • National 5-a-Day Week
3rd Week • National Flower Week
Last Full Week • National Dog Week

Days to Celebrate

1st Monday • Labor Day
1st Sunday after Labor Day • Grandparents Day
4th Sunday • National Good Neighbor Day

7	Backwards Day (or Yad Sdrawkcab)
9	Party Party Day
18	National Play-Doh Day
20	National Student Day
22	National Family Day
22/23	First Day of Autumn
26	Johnny Appleseed's Birthday
29	Pumpkin Day

American Newspaper Month

Want to relax with coffee and a newspaper on Saturday morning? You may not have that luxury, so use the newspaper to have some family fun.

Celebrate with Fun

- Cut out several human-interest pictures from the paper. Can family members guess what the pictures are about? Is it true that "A picture is worth a thousand words"?

- Read the obituaries to see the full, rich lives most people lead. Children may be surprised to know the newspaper publishes death notices. Discuss a Christian's view of death and how we'll be with Jesus when we die.

- Celebrate National Newspaper Month with a neighborhood "Giant Newspaper Fight." Find a level backyard playing area and divide it in half with a net or barrier. Place half the participants and half the newspapers they've saved for weeks on 1 side and half on the other. Each team wads sheets of newspapers into balls till both sides have huge stacks. On "Go!" Team A tries to throw all their paper balls across the net, while Team B does the same. Play for 5–10 minutes to see if one team actually gets most of their newspaper balls on the opposite side. This event gets so wild you might want to contact your local newspaper to write a story about how you are celebrating National Newspaper Month.

Celebrate with Crafts

Make some newspaper floogles, paper sculptures that add a new element to your home décor. Spread a double sheet of newspaper on the floor. Roll it up beginning at 1 side. For the last 4 inches, slide another piece of newspaper on top, overlapping the edges. Roll again and add 1 more sheet as before. Roll that piece to the very end. Cut 6 slits down 1 edge of the rolled paper, about 6 inches down. Hold the uncut end of your floogle and gently pull up on the cut strips. The floogle will get longer and longer as it spirals and twists.

Celebrate with Food

Most newspapers feature a weekly food section containing cooking tips and recipes. Collect the recipes from several weeks of newspapers. Which dish appeals to your family? Buy the ingredients and spend time together making the new recipe. Pretend you are food critics. On a scale of 1 to 5, how would you rate the recipe?

Better Breakfast Month

Does your family enjoy leisurely breakfasts of fresh fruit, yogurt, and homemade crepes? Or does everyone race around grabbing a cold piece of toast as they bolt out the door? Use this month to get in the routine of serving healthy breakfasts this school year.

Celebrate with Fun

- Make sure children are hungry for breakfast. Pick one day this month to wake everyone an hour early for a brisk bike ride or walk before breakfast. They'll eagerly come home to a healthy meal.

- See if your children can figure out these egg-related puns. What word is created by adding the 2 words together?

Eggs plus picture of plane	(explain)
Eggs plus picture of coins/change	(exchange)
Eggs plus picture of 2 people hitting	(exit)

- Plan a week's worth of healthy breakfasts in advance. It's easier to serve a nutritious breakfast if you know what ingredients you need ahead of time. Give children input into their good-for-you breakfasts.

- Who says breakfast has to be cereal or pancakes? A hearty bowl of chicken noodle soup is a great way to start the day. Break out of the boring breakfast food routine by serving an untraditional food like leftover pizza or grilled cheese sandwiches. If children insist on pancakes, serve a stack for dinner!

- Add a festive atmosphere to your morning meal by having a formal breakfast. Light candles, dig out the good china, and eat breakfast in the dining room. Wear clean pajamas instead of tuxedos.

Celebrate with Crafts

Set the stage for a month-long focus on healthy breakfasts by making your own breakfast bowls. Check if your community has a "decorate your own pottery" store. Take the family to paint their own bowls. A week later, return to pick up your dishwasher-proof designer bowls.

Celebrate with Food

Instead of slicing a banana in cereal, turn it into a breakfast popsicle. The night before, have children push a wooden craft stick into the bottom half of a banana. Spread peanut butter on the banana. Roll the sticky banana in granola or crushed cereal. Freeze on waxed paper. For breakfast, let defrost for 10–15 minutes, then enjoy your banana on a stick.

National School Success Month

Each September, children full of anticipation head off to school with new clothes and backpacks. This month celebrate ways to assure your children of success in school.

Celebrate with Fun

- The day before school starts, plan a special Family Fun Night. Let children show off their new lunch boxes and model some new clothes. Play some games, then set the school supplies by the front door to avoid the last-minute rush. Pray for your children, their teachers, and classmates.

- Try not to ask, "How was school?" the minute children come home. Wait an hour, then ask open-ended questions like "What did you do at recess today?" or "What kind of dioramas did your classmates turn in?" You're more likely to get intelligent answers if children have some time to "decompress" first.

- The school year offers countless opportunities to sign up for soccer, wrestling, art classes, gymnastics, . . . Avoid overscheduling. Success in school results from children being well rested and having plenty of free time to use their imaginations.

- Have children who are studying for a test play "Stump the Parents." They review by asking you questions. They'll enjoy seeing you squirm when they ask, "What year did the Civil War end?"

- Make learning fun by giving your young reader plastic fingernails to wear as they point from word to word. Party supply stores sell fingernails that glow in the dark or look like spiders.

Celebrate with Crafts

School projects often require children to make models or displays. At the last minute it can be a frantic scramble to look for glue and supplies. Designate a place for craft supplies. Stock it with colored markers, tape, glue, paintbrushes, small boxes, paper, and rulers. No more frantic last-minute searches!

Celebrate with Food

Prepare a special breakfast for the first day of school. Children are often too excited to eat, so a treat will entice them. How about minibagels with assorted cream cheese spreads? Use toothpicks to skewer a few pieces of fruit for easy fruit kabobs.

More ideas: Parenting without Pressure 407-767-2524

Children's Good Manners Month

Your children always say "please," use a napkin, and write thank-you notes, right? Then urge the neighbor kids to brush up on their manners this month!

Celebrate with Fun

- Make manners fun. If your child burps at the table, have her do 5 sit-ups while singing "Row, Row, Row Your Boat." (That's what they do at camp.) Silly punishments are more effective than constant nagging.

- Tell children what to expect in a new social situation. Explain how to shake hands with people at church and the importance of being very quiet during a wedding ceremony.

- Let children know about etiquette in medieval times. Back then, children were limited to 2–3 glasses of wine a day! Other basic rules included not throwing sticks at horses, not imitating adults behind their backs, and learning to toss bones on the floor after eating off the meat.

- Role-play situations requiring proper manners. Write scenarios on note cards so children can pick. Try these: You feel a big sneeze coming on during prayer time at church. Grandma knits you a babyish sweater with a pink and yellow bunny on it. She wants you to wear it. Let more than 1 child act out the scenes. Discuss how they handle them differently.

- Make an effort to model good manners yourself. Do you yell at someone who cuts in front of you on the freeway? Do you make a snide remark when the store clerk is too slow? Do you interrupt your children?

Celebrate with Crafts

Make a place mat to help children learn how to set the table. On construction paper trace around a plate, glass, knife, fork, and spoon. Cut out the paper utensils. Glue them in the proper positions on a place mat–sized piece of cardboard (the fork on the left, the knife and spoon on the right). When children set the table, they simply place the actual dishes on top of the paper cutouts.

Celebrate with Food

After reviewing proper table manners, plan a formal dinner. Set the table with your best linens and china. Light candles, bring out flowers, and fold swan napkins. After everyone is dressed in their Sunday best, begin the meal. Have polite conversation while passing food to the right. Watch everyone chew with closed mouths. Could you eat like this every night?

Play Days

On Labor Day, we honor people who labor at their jobs every day. This week, do the opposite. Spend the week playing as often as possible.

Celebrate with Fun

- Bring out the video camera and put on a talent show. Your children have probably seen TV talk shows. (Hopefully not Jerry Springer!) Move the living-room furniture so it looks like a talk show set. Appoint a "host" to do an opening monologue and interview world-famous guests. Viewers will be thrilled to watch a 5-year-old tie her shoes and a mother show how to make cookies. Your family is sure to love watching the video over and over.

- Make your own Twister game. Buy an inexpensive plastic tablecloth or shower curtain. Family members draw their faces or other designs on the cloth so that there are 5 designs going down and 4 across. Instead of saying, "Right hand, blue," you would say "Left hand, Ryan's face." Play the game as usual until the family collapses in a heap.

- Play Alligator Tag. Designate an area as the alligator tank. Everyone lies on their stomach inside the tank. The person who is "It" slithers on their stomach, trying to tag other people before they slither away. If a person is tagged, they become the attacking alligator.

Celebrate with Crafts

Make squeezable paint in an old plastic squeeze bottle. Mix ½ cup salt, ½ cup flour, and ½ cup water. Add a few drops food coloring. Lay out heavy paper so your children can make designs by squeezing the paint bottle over the paper.

At a home improvement store, ask for some free outdated wallpaper sample books. These (heavy!) books provide hours of creative fun and include bright pictures and bold patterns. Children can freely use the paper samples without an adult saying, "Don't waste paper."

Celebrate with Food

Make some playful sandwiches this week. Slice a banana into 6–8 "rounds." Spread half the slices with peanut butter. Add 3–4 raisins and top with another banana slice. There you have it—a smooth, round sandwich.

Want a l-o-o-o-n-n-g sandwich? Use a bamboo skewer to make a shish kebab sandwich. Cut up chunks of bread, cheese, cherry tomatoes, meat, and even lettuce. Slide the food on the skewer to make a fun, long sandwich.

National 5-a-Day Week

Sadly, most of our diets consist of fast-food fries and processed foods. Take a day to discover the joy of eating healthy fruits and vegetables.

Celebrate with Fun

- Look up the new Food Pyramid designed by the U.S. Department of Agriculture at www.nal.usda.gov.
- Show your children how many servings of fruits and vegetables they should be eating. Make an effort to eat 5 servings every day this week.
- Plan a family trip to the grocery store to spend some time in the fruit and produce sections. Instead of just buying apples and bananas, try a kiwi or star fruit. How about a pomegranate? You may need to ask the grocer how to prepare jicama! Your family might decide fruits and vegetables aren't so bad.
- Plan an apple-tasting contest. Purchase several types of apples, keeping track of which is which. Peel and slice the apples on separate plates. Have family members taste and rate them according to flavor.
- Make a chart listing how many fruits and vegetables each family member eats daily for a week. Your chart will graphically show if you need to cut back on chocolate and increase the blueberries.

Celebrate with Crafts

Use your abundance of fruits and vegetables for some printmaking. Set out several paper plates with a thin layer of paint spread on them. Cut pieces of mushroom, peppers, or carrots. Dip the vegetables in the paint and then press onto paper. Design your own greeting cards or wrapping paper.

Celebrate with Food

Relive your memories of summer camp by making foil dinners over your barbecue (or over a real campfire). Slice up onions, carrots, potatoes, broccoli, and peppers. Have everyone place assorted vegetables on a 15-inch piece of heavyweight foil. Top with salt, pepper, and butter. For extra flavor, add a few meatballs. Wrap foil tightly and barbecue for about 20 minutes. Make sure an adult unwraps the foil meals. Enjoy your healthy vegetable dinners!

More ideas: www.5aday.com

National Flower Week

As summer comes to an end, enjoy the last brilliant blooms from flowers in your backyard or local farmer's market.

Celebrate with Fun

- Find a local U-pick flower center. Many places offer rows of dahlias and other flowers for you to pick. Pick an extra batch to drop off at a local nursing home on the drive home.
- Send a "flower message" to family or friends. Buy flower stickers or draw pictures of flowers to convey a specific message. (If the budget allows, purchase real flowers to go along with your message.)

Asters	love, daintiness
Red roses	I love you
White camellias	You're adorable
Crocus	cheerfulness
Begonia	beware
Bluebells	humility

- How many songs can you sing about flowers? Try "Yellow Rose of Texas" and "Daisy, Daisy."
- Read Matthew 6:28–29. Discuss how we can trust God with our lives since he takes care of the "lilies of the field."
- Visit a local florist or farmer's market. Ask about the unusual flowers sold there. What is the most expensive flower they sell? Which is the most popular? Set a budget and see what type of bouquet you can put together with that amount of money.

Celebrate with Crafts

Since bumblebees like flowers, make your own bee from a flowerpot. Paint a ceramic clay pot with yellow paint. When dry, use black paint to decorate your bee's body with stripes. As paint dries, form the bee's head by gluing wiggle eyes onto a large black pom-pom. Add 2 chenille stems as antennae. Place the flowerpot upside down, then glue on the bee's fuzzy head.

Celebrate with Food

Did you know some flowers are edible? Just make sure the flowers are specifically grown without pesticides. Try adding a few nasturtium petals to salads. They have a sweet, spicy flower. Marigolds have a citrus-flavored flower, while gladiola petals taste like lettuce.

National Dog Week

This week is set aside to promote the relationship of dogs and people. It also emphasizes the importance of caring properly for your dog.

Celebrate with Fun

- Test your dog's intelligence. Have your dog sit and show her a favorite toy. Place it on the ground where she can see it. Cover the toy with a towel and say, "Find it." Does your dog try to get to the toy? Some dogs quickly forget where the toy is because it's out of sight.

- Dogs like playing Hide and Seek. Have your dog "stay." (Or have someone hold him.) Hide behind a couch or tree, then call your dog. See if he can find you. Since Rover is a popular name for dogs, next gather some kids and play "Red Rover, Red Rover." Let Rover play too.

- Some dogs are so pampered they have private chefs who cook their meals. While your dog probably eats store-bought food, you can fantasize what it would be like to treat your dog like royalty. Let everyone sketch the most luxurious doghouse they can imagine, complete with amenities like an indoor swimming pool and dog biscuit–shaped windows.

- Give your dog's sleeping area a thorough cleaning. Sweep out the doghouse while replacing the bedding. If your dog sleeps inside, wash his blanket so everything is clean and comfortable.

- In America, 76 percent of dog owners say they celebrate holidays and birthdays with their dog and give it presents. How about your family? Make your dog feel extra special today with a new doggy toy.

- When was the last time your dog had a checkup at the vet? Make sure your beloved pet's shots are all up-to-date.

Celebrate with Crafts

Make a dog biscuit pin in honor of your dog. A small-sized dog biscuit will be your dog's "face." Glue 2 felt ears at the top. Add wiggle eyes. Use a bead for the nose and black embroidery floss for whiskers. Glue a pin back (available at craft stores) on the back and wear your doggy pin. This is one dog biscuit your dog can't eat!

Celebrate with Food

You enjoy eating animal crackers, don't you? Go to a pet store and buy a box of "people crackers" for your dog to enjoy munching.

Labor Day

Back in 1894, labor unions played an important role in American life. Labor Day became a national holiday to honor workers. Today we often celebrate the day with end-of-summer picnics.

Celebrate with Fun

- Invite friends over for a Labor Day barbecue to which everyone needs to bring an item representing the job they do. Have a "show and tell" during which your firefighter neighbor shows his fire boots and your nurse friend shows her stethoscope.

- Do some physically hard labor today. Clean the garage, restack the woodpile, or scrub the lawn furniture. Children today often think all jobs are done sitting at a desk and working on a computer.

- Show your children how you punch in and out with a timecard at work. Borrow one if your company doesn't use timecards. Set up a mock timecard for children. Assign them an hour of yard work or half an hour of reading. They sign or punch the timecard when they begin and end.

- Show children the classified ads. Read some help-wanted ads out loud. Are there positions available your children would like someday? Explain the job application process.

- Make up family member resumes. No, you're not sending your 4-year-old to work at McDonald's, but explain how resumes document a person's experience and qualifications. Children can write out their skills, volunteer experiences, and special strengths. They can include their ability to ride a bike, memorize Bible verses, feed the cat, and help in the church nursery. Type up the "resumes." Every 6 months, look back and notice how the accomplishments have changed.

Celebrate with Crafts

Set out a plain-colored plastic tablecloth divided into sections equal to the number of people. Give everyone permanent markers. Assignment: Draw your current occupation. Next to that, sketch your ideal dream job. This can be an eye-opening experience for adults!

Celebrate with Food

Have children set up a lemonade stand to learn about running a business. (You provide coaching; they provide labor.) Show them how to make advertising signs. Float children a loan for the initial purchase of lemonade and cups. "Rent" them the table and chairs. They'll probably make some money, but they'll also learn it isn't all profit.

Grandparents Day

Celebrate this special day with real grandparents or with "adopted" seniors in your area who would love to be around children.

Celebrate with Fun

- Brainstorm ways to celebrate this day with your grandparents, real or adopted. Should they come to your house for their favorite dessert? How about a picnic at their favorite park? Increase anticipation by sending an invitation to them. Decorate it with stickers and glitter.

- Create a festive atmosphere with balloons and streamers. Have children make a gift ahead of time for grandparents, wrap it in festive paper, and present it with a kiss.

- Have children make a list of why their grandparents are "grand." Display the list for everyone to see.

- Spend time asking the honored guests questions. What was school like when they were little? What did they do in their free time? What's their favorite vacation memory? What pets have they had?

- Give grandparents a coupon book with redeemable coupons for children to give hugs, send pictures, or call Grandma on the phone.

- If grandparents live far away, celebrate by calling them and singing "For She's [or He's] a Jolly Good Fellow." Make a family video highlighting everyone's accomplishments. Doting grandparents love seeing grandchildren do somersaults or recite a poem. Send to Grandma with a big note saying, "Do Not Open until Grandparents Day!"

Celebrate with Crafts

Select a craft to work on together to give grandparents. Set out a solid-colored vinyl tablecloth and permanent markers. Have everyone draw pictures for the special grandparents. Older children can write things like "Thanks for taking me to the movies, Grandpa." Your grandparents will have a special tablecloth to use year-round.

Celebrate with Food

Make your favorite sugar cookie recipe. (Or take the easy way out and buy cookie dough at the store.) Use a gingerbread person cookie cutter to cut out Grandma and Grandpa body shapes. Let everyone use frosting to make their cookie look like their favorite grandparent.

More ideas: www.grandparents-day.com

249

National Good Neighbor Day

This is a day to develop a positive relationship with your neighbors . . . even if their dog's barking keeps you awake at night.

Celebrate with Fun

- Print a neighborhood newspaper describing local activities. Ask neighbors if you can share the hot-breaking news on Mrs. Johnson's new cat and the Clark family's Disneyland vacation. Use your computer to print up the newsletter. Deliver it personally.

- Plan a neighborhood block party. Use a neighbor's large driveway, or if possible, block off a cul-de-sac. Everyone brings a potluck dish starting with the first letter of their last name. You'll get pie from Petersons, salad from Swansons, and of course, Jell-O from Johnsons. Set up a stereo system and set an upbeat mood by playing '50s music. Play People Bingo. Make up cards with 9–12 squares. In each square write a description like "A person with 4 siblings" or "A person who snores." Everyone gets a Bingo card and races around to find the names of neighbors who fit the descriptions. First one with a full card wins!

Celebrate with Crafts

Make crazy name tags at the block party. Set out paper scraps, glue, glitter, stickers, and markers. Encourage people to design innovative name tags to introduce themselves.

Celebrate with Food

Before guests arrive, cut peeled bananas in half (not lengthwise). Slide wooden sticks in pieces. Freeze 1–2 hours. Let guests decorate frozen bananas. Microwave 2 cups chocolate chips and 2 Tbs. butter 30 seconds, stir, then melt at 20-second intervals until chocolate is smooth. Guests dip bananas in chocolate, then roll in assorted toppings like crushed cereal, chopped nuts, or sprinkles. Eat immediately or return to freezer for another hour.

Use that same melted chocolate to make edible shells out of paper cupcake liners. Use a basting brush to spread a layer of melted chocolate on the inside of the liners. Chill the cups in the refrigerator for 1 hour. Slowly peel off the paper. Use the chocolate cups to hold small candies or fruits.

More ideas: www.natgoodneighborday.org

Backwards Day
(or Yad Sdrawkcab)

Today's the day to do everything in a different way. Nothing normal happens on Backwards Day!

Celebrate with Fun

- As you wake children up, sing lullabies. Tell them, "Get a good night's sleep. Sleep tight!"
- As children get dressed, turn out their lights while saying, "Time to get in your pajamas." (By this time, your children will be thoroughly confused.)
- Encourage everyone to brush their teeth with their nondominant hand. Have them do the same with eating breakfast and brushing their hair. Have them try writing their name and a short message with their "opposite" hand. Can you read Michael's request for a new bike?
- Show children how to write backward. Print a few words, then hold the paper up to a mirror. Write down what the mirror shows. Now write something backward first, then to interpret the message hold the paper up to a mirror.
- If the bathroom mirror is foggy after someone takes a shower, write a backward message in the steam. (Some people write with lipstick!)
- Wear some backward clothes. It might be awkward to put a suit on backward, but you certainly could wear socks inside out or slip on a T-shirt so the front is in the back.
- Hand children a completed puzzle. Tell them to take it apart piece by piece.

Celebrate with Crafts

Find puppets or other craft items at a garage sale. Do a backward craft by having children take the item apart! Remove the puppet's hair and eyes. Dismantle a flower wreath so you're left with separate flowers.

Celebrate with Food

Serve backward meals today. Have soup for breakfast. It's nutritious and easier than making French toast. For lunch, pack cereal in plastic bowls for your children to eat with their milk. (Yes, they'll be embarrassed, but they'll survive. Maybe their friends will even think it's cool that they are celebrating Backwards Day.) Plan a tasty dinner of scrambled eggs, pancakes, and orange juice. Pour syrup on the plate first, then place pancakes on top.

251

Party Party Day

This day is celebrated every month when the actual date corresponds to the number of the month, so you can technically celebrate it on January 1, February 2, March 3, April 4, May 5, June 6, July 7, August 8, September 9, October 10, November 11, and December 12. Celebrate however you want!

Celebrate with Fun

- Invite your friends over for an egg-dropping contest. Have them bring a raw egg packed in a container. The catch? You're going to drop each container off the roof to see if the egg withstands the fall. (Obviously, it is an adult's job to be on the roof.) You'll be amazed at the creativity. Some people put the egg inside a stuffed animal or surround it with packing peanuts. How about mixing up a concentrated solution of Jell-O in a plastic bowl? Let the egg rest inside the Jell-O. Complete your "party party" by serving egg salad sandwiches.

- Bring back childhood joys—play backyard games. Try Hide and Seek or draw Tic-Tac-Toe on the sidewalk. Play Kick the Can. The goal is to have fun with little expense or preparation.

- Make party hats—no matter how silly. Set out paper plates, construction paper, ribbon, glitter, and foil. See who can create the most whimsical hat. Are you brave enough to walk down the street wearing them? Decorate the front door with balloons and streamers so all the neighbors know you are celebrating Party Party Day.

- Why should kids be the only ones who dress up? Divide into pairs. Each group gets the name of a TV show, Broadway musical, cartoon, or book. They have to dress in character and present a scene from their selected topic.

Celebrate with Crafts

Find a cardboard or wooden frame with a wide border. Looks pretty plain, doesn't it? Add a party party look with plastic colored paper clips. Glue on these avant-garde clips for an instant frame designed to hold a picture of you as the life of the party.

Celebrate with Food

Plan an old-fashioned barbecue with traditional foods like hot dogs, baked beans, potato salad, chips, corn on the cob, coleslaw, pretzels, popcorn, ice cream, and fruit cobbler. Bring out the party party food!

More ideas: www.ssww.com

National Play-Doh Day

We all remember the smell of a newly opened container of Play-Doh. Have fun squishing and playing with this versatile clay.

Celebrate with Fun

- Buy some new Play-Doh. Give everyone 2 colors and allow them 5 minutes to create a self-sculpture. Bring out toothpicks and plastic knives to help make shapes. Don't forget to squeeze some Play-Doh through a garlic press to make great wavy hair.

- Ask people to mix colors together and create their own new colors. Come up with creative titles such as "burnt toast" or "sunflower yellow."

- Give people equal amounts of Play-Doh. Who can make the longest clay snake? See who can form the doughnut with the largest hole. Sculpt an exotic animal and let people guess what it is.

Celebrate with Crafts

Make a batch of homemade play dough using this easy recipe: Combine 1 cup flour, ½ cup salt, 2 tsp. cream of tartar, 1 Tbs. salad oil, 1 cup water (add food coloring to water if desired), and dash of peppermint oil if a scent is desired. Stir constantly over medium heat for several minutes. It will stick together suddenly and can then be stirred into a ball. Keep stirring a few more seconds. Turn onto a lightly floured surface and knead after it cools. Keeps a long time refrigerated in a covered container! For a smelly variation, mix 1 package unsweetened Kool-Aid into the water. This gives your dough a deep rich color along with a pleasant scent.

Try salt dough: Mix 4 cups salt and 1 cup cornstarch with enough water to make a thick paste. Cook over medium heat. Let cool, then use as modeling clay. Items can be air-dried.

Celebrate with Food

Here's an edible play dough recipe: Mix together 9 oz. creamy peanut butter, 3 Tbs. honey, and ⅜ cup powdered dry milk. (May need more dry milk to get smooth consistency.) After they wash their hands, let children mold the clay into tiny bugs or cute shapes, then eat their creations!

More ideas: www.hasbropreschool.com/playdoh

National Student Day

Today is set aside to honor all students—from preschool through college. Let the students in your life know you appreciate their academic efforts.

Celebrate with Fun

- Contact your children's school or PTA. See if they'll help celebrate this important day by planning special events at school. It could be as simple as hanging balloons at the school entrance or serving cookies for a midafternoon treat.

- Send a Care package to a college student. Fill it with items like postage stamps, a phone card, homemade cookies, and extra batteries for their Walkman.

- Make homework a special occasion today—offer a little more help than usual. Set out a small gift for each child to open when homework is completed.

- Take time to reminisce about school in "the olden days." Your children will roll their eyes, but also be amazed that you used card catalogs and never surfed the net. Try to explain how exciting it was to walk into class and see a filmstrip projector ready for that day's lesson.

- Ask grandparents to call up and congratulate their student grandchildren.

- Decorate the house with banners and streamers. Put up posters saying, "This family has two terrific students!" or "Allan knows his multiplication tables!"

Celebrate with Crafts

Since your students are busy discovering new ideas at school, let them discover some old bones at home. While they are at school, boil some chicken and remove the bones. Spread the bones outside over a rock or other hard surface. Pour plaster over the bones and let harden. Encourage your budding archaeologists to use screwdrivers or garden tools to carefully chip away the plaster to reveal the bones.

Celebrate with Food

If your children take the bus to school, plan a "Bus Stop Buffet." Let parents know you'll be serving breakfast at the bus stop. (Ask them to contribute if they like.) Bring bagels, granola bars, and some fruit to the bus stop. Let kids eat while adults congratulate them on being hard-working students.

More ideas: www.collegeknowledge.com

National Family Day

Do you have 8 children, 2 parents, and Grandma living with you? Or does your family consist of 1 adult and 1 child? Whatever the makeup of your family, celebrate today!

Celebrate with Fun

- Begin the day with a group hug before everyone goes their separate ways.

- Bring out some baby pictures of the adults in your family. Share stories from your childhood with your children. Don't forget to tell how you had to walk 14½ miles to school—barefoot—in 3 feet of snow!

- Take turns dressing as different family members. Mom dresses toddler style, while Dad gets to look like a 13-year-old.

- Take turns playing your favorite games. Play Twister, Hide and Seek, Tag, or the ever popular Candyland.

- Try playing "Giggle, Giggle, Spit." Give everyone a glass of water and a washcloth or towel. The person who is "It" stands in front as everyone takes a big sip of water and holds it in their mouths. "It" then makes disgusting sounds or tells a silly joke, trying to get family members to laugh. People unable to keep from laughing spew water out of their mouths. (That's why you all have towels.)

- Even if it gets mushy, take time to share why each family member is special. Take turns sharing positive things about each other.

Celebrate with Crafts

Create some 3-dimensional family can sculptures. Give everyone an empty soup can (or coffee can if you like large-sized crafts!). Cover the can with solid-colored paper to make a smooth surface. Using buttons, lace, and paper scraps, embellish the can so it looks like you. Glue on pipe cleaners to represent arms and legs. Display your finished family cans and use them to hold pencils or other household items.

Celebrate with Food

Ahead of time, ask each family member to write down their 3 favorite foods on 3 pieces of paper. Toss the paper strips into a hat. Take turns selecting pieces of paper. When you've all picked some, that's your menu on Family Day! You might end up with a meal of pancakes, mashed potatoes, salsa, and popcorn!

First Day of Autumn

If you're lucky enough to live in New England, you can enjoy the fall season with traditional colored leaves, fresh apple cider, and cool evenings. Wherever you live, celebrate the transition between summer and winter.

Celebrate with Fun

- Take a "Family Fall Walk." Notice signs of fall: leaves changing colors, autumn wreaths on doors, and your dog getting a thicker fur coat.

- The days are getting shorter. Spend the evening reading a new book by candlelight. If there's a lot of dialogue, try "Readers' Theater." Different people read various characters out loud. Use dramatic voices for the biggest impact.

- Collect "Four Seasons" photographs of your house. On the first day of autumn, take a photograph of your house from a specific location. Save the picture. (That's the hard part!) Take photos from that exact location on the first day of winter, spring, and summer. Display the photos in frames and note the differences in flowers and trees around your house each season.

- Check the newspaper for fall harvest events. Local farms may open up for apple picking, and some have a corn maze where you try to find your way through a complex series of paths. Pick a pumpkin at the local pumpkin patch.

- If you can't go camping tonight, plan an indoor campout. Set up a miniature pup tent in the living room (or drape a sheet over furniture). Bring out the sleeping bags. Tell semiscary stories before singing some campfire songs. Then roll over and go to sleep, safe and dry in your indoor tent.

Celebrate with Crafts

Purchase several yards of different-colored rip-stop nylon at a fabric store. Make a fall banner to hang on your front door. The nylon withstands rainy fall days. Cut out leaves or pumpkins and glue to your banners. Use heavy-duty waterproof or carpenter's glue to attach pieces. Display until December 22, the first day of winter.

Celebrate with Food

So often, we barbecue only in summer. Even if the weather is cool, celebrate fall by having a traditional barbecue. Make hamburgers, find end-of-the-season corn on the cob, and if you feel really creative, make homemade ice cream. Add lemonade to bring back that feeling of lazy summer days.

Johnny Appleseed's Birthday

John Chapman walked barefoot through the Midwest. He was easy to spot since he wore a cooking pot on his head and carried a bag of apple seeds. Is it any surprise people began calling him Johnny Appleseed?

Celebrate with Fun

- How's this for a breakfast menu? Pancakes with applesauce, along with some apple slices. Don't forget the apple juice!

- Buy several varieties of apples. Cut each apple in thin slices and place on a plate. Sample each variety and vote on the "Family Apple Favorite." Challenge a family member to close his eyes and plug his nose. Have him take a small bite of onion and a bite of apple to see if he can tell the difference.

- It might be too dangerous to shoot an apple from your child's head. Instead, have your child stand with an apple balanced on his head and use a lightly wadded up piece of newspaper instead of an arrow to try to hit the apple. See how much your child really trusts you! Do they flinch? Now reverse the game. You stand with an apple on your head while your child tries to hit it with wadded newspaper. Will you flinch?

- Cut out the centers of 4–5 paper plates to make cardboard rings. Place several apples on a table. Try to throw the rings over the apples.

Celebrate with Crafts

Mix 1 cup cinnamon and ¾ cup applesauce until it forms a sticky ball. Knead several times and roll out about ¼-inch thick on a flat surface. Cut dough into shapes with cookie cutters. Use a straw to poke a hole in the tops so you can hang them wherever you want a nice cinnamon smell. Let dry over a heating vent or outside in the sun for several days. Enjoy your applesauce ornaments all year long.

Celebrate with Food

Fill a bucket or the kitchen sink with warm water. Toss in a few apples and take turns trying to pick up an apple with only your mouth. Guaranteed to produce water up your nose and wet hair. Eat the apples as a healthy snack.

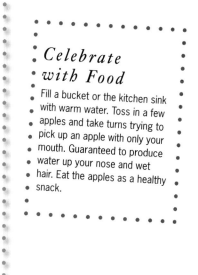

More ideas: www.appleseed.net

257

Pumpkin Day

Traditionally fall is a time to eat pumpkin pie, carve pumpkins, and roast pumpkin seeds. See what other fun things your family can do with pumpkins.

Celebrate with Fun

- It's not too late to make your mark on a pumpkin. Go to your garden or find someone who is growing pumpkins. Ask if you can carve your name in a pumpkin. By the time the pumpkin grows for another month, your name will be larger and more distinct.

- Pretend you are a pumpkin growing in a large pumpkin patch. People are walking around looking for that very perfect pumpkin to take home and carve into a jack-o-lantern. Oh no! A family is going to cut you from the vine and take you home. Quickly give a passionate speech to the unsuspecting family, telling them why they should not choose you for their jack-o-lantern.

- When selecting a pumpkin to carve, don't just look for the "perfect" pumpkin. Find a lopsided, misshapen pumpkin to take home and decorate. You'll end up with a whimsical jack-o-lantern.

Celebrate with Crafts

Ordinary paper bags make adorable pumpkins. Select any size paper bag and stuff with crumpled newspaper so pumpkin is "chubby." Tie the top shut with a piece of yarn or a twisty tie. Cut slits in the top section to look like vines. Paint pumpkin with orange paint. When paint dries, add black facial features. Paint top of the pumpkin green.

Celebrate with Food

After carving your pumpkin, rinse off the seeds to make roasted pumpkin seeds. Spread seeds on a lightly greased cookie sheet. Sprinkle with salt and bake 40 minutes at 250 degrees. Want something more complicated? Add ¼ cup salt to 2 quarts water. Add 2 cups pumpkin seeds. Simmer 2 hours. Drain, place on a cookie sheet, and bake 30–40 minutes at 300 degrees. Try both recipes. See if your family can taste any difference between them.

Make an easy pumpkin ice cream. Soften 1 quart ice cream. (Or, if you really like ice cream, soften a gallon.) Mix in ½ to 1 cup complete pumpkin pie filling (with seasonings and sugar already added). Put ice cream back in freezer to harden for 1 hour. Enjoy!

OCTOBER

Popcorn Popping Month
Family History Awareness Month
National Pasta Month
National Apple Month
Month of the Young Adolescent
Oktoberfest
Clergy Appreciation Month
Eat Better/Eat Together Month

Weeks to Celebrate

1st Full Week • Get Organized Week
2nd Week • Teen Read Week
Week of October 9 • Fire Prevention Week

Days to Celebrate

Wednesday of 1st full week • Walk to School Day
1st Saturday • Frugal Fun Day
2nd Sunday • National Children's Day
2nd Monday • Columbus Day
Mid-October • Lee Jeans Denim Day
3rd Saturday • Sweetest Day
4th Saturday • Make a Difference Day

  1 World Vegetarian Day
  2 National *Peanuts* Day
  8 Silly Day
10 Stamp Collecting Day
12 World Farmer's Day
13 "The Un-Birthday" Day
15 National Grouch Day
16 Dictionary Day
18 Watch a Squirrel Day
18 Boost Your Brain Day
22 Pretzel Day
31 Halloween

Popcorn Popping Month

Start a new month by celebrating with a big bowl of popcorn. Then get creative and try some "popping fun." The average person eats 59 quarts of popcorn per year!

Celebrate with Fun

- Fill a small jar with unpopped popcorn. Family members guess how many kernels are inside. After everyone writes down their guess, count the kernels together. Person closest to the actual amount gets a prize.

- Collect 6 clean socks and fill with ½ cup unpopped popcorn. Tie a knot in the tops. You've just made beanbags! Use them for a "beanbag toss" similar to an egg toss. Set an empty wastebasket in the middle of the room. Stand behind a designated line and try to throw your popcorn-filled socks into the basket. Set up a mini obstacle course in a hallway or family room. Place 3–4 objects like a chair, pillow, or shoe on the ground between points A and B. Take turns standing on the start line with the beanbag sock balanced on your head. Time each other. Who can go through the obstacle course fastest without losing the beanbag?

- Give everyone a spatula or wooden spoon. Toss a kernel of popped popcorn in the air. Try to keep the popcorn in the air by hitting it with your spatula. You'll find yourself moving all over the room to keep the popcorn from touching the ground.

- Use a spatula to see who can bounce a piece of popcorn the most consecutive times.

Celebrate with Crafts

To make edible bird necklaces, let a bowl of popcorn sit out overnight. This makes the popcorn easier to string. Thread a large-eyed needle with dental floss or embroidery floss. "Sew" pieces of stale popcorn on the thread. Hang on trees for a tasty bird treat.

Celebrate with Food

Most people enjoy popcorn with butter and salt. Europeans, though, enjoy sugar on their popcorn. Set up a popcorn-tasting station and experiment with different flavors. Give each person 2 paper lunch bags filled with 1 cup popped popcorn. "Secretly" have each family member flavor their bags of popcorn. Try cinnamon and sugar, garlic powder, lemon pepper, and Cajun seasonings. Sample each bag and vote on your favorite flavor.

Pop a batch of microwave popcorn and a batch the "old-fashioned" way in a pan on the stove. Can your family tell which is which?

More ideas: www.popcorn.org

Family History Awareness Month

Knowing your family history creates a sense of belonging. It's fun knowing Uncle Karl's interest in motorcycles began when he was 10 — the same age your son began begging for his own motorcycle.

Celebrate with Fun

- Make a family time line. Use a roll of adding paper to make a long graph showing important events in your family's history. Include the day Gabby lost her first tooth as well as the day Grandma Helga arrived as an immigrant from Germany. Display the time line down the hallway, and leave room to add events when relatives come over and tell you when Uncle Joseph opened his first bakery in New York. Keep a world map handy this month to point out where your family's history began.

- Send a letter or e-mail to relatives asking for their favorite family recipe. Compile all the tasty treats for your very own "Schwartz Family Cookbook." Print copies to give to the contributors as holiday gifts.

- Have relatives send you their childhood photos. Label the photos and make a family collage. A quick printer can duplicate the collage. Send it to a relative who will enjoy seeing pictures of Aunt Edna as a baby.

- Encourage family members to keep in touch with each other. This takes some work, but track down names, addresses, birthdays, and e-mails of as many family members as possible. After compiling the list, send it out to everyone so they have an up-to-date directory of relatives to help them keep in touch with distant family members.

Celebrate with Crafts

Make a giant family tree on a large piece of poster board. Have children cut out construction paper leaves. Sketch the family tree, beginning with your family at the top. Write the name of each family member on a leaf and attach it on the proper place. Start making phone calls to relatives to ask, "What was the name of Uncle Joseph's second son?" Continue adding leaves until you have a complete (or semicomplete!) pictorial representation of your family history.

Celebrate with Food

Celebrate your heritage by making a traditional meal like your ancestors made. Find a new recipe to try along with traditional family favorites. Dress in costumes your ancestors wore to add to the effect. Invite relatives over to share memories while you share food.

National Pasta Month

When today's parents were young, they ate plain old macaroni. Now "pasta" comes in a variety of shapes, textures, and flavors. Celebrate October as Pasta Month by making pasta a regular part of your meals.

Celebrate with Fun

- This month, remind your children to do their chores by writing messages on large dry lasagna noodles. Hand out the noodles and watch the kids' faces as they read, "Don't forget to feed the dog before soccer practice."

- Go to a gourmet grocery store and check out the pasta available. Purchase a pasta that is a unique shape or offers a special seasoning.

- Many types of pasta now come in flavors such as broccoli or spinach. Serve a batch of "green" pasta and see if your family can guess the source of color.

- Do you know how experts test if spaghetti is done? They toss a piece on the ceiling! If it sticks, it's ready to eat. Boil some spaghetti and let your family enjoy tossing it on the ceiling. Don't worry, cleanup is easy. Just reach up and remove any pasta.

- Set out 24 pieces of round spaghetti. Play a game of pick-up sticks using the pasta instead of regular plastic or wooden sticks.

- Purchase some inexpensive pasta. Cook and drain. After pasta has cooled, transfer it to a dishpan. Add a few marbles. (No, this isn't a new pasta recipe!) Have children use their bare feet to try to remove the marbles with their toes. Slippery, slimy fun!

Celebrate with Crafts

Make pasta necklaces to wear as you eat your pasta dinner. Purchase a package of ziti pasta. The shape is ideal for stringing necklaces. Use poster paint to decorate the ziti with polka dots, stripes, or other designs. Let dry, then string on yarn for necklaces.

Celebrate with Food

Plan a neighborhood Pasta Party. Ask several families to prepare their favorite pasta and sauce. Travel from house to house sampling small servings of the dishes. Use paper plates for easy cleanup. Get someone to make a noodle kugle for dessert. This sweet dish is also made with pasta.

More ideas: www.ilovepasta.org

National Apple Month

Are Golden Delicious or Granny Smith apples more popular at your house? Don't worry if you can't decide between the 7,000 varieties of apples.

Celebrate with Fun

- Ask children to guess how many seeds are inside an apple. Cut it open to see whose guess was closest.
- Make an acrostic from the word *apple* with words describing apples:

  A—wesome
  P—retty
  P—ippin
  L—uscious
  E—arthy

- Ever wonder why apples float when you bob for apples? Fresh apples are 25 percent air. Bob for a few apples with your family.
- The National Apple Museum is in Biglerville, Pennsylvania. The world's largest apple was grown in England. It weighed a hefty 3 lb. 1 oz.! That's what a whole bag of apples usually weighs! Go buy the largest apple available, then find the smallest, most red, and most unusual.
- Slice 2 apples and put in a plastic bag. Weigh the bag. Let the apples sit out in the air for 2 days. Weigh again and notice how much lighter the apples are because their water has evaporated.
- Set out an apple pie and ask your family, "How can we cut this into 8 equal pieces using only 3 straight cuts?" Cut the pie in half, then half again. That's 2 cuts. Now stack all the pieces on top of each other and make 1 more slice to cut those pieces in half!

Celebrate with Crafts

Make a shrunken head. Peel an apple to give your "head" a smooth appearance. (At least for now!) Carve indentations for the eyes and mouth. Carve around the nose so it's raised. Pour lemon juice over the entire carved face. Tie a string from the stem and hang in a warm, dry place for 3 weeks. Try not to peek at your apple head. You'll be surprised at how shriveled and "full of personality" your head will be.

Celebrate with Food

Make a crunchy apple sandwich. Peel and core an apple. Slice the apple into 4–5 "rings." Spread the layers with peanut butter topped with a few raisins. Put the apple together again. Now slice your crunchy sandwich as if it were a piece of cake. Healthy and tasty!

Month of the Young Adolescent

Many parents dread the teen years as children struggle to discover who they are. Take advantage of your children's early adolescence by enjoying their energy and their desire to assert their independence.

Celebrate with Fun

- Plan special outings with your young teen. They may act as if they don't want to be seen with you, but secretly they'll enjoy the attention. Make an invitation to a mystery restaurant out of magazine letters so it looks like an old-fashioned ransom note. Toss a paper airplane to your child with a note on it inviting her on a bike ride to get ice cream.

- Your teens strive to be mature but still need close parental contact. This month tell your child how much you love her. Point out her positive traits. Is she hesitant to talk? Try evening walks. The darkness and lack of direct eye contact encourage children to open up and share their feelings. Try not to give a lecture on every topic your child brings up!

- Do something special with your young teen and his/her best friend. A movie or bowling "for no reason" conveys that you think your child is special.

- Take time to express interest in your children's choice of music. In a casual way ask them what the words mean or why they like that particular group. Avoid making judgments unless the music is totally inappropriate.

- Spend time this month praying for your child. Pray they'll make wise choices in their decision to serve God.

- Teen author Sondra Clark has written *You've Got What It Takes!* to help young teens set goals and gain self-confidence.

Celebrate with Crafts

Encourage your children's craft skills by having them add a homemade touch to their room. Help your daughter paint a mural on her wall or add fringe to curtains. Your son could decorate a frame for his favorite poster.

Celebrate with Food

Teens love pizza, so celebrate with a pizza party. While kids munch pizza, bring out the "pizza cake" dessert. Bake a round yellow cake. Use red frosting "sauce." Every pizza needs olives, so mix a tiny bit of green, blue, and red food coloring to create black. Quickly dip cheerios in the black dye, let dry, and use for olives. Cut the inside of a 3 Musketeers bar to resemble mushrooms. Place shredded coconut in a plastic bag with orange food coloring. Shake. You have your cheese!

More ideas: www.nmsa.org

Oktoberfest

How would you like to attend a 2-week wedding? The guests had such a great time at the wedding of Bavarian King Ludwig I in October 1810 that the party continued . . . and continued. Evidently the party never ended—people continue to celebrate Oktoberfest with many community events.

Celebrate with Fun

- It's a German Oktoberfest tradition to link arms with the person next to you, sway back and forth, and sing loudly. The song doesn't matter as long as it's loud. Periodically link arms at dinner and sing. (Try some songs from *The Sound of Music* with a German/Austrian feel.)

- Work German words into your conversations. Almost everyone knows *guten Tag* (good day), *gesundheit* (good health), and *auf Wiedersehen* (farewell). Try "Guten Tag, Jacob. You sneezed. Gesundheit. I have to make dinner now. Auf Wiedersehen."

- German men traditionally wore lederhosen, leather shorts with suspenders. At a thrift shop buy inexpensive suspenders, or make your own using narrow strips of fabric and pinning the ends to the front and back of your pants.

- German women wear dirndls at Oktoberfest. These dresses include colorful aprons. Use scrap fabric to make aprons for girls to wear.

- Ask a travel agency for old posters or travel brochures from Germany. Display them around the house. Plan a fantasy trip to Germany. Look at Internet airfares. Where would you visit? What would it be like to sleep in a castle on the Rhine River?

Celebrate with Crafts

In Germany, Oktoberfest celebrations involve drinking large quantities of beer. This is not a recommended activity! The German beer halls always use coasters under the huge steins of beer. Make coasters out of plain-colored 4" x 4" tiles. With acrylic paint, decorate tiles with October or fall designs. Coat with a clear seal or decoupage. Glue felt scraps on the bottom and use when drinking root beer.

Celebrate with Food

A traditional German meal consists of sausage, potato salad, and sauerkraut. The secret to German sauerkraut is to cook it for hours! While sauerkraut in the United States has a bit of a "bite" to it, Europeans like theirs almost mushy. Cook your sauerkraut over low heat for several hours to get that authentic German Oktoberfest taste. (Then it will take another couple of hours to get the sauerkraut smell out of the house!)

Clergy Appreciation Month

Week after week, pastors, ministers, and other clergy work hard to serve the needs of their people. This month give some much-needed recognition to the clergy at your house of worship.

Celebrate with Fun

- Decorate the pastor's office with balloons and streamers. Why stop there? Decorate the church entrance also. Put signs out front that read "Our Pastor Is the Best!" and "Our Preacher Is Our Best Feature!"

- Organize a card shower. People all send cards by e-mail or snail mail on a certain day. The more cards, the more your pastor feels appreciated. Have children in Sunday school make glittery "I Love You" cards.

- Decorate a bulletin board acknowledging your pastor. Decorate with cute borders and bright cutouts. Display pictures of Pastor as a baby, on his or her first date, and graduating from seminary.

- During a service, pass out paper for people to write why they think the pastor is special. Collect the notes with the offering. Present the notes in a satin bag or special box.

- While the pastor is hard at work in his office, secretly wash and wax his car. Vacuum out the cracker crumbs and add a cute air freshener for that professional car wash touch.

- During a service, arrange a "surprise" testimony time so people can share their feelings about the pastor. Or videotape people's testimonies ahead of time, then play the video during the service.

- Pass around a calendar for the month so people can take turns praying for the pastor on a daily basis.

Celebrate with Crafts

Make a giant "Thank You" card. Hinge 2 pieces of 4′ x 8′ plywood. Sand and paint with a solid color. Have people use permanent markers to write large thank-you notes to the pastor.

Celebrate with Food

Purchase gift certificates for food. Your pastor might enjoy a meal at a nice restaurant. Give certificates for ice-cream sundaes, fruit smoothies, or submarine sandwiches. If there's a certificate for an evening at a restaurant with his or her spouse, add a coupon to pay for the babysitter too.

More ideas: christianitytoday.com/holidays/clergy

Eat Better/Eat Together Month

Does your family eat in staggered shifts, barely talking to each other while racing from one activity to another? This month reschedule activities to allow more time for family meals.

Celebrate with Fun

- Extend the time your family sits at the table with some story stretchers. On slips of paper, list topics for family discussions. Examples: Tell about a time you played a trick on someone. Describe a time when you shared your faith. Have you ever eaten an unusual food? Tell about a time you tried something new—and succeeded!

- Give everyone a glass of water with several ice cubes and a 12-inch piece of embroidery floss with a loop at 1 end. See who can "lasso" their ice cube. Then demonstrate your lassoing skills. Lay the thread on top of an ice cube. Sprinkle 1 tsp. salt on the loop. Wait 20 seconds. Slowly lift up on the string, which will have the ice cube attached to the end. The salt freezes the string to the ice cube.

- Just as everyone gets ready to sit down at their usual places, announce, "Switch seats!" Everyone sits at a different place. Sounds simple, but you'd be amazed at how people feel ill at ease in a different chair.

- Get a jokes and riddles book. Take turns passing it around after dinner so everyone gets a chance to make others laugh.

Celebrate with Crafts

Make designer plates to use throughout the month. Purchase solid-colored plastic plates at the dollar store. Use permanent markers to decorate the plates with family self-portraits, or in the case of your 2-year-old, scribbles. Enjoy family dinners as you eat off the plates.

Celebrate with Food

Celebrate this month of family mealtime togetherness by trying a few new recipes. Get children involved in cooking. Picky eaters will be more likely to eat a new dish if they helped prepare it.

Do your children play with Legos? Make an easy Lego cake. Bake a 1-layer sheet cake in a rectangular pan. Remove and place on a tray. Cut the tops off of 6 cupcakes to form Lego "knobs." Place cupcake bottoms evenly spaced on the cake. Frost cake and cupcakes in the same color to resemble a Lego.

Get Organized Week

1ST FULL WEEK IN OCTOBER

This entire week is set aside to reduce the clutter in your life. Choose at least one day this week to get organized. More organization means less stress!

Celebrate with Fun

- Begin with a family "clutter walk" through the house. Figure out where most clutter accumulates. Is it by the front door? At the bottom of the stairs? Take pictures of the junk piles so you'll have "before" and "after" photos. Unclutter one prime area. These tips might help:

  Create a "take-out area"—not a fast-food restaurant, but one central location to put items that need to go out. All backpacks, lunch pails, and notes for school go in this location. That way mornings are less chaotic. Children pick up their things as they go out the door.

  Get each family member color-coded baskets. Toss loose items into appropriate baskets. Kids may get tired of looking through their basket of jumbled items and actually put their shoes away!

  Spend just 5 minutes a day organizing 1 drawer or closet. Every bit helps unclutter. Do you really need 4 nail files and 3 bottles of dried glue in your kitchen drawer?

- Simplify daily organization by having children lay out school clothes the night before. It makes mornings easier! Let younger children decorate a paper plate to look like their face. Place it on the floor at bedtime with the next day's shirts and pants spread out to make a "body."

- Organize your schedule by setting up a large calendar listing all family activities. Color-code each person so it's easy to see that Sarah has soccer practice and Brandon goes to karate on Wednesday.

Celebrate with Crafts

Purchase a hanging shoe bag for a closet. Using permanent markers or puff paint, let each person write their name on and decorate 1 or 2 pockets. Hang in a handy location. Use to store permission slips, gloves, and other small items —or even shoes.

Celebrate with Food

Make a family event out of organizing a cupboard or pantry. Remove food items and wipe down shelves. Have family members make labels for "soups," "vegetables," or "pasta." Throw away that package of generic tuna noodle delight that's been in the cupboard for years. When finished, make a meal from the items in your newly organized pantry.

More ideas: www.napo.net

Teen Read Week

We place great emphasis on reading to young children and having them read independently. Teens also need encouragement to develop a love for reading.

Celebrate with Fun

- Treat your teen to a trip to the bookstore. Let her pick out a "just for fun" book. Teens often get bogged down in only reading required textbooks.
- Plan a family reading night. Pick a general interest book or even a *Reader's Digest* magazine and take turns reading out loud.
- Let your teen see you read for fun. You may not be popular at first, but restrict TV or computer time so your teen has an opportunity to read for enjoyment too.
- Start a tradition of purchasing a high-quality "coffee-table" book on your children's birthdays. As they approach the teen years, they'll have a collection of books reflecting their ever changing interests.
- Invite your teen's friends over for an impromptu book club. Ask them to come with their favorite book and share why they find their book special. They may also trade books so friends can read them.
- Ask your teen to read a portion of a book out loud as quickly as possible. Can the rest of the family understand her? Have other family members speed-read for a few laughs also.
- Teens sometimes feel stressed out. Suggest they make some stress reducers. Stretch a sturdy balloon over the end of a funnel. Pour in as much flour as possible. Tie balloon securely. Stretch another balloon over the first, covering the tied end. The poured flour gives a firm yet squishy feel. Squeeze as a stress reduction toy.

Celebrate with Crafts

Give your teen a journal. Most stationery and craft stores sell a variety of journals. Teens can add stickers, photos, and other mementos. Include a new set of fancy gel pens to encourage literary prose.

Celebrate with Food

What better way to celebrate your teen reading than with pizza? Let him choose his favorite pizza to eat while reading, even if no one else in the family likes anchovies, olives, onions, and pepperoni.

More ideas: www.ala.org/teenread

Fire Prevention Week

Since 1925 Fire Prevention Week has been celebrated by presidential proclamation. Children are involved in starting over 100,000 fires a year. Use this week to teach children about the dangers of fire.

Celebrate with Fun

- Children are naturally curious about matches and fire. Set up a very controlled situation in which children use matches. Begin with large wooden matches. Show children how to strike them away from their bodies. Let them experiment with lighting the match and a candle. Knowing how matches work takes the mystery out of using them. Stress the importance of using matches only with adult supervision.

- Check the paper for community workshops on fire safety. Some fire stations offer tours this week. If your children's school offers a fire safety assembly, attend so you'll be up-to-date on the latest prevention ideas.

- After completing a home safety check and a practice fire drill, award certificates to family members. Pass out awards that say, "Jason knows how to call 9-1-1," or "Samantha knows how to stop-drop-and-roll."

- Remember the basics of fire prevention: Make sure pot handles are not out in front of the stove; make sure no rugs are placed over electrical cords; never let young children push in electrical plugs; dust smoke detectors and check batteries regularly. "Spring ahead—Fall back" defines daylight savings time. Change batteries in your smoke detector whenever daylight savings time occurs.

- Read *The Cow That Destroyed Chicago* about Mrs. O'Leary's cow. The cow supposedly kicked over a lantern that started a fire that burned 2,000 acres in Chicago.

Celebrate with Crafts

Turn the top of a cardboard egg carton into a fire truck. Cut off the lid and paint it bright red. When dry glue on 2 black paper tires. Cut pictures of faces out of a magazine and glue behind the "holes" in the egg carton to look like firefighters.

Celebrate with Food

Try some "hot" foods today. Serve salsa with chips. Challenge your family to take a bite of a semihot pepper. (Use milk to counteract your burning mouth.)

More ideas: nfpa.org/fpw/index.asp

Walk to School Day

Even if you don't have children to walk to school, this is still a good day to get some exercise. Some communities use the entire week as "Walk to School Week."

Celebrate with Fun

- Do your children normally ride the bus? Can they get up earlier and have you walk them to school? If it's still too far, drive them within a mile and then walk. (Yes, you'll get extra exercise as you walk back to your car.)
- If walking your children to school isn't possible, find some other way to exercise with them today. Go to a park and play Tag with them on the playground. They'll love chasing you up and down the slide as other adults marvel at your endurance.
- Talk to other parents ahead of time about organizing a "walk to school parade" today with children.
- Feeling silly? Divide your family in half. (In number, not their bodies!) Stand by your front door. Have half the family walk briskly to the right and the other half walk to the left. Each group walks several times around the house, greeting each other enthusiastically when the groups overlap.
- Take a one-on-one walk with your children or spouse. Even a tongue-tied preteen opens up when walking with an adult at twilight.
- Play Follow the Leader while taking a walk. Take turns being the leader and having the rest of the group hop, skip, and pirouette behind you.

Celebrate with Crafts

Make your own treasure hunt game. Give each person 6 index cards. Ask them to draw an item found outdoors on each card—a dog, a brown house, a VW. Collect the pictures, shuffle them, and distribute them evenly to everyone. Go outside with your cards and walk around the neighborhood. See who can find the items on their card first.

Celebrate with Food

Plan a "Walking Dinner Picnic." Have everyone help pack a picnic dinner. Load up a few backpacks and head out for a walking adventure. Hike 3 or 4 blocks and find a place to eat your first course, maybe sandwiches or carrot sticks. Walk to another location and eat your pretzels. Continue walking and eating until everyone is full.

More ideas: www.walktoschool-usa.org

271

Frugal Fun Day

It doesn't take an expensive trip to Disneyland to laugh together as a family. Try these ideas for low-cost fun.

Celebrate with Fun

- Leave small invitations at everyone's breakfast plate: "You are cordially invited to attend a family game night this evening at 7 P.M." When everyone gathers, vote on which games to play. Vary quick and easy games with a longer game of Monopoly Jr.

- Depending on the weather, have an indoor/outdoor scavenger hunt. Put together a list of items to find within a designated amount of time:

Indoor hunt	Outdoor hunt
Dirty sock	Largest leaf
Book with animal pictures	Twig shaped like an L
Picture of yourself	Smooth stone
Broken crayon	Smallest pinecone
A toy with wheels	Piece of litter
Magazine	Blades of grass
Stuffed animal	Something representing fall

- Play Flashlight Tag. Go outside and try to "tag" people running from one hiding place to another. Inside, remove your valuable Ming vase and play the same way, running from room to room without being tagged by a flashlight.

Celebrate with Crafts

Write your names on paper and have 1 person collect, shuffle, and pass out the papers again. Spread around the room so no one can see anyone else's paper. Spend 10 minutes drawing a picture of the family member listed on your paper.

Celebrate with Food

Plan a mixed-up dinner. Eat ice cream first, then something simple like grilled cheese sandwiches.

Get ready to eat an ordinary meal with out-of-the-ordinary utensils. At dinner, pass around a box filled with soup ladles, spaghetti forks, wooden spoons, and so on. (No knives though!) Without looking, each person reaches into the box and selects a utensil. That's what they'll use to eat with! Messy, but fun.

More ideas: www.frugalfun.com

National Children's Day

This special day recognizes the value, dignity, and inherent worth of children everywhere. Take time to let the children in your life know they are special.

Celebrate with Fun

- Ask your child, "What would you like to do this afternoon?" Most likely a trip to Disneyland isn't an option, but you might be surprised at what your child chooses. Maybe she wants to work on a puzzle with you or go on a bike ride. Try to do what they want, even if you don't feel like playing in their backyard fort.
- Buy a new game, book, or craft project. Wrap in colorful paper and give to your child as a gift the family can enjoy together.
- Play "Hot-Cold-Clap-Clap." Remember how you hid an item and a person tried to find it? To help the "seeker" you'd say, "You're getting warmer, warmer, no—you're getting cold." This game is similar. Hide an item while "It" is out of the room. As "It" looks for the item, the rest of the group claps the closer "It" gets, and the closer, the louder the group claps. This popular game causes sore hands!
- Make up an acrostic for each child. Use the letters of their name to describe a positive trait they have:

S—mart
O—ptimistic
N—ice to others
D—ependable
R—esponsible
A—lways has a sense of humor

Celebrate with Crafts

Lay out a large piece of butcher paper or newsprint on the floor. (See if your local newspaper gives away roll ends.) Have your child lie on the floor while you trace his or her body. While children use markers to draw their hair and faces, decorate their shirt areas by writing "slogans" such as "Jenni is great at riding a bike" or "Mike can count to 29."

Celebrate with Food

Ask your children what they'd like for dinner. Serve their favorite meal, along with a coupon that says, "No Chores Today!"

More ideas: See also National Kid's Day—Aug. 1 (www.kidsday.org); (www.holidaysmart.com/10_nationalchildrensday.htm)

Columbus Day

Most school children know the short poem "In 1492, Columbus sailed the ocean blue." While there is controversy about its historical accuracy, we still celebrate Columbus Day on the 2nd Monday in October.

Celebrate with Fun

- Columbus was one of the few people in his time who believed the world was round! How shocking! We all know the world is flat—just look at how the ocean "drops off." Divide family members into 2 groups. One group gives reasons why the world is flat. The other presents reasons why the world is round. Which group is more convincing?

- Columbus took risks by exploring new territories. Take a risk by enjoying a new experience with your family. Travel to a nearby community for ice cream. Attend a different church next week. Spend an afternoon visiting a new museum.

- Talk with children about inappropriate and appropriate risks. Act out different situations to see how children respond. Discuss which of these are appropriate risks:

A friend dares you to ride your bike down a steep hill without a helmet. What do you do?

The dog next door is growling and baring his teeth as you walk up to him. What do you do?

You are at the candy store with a friend. He puts the candy bar in his pocket without paying for it. What do you do?

More ideas: www.surfnetkids.com/columbus.htm

Celebrate with Crafts

Columbus didn't know what kind of people he'd find on his explorations. Make some silly balloon buddies. Blow up large balloons, one for each family member. Cut out magazine pictures of eyes, noses, hair, and other facial features. Make wacky self-portraits by gluing the pictures to the balloon. Cut long strips of magazine pages for hair. Wrap the strips around a pencil if you need curly hair.

Celebrate with Food

Columbus was born in Italy. Make some homemade Italian pasta today. Try this recipe and compare the taste with store-bought pasta. Beat 2 large eggs until "frothy." Set aside. Pour 1 cup semolina flour, 1 cup white flour, and a pinch of salt in bowl. Mix well. Make a "well" in the middle of the flour and add eggs. Mix well. Roll ⅛-inch thick on floured surface. Cut into thin strips. Boil as usual.

Lee Jeans Denim Day

What better way to celebrate today than by wearing your very favorite jeans? Enjoy activities centered around America's most popular clothing item.

Celebrate with Fun

- Have an old-fashioned "jean walk." Have everyone collect all their jeans and jean skirts. Fold each one into a neat square and place on the floor about a foot apart in a circle. Use a sticky note to number each pair. Assign 1 person to play lively music as everyone marches around barefoot stepping on the folded jeans. When the music stops, call out a number. Whoever is standing on that number gets a small prize.

- Give out awards for various "jean categories" — 1st prize for most faded jeans! 1st prize for newest jeans! 1st prize for smallest pair of jeans!

- Have a family jeans fashion show. Ask everyone to put together an outfit that includes a pair of jeans. Maybe it's a cozy pajama outfit or an evening outfit with a glittery top and blue jeans. Take turns walking down a "runway" just like professional models.

- Use a pair of jeans to make your own Wicked Witch of the East. (Remember when the house landed on her?) Stuff a pair of jeans with newspaper. Stuff the leg ends into a pair of shoes. Put the waist end next to the outside wall of the house. It looks like the house landed on a person.

Celebrate with Crafts

Use some of your outgrown jeans to make handy jean-pocket purses. Cut the back pockets out of an old pair of jeans (both front and back of the pocket). Trim loose threads. Decorate the pockets with puff paint or sew on fancy buttons. Add a row of trim along the bottom if you want an extra-fancy purse. Cut a 24-inch ribbon. Sew or use hot glue to attach the ribbon to each side of the pocket for the handle. Use smaller jean pockets to make minipurses for dolls.

Celebrate with Food

Since you've made purses out of jean pockets, now make sandwiches out of pita pocket bread. Show children how to gently split open the "pocket." Fill with a variety of fillings. Try tuna fish, lunch meat, cheese, or even peanut butter and jelly. Be sure to wear jeans while eating pocket sandwiches!

More ideas: www.denimday.com

275

Sweetest Day

Herbert Kingston began this holiday in Cleveland to distribute candy to orphans, shut-ins, and the homeless. Do something today so people say, "Oh, how sweet!"

Celebrate with Fun

• Play an exaggerated game of "You're so sweet!" Let children act out supernice, very considerate, incredibly kind actions. They might say, "Mother dear, would you like me to massage your feet?" They rub your aching feet, and you say, "You're so sweet!" Children might say outlandish things like, "Dear Dad, you need a break. I'll use my babysitting money to hire someone to mow the lawn." Naturally, Dad responds with, "You're so sweet!"

• Sweetest day is a perfect time to make sugar rock-crystals. In a saucepan, heat 2 cups sugar with 1 cup water. Slowly add another 2 cups sugar and melt thoroughly. Mixture should be clear. Pour into a glass. Tie an 8-inch string to a pencil. Place pencil on top of glass with string in sugar mixture. Within several hours, sugar crystals will form and make candy. Let sit overnight before eating the sweet candy!

• See if your family can tell the difference between white sugar, honey, brown sugar, and molasses. Make several cups of tea. "Secretly" add 1 of the sweeteners. Have family members sip to determine the sweeteners.

Celebrate with Crafts

Use chocolate "kisses" to make someone say, "Isn't that sweet!" Using a low-temperature glue gun, spread glue on the bottom of each kiss. Press kisses on a 4-inch Styrofoam ball until entire ball is covered. Attach a ribbon loop to a kiss to serve as a hanger. Give to someone who could use a little chocolate!

Make sweet LifeSaver wreaths. String various colors of LifeSavers on a chenille stem. When complete, twist 2 ends together in a loop. Hang your sweet wreath in a window where the sun can shine through the translucent candy.

Celebrate with Food

Make sweet pretzels today. Preheat oven to 350 degrees. Separate refrigerated breadstick dough. Carefully unwind each breadstick so it is a long rope. Form into a heart shape and place on ungreased cookie sheet. (Combine the ends of 2 ropes if you want an extra-large pretzel.) Beat 1 egg white until frothy, then brush on each pretzel. Top with cinnamon sugar or tiny sprinkles. Bake 12–16 minutes.

Make a Difference Day

This national program encourages individuals and teams to participate in a volunteer activity that "makes a difference." It is a national day of volunteering by yourself or with a group.

Celebrate with Fun

- Get friends together to work on a group volunteer project for Make a Difference Day. You might win the $10,000 donated by Paul Newman to give to your favorite charity.
- Check out www.makeadifferenceday.com. Its "idea generator" helps you identify the volunteer opportunity best suited to your interests and time schedule.
- Collect Halloween candy to give to children's group homes or shelters. Collect new or "gently used" teddy bears to give to firefighters and police officers. They give the bears to lost or hurt children.
- Find a senior citizen who needs help cleaning up their yard. Gather a group of people who can mow the lawn, trim bushes, and repair broken steps.
- See if your local downtown association needs help repainting park benches or flower boxes. Clean up trash along a stream or beach in your area.
- Build and paint a number of birdhouses. Put them up at a nursing home where residents can enjoy the birds flocking to their new homes.
- Contact your local Association for the Blind. Offer to read books or magazines on tape for their clients.
- Visit local dentists to ask for donations of toothbrushes and toothpaste. Donate supplies to a homeless shelter.

Celebrate with Crafts

Collect fabric or yarn to donate to a group that will make quilts or toys from the supplies.

Make colorful bookmarks and sell them in front of a bookstore (with manager's permission, of course). Donate money to a charity.

Celebrate with Food

Have an old-fashioned bake sale for a charity. Sell the goodies at a community event like a sports game or concert where large numbers of people are present.

Deliver homemade cookies or brownies to local firefighters or police officers as a way of thanking them for their work.

World Vegetarian Day

Most everyone loves a thick hamburger or a juicy steak. Today, on World Vegetarian Day, change your eating habits and try a vegetarian menu.

Celebrate with Fun

- Check a food pyramid chart to see how you can have a balanced diet without meat portions. Does your family eat the daily recommended portions of grains, breads, and fruit? Are your diets high in sugar and fat portions?

- Take a family trip to the grocery store. Purchase a unique fruit, vegetable, and grain to take home. Experiment with different ways of preparing and serving the food.

- Watch a *Veggie Tales* video while eating vegetables and dip.

- See who can think of the most fruits and vegetables. The first person names a fruit like a banana. The next person needs to say the name of a fruit or vegetable that begins with A, because that's the last letter of *banana*. If someone says, "apple," the next person says a fruit beginning with E. Continue until you can't think of any more names.

Celebrate with Food

Try a few new foods today in honor of National Vegetarian Day. Start with some erupting potatoes. Follow your usual recipe for mashed potatoes. Scoop the potatoes on plates. Ask everyone to shape their potatoes to look like a mountain with a high peak. Use the fork tines to make ridges down the sides of the potatoes. Shred 1 cup cheddar cheese. Place in a microwave bowl and mix cheese with ¼ cup milk and 2 Tbs. butter. Heat 30–60 seconds until cheese melts and mixture is smooth. Pour over top of each potato mountain and let the "lava" flow down the sides.

Go to a health food store to buy some soy burgers or hot dogs. Barbecue them like regular meat and compare the texture and flavor. Some people find they like the flavor of vegi-burgers or other nonmeat substitutes.

Make a tofu smoothie. In a blender, mix 5 oz. silky tofu, 1 cup orange juice, 2 ripe bananas, and 1 grated carrot. Blend until smooth and foamy. Enjoy!

Celebrate with Crafts

Cut a carrot into ¼ inch slices. Use a small Phillips screwdriver to poke a hole in the center of each slice. Insert a toothpick to keep the hole from shrinking shut. Let dry in a warm place 3 to 4 days. Use these "coral" beads to make one-of-a-kind jewelry.

More ideas: www.vegsoc.org

National *Peanuts* Day
(Comic Strip)

In 1950 Charles Schulz published his first *Peanuts* daily comic strip. Schulz went on to draw 18,250 cartoon strips that appeared in 2,600 newspapers.

Celebrate with Fun

- Invite friends over for a *Peanuts* character look-alike contest. Dress up and act like your favorite character. Here's your chance to be extra bossy like Lucy.

- Speaking of Lucy, take her advice. Designate 1 person as "Psychiatrist Lucy." This person sits behind a desk, ready to help anyone with a "problem." Other family members go to Lucy for advice. Some situations for Lucy: How to handle being "way too popular" at school. What to do about having too much money.

- Poor Charlie Brown always gets tricked when he tries to kick the football. Take turns seeing who can kick the football the farthest. (No fair moving the ball just as someone gets ready to kick.)

- Charlie Brown looks for shapes in the clouds. Linus, Schroeder, Sally, and Lucy see aardvarks, the Statue of Liberty, and a rare blooming orchid. Charlie Brown sees duckies in the clouds. What shapes do your family members see?

- Snoopy enjoys sitting on his doghouse. Be extra kind to your dog today by taking him on a long walk.

- Have a peanut race to see who can push a peanut to the finish line—with their nose! Try another race in which you each put peanuts on the toes of your shoes and race for the finish line without the peanuts falling off.

Celebrate with Crafts

Use a white paper plate to make your Snoopy puppet. Draw eyes and nose on the plate. For ears, blow up 2 long, narrow black balloons. Attach balloons to the top of the paper plate so they flop around like ears. Have your Snoopy puppet explain what it's like to wait for someone to bring your dog food.

Celebrate with Food

Linus loves his blanket. Ask everyone to bring their favorite blanket for an indoor picnic. Spread blankets on the floor and enjoy peanut butter and jelly sandwiches. Crack open peanuts from their shells. If you haven't had your share of peanuts, add a Reese's peanut butter cup for dessert.

More ideas: www.schulzmuseum.org/

Silly Day

Children have no problem celebrating Silly Day. It's all too easy to get the giggles over burping and silly knock-knock jokes.

Celebrate with Fun

- Fill a plastic resealable bag with water. Tell your children since it's Silly Day, you will perform a silly trick. Quickly poke a sharpened pencil through 1 side of the bag and out the other. Your children will assume the water will flow out. Not so. Repeat several times as you amaze your children by poking pencils in the bag without losing water.

- Dress silly today. Drive children to school wearing a sun hat, mismatched socks, and your most outlandish shirt.

- Get your children involved in telling knock-knock jokes. After everyone has tried it, say, "I have another great knock-knock joke. It's so funny! You go first." Your child will start in, "Knock, knock." You excitedly ask, "Who's there?" At this point they look bewildered because they just realized they don't have the conclusion to the joke. Try this one. It's much funnier to do than can be described on paper.

- Tell children each person's hair has a chemical makeup that causes hair to "fight." Pour water in a dinner plate and have 2 people pull out 1 strand of hair. With a great flourish, put the 2 hairs on the water. Announce, "Look closely. Watch what happens when the hairs touch. They'll start twisting and turning." As family members closely examine the hairs, bring your hand down in the water to splash everyone!

Celebrate with Crafts

Make a few silly-willy creatures. All you need are chenille stems and wooden beads. Bend chenille stems to form a body. Wooden beads are the head of your creature. Add several heads or 4 legs by using more chenille stems. Come up with silly names for your creatures.

Celebrate with Food

Get silly with dinner. Make your favorite meatloaf recipe. Instead of forming meat into 1 loaf, divide into muffin tins for minimeatloaves. When meat is done, "frost" with icing, a special icing, of course. While mixing mashed potatoes, add a few drops red food coloring to make pink "frosting." Spread colored mashed potatoes over meatloaf and serve as "cupcakes."

Stamp Collecting Day

In reality, all of October is National Stamp Collecting *Month*. We'll just take a day to honor this popular hobby.

Celebrate with Fun

- Get your children involved in collecting stamps. Call 1-888-STAMPFUN to get free magazines and posters about stamps.
- Visit a stamp store. You'll be amazed at the horse stamps put out by Vietnam and the flower stamps from Iceland. Purchase a package of 200 or so mismatched stamps for a few dollars. Your children will enjoy sorting and classifying them.
- Post offices carry unique stamps. Ask to see any special editions of cute teddy bear or animal stamps.
- Check the day's mail and look at the stamps. Which design is most popular?
- Set up a miniature post office and let children enjoy sorting through junk mail. Use a shoe box with a slit in the top as a mailbox so children can pretend to mail letters.
- Decorate your mailbox for today. Add some balloons and streamers so your neighbors wonder why you're happy that you're getting bills delivered.
- Speaking of junk mail, as you sort the day's mail, here's an easy way to get rid of unwanted mail. Put a wastebasket in the middle of the room. Stand about 5 feet away. Take turns trying to toss junk mail into the wastebasket.

Celebrate with Crafts

Save the stamps from a week's worth of mail. To remove the stamp from an envelope, dampen slightly. Put in the microwave for 15–20 seconds. The stamp will easily lift off the paper. Dry the stamps. Use them to make a stamp collage for a notebook cover. Glue the stamps on the front of the notebook. Cover with a thin layer of glue. Don't worry! The glue dries clear and provides a shiny cover for your new notebook.

Celebrate with Food

Start the day by making an edible stamp. Set out 3–4 small bowls filled with 1 Tbs. evaporated milk. Add a few drops food coloring to the milk. Mix well. With a clean paintbrush, paint with the colored milk. Paint a "stamp" design on white bread. Toast the bread lightly to reveal your stamp pattern.

More ideas: www.usps.gov

World Farmer's Day

Look in your refrigerator. The majority of your food would not be available if it wasn't for farmers. Take a day to acknowledge the hard work of farmers who give us so much food.

Celebrate with Fun

- Visit a farmer's market. Ask about unusual fruits or vegetables. How do they grow and harvest kale? What steps are needed to get wheat from the field into wheat flour?

- Don't have 400 acres to plow? Start an herb garden on your windowsill. Try growing parsley or other easy herbs. Put children in charge of watering.

- Be sure to sing "The Farmer in the Dell" today.

- Set out various foods like ketchup, cereal, jelly, and butter. Ask your children which animal or plant had a part in providing that food. They will be surprised to find out they are eating thiamin hydrochloride in their cereal!

- Help children appreciate the hard work of harvesting food. Check if your community offers a "gleaners" program. Gleaners glean any extra crops farm machines have overlooked. Take children to dig up leftover potatoes or pick the last of the apples. The gleaned food is donated to local agencies serving the needy. After a day of gleaning, your children will appreciate the work farmers do daily.

- See if local farms offer dairy production tours or let families see how giant combines work. After seeing cows milked, ask children, "What happens to the cows if the farmer and his family want to take a vacation?" It's eye-opening to see how farmers must work around the clock.

Celebrate with Crafts

Make your own watering can. Wash and dry a 1-gallon plastic milk jug. Use acrylic paint to draw a farm scene on the jug. Add a cheerful sun along with cows and chickens. Have an adult poke 6–8 holes in the top of the jug, opposite the handle. Fill with water. Simply hold the jug by the handle and "tip." The water will flow out of the holes.

Celebrate with Food

Prepare a totally natural farm-fresh meal. Serve baked potatoes, fresh carrots, apple slices, and salad with radishes and tomatoes. Avoid any processed or canned foods. Drink 100-percent juice. Serve buttermilk and explain how the "butter" is removed to make the milk children usually enjoy.

"The Un-Birthday" Day

There's nothing much happening on October 13, so celebrate with an "un-birthday" party. Have a good time at a party for no special reason.

Celebrate with Fun

- At breakfast, sing "The Un-Birthday Song" to the tune of "Happy Birthday":

    "It's not your birthday today,

    It's not your birthday today,

    It's not your birthday, Allan,

    It's not your birthday today."

    Repeat several times so everyone's name is included in the song.

- Hang balloons all over the house—unblown, of course. Tape them up in strategic locations, but save your breath (and save the balloons for the next real birthday).

- You also need streamers at your un-birthday, but don't get fancy twisting streamers from 1 end of the room to another. Just tape a streamer to the ceiling and let it hang to the floor.

- Instead of playing "Pin the Tail on the Donkey," try "Pin the Whiskers on the Donkey." Since this is an un-birthday, no one wins prizes for the games!

- Do something untraditional: Go outside and play basketball. Ask kids to bring their in-line skates. Skate in the basement or around the block.

- Ask friends to come to the un-birthday party with a gift—a gift of food, that is. Collect canned goods to later donate to a food bank.

Celebrate with Crafts

Almost every birthday party involves children making a cute craft project, but this is an un-birthday. No glitter! No glue! No crafts!

Celebrate with Food

Birthday cakes are usually elaborately decorated and center on a specific theme. Make your un-birthday cake plain and ordinary. Bake a cake and serve it. That's right, serve just a cake without frosting. If you must have icing, use gel frosting to write "Un-Birthday Cake."

Serve refreshments in plain, ordinary dishes. No fancy coordinated Cinderella napkins and plates. Instead, use white paper plates with "Un-Birthday" written on them.

National Grouch Day

OCTOBER 15

We all like to be around friendly, upbeat people. But what about the grouches? Take National Grouch Day to teach children they have the choice to be positive or just plain grouchy.

Celebrate with Fun

- Take pictures of each family member making the grouchiest face possible. Then take pictures of pleasant expressions.
- Wash out a large trash can. Have a volunteer sit inside it as Oscar the Grouch. Family members cheerfully talk to Oscar, who gives grouchy answers. Can anyone convince Oscar to come out of his trash can?
- Buy some supersour candy. Have everyone in the family (except toddlers) put the candy in their mouths at the same time. See who can keep from spitting out the sour candy.
- Role-play typical situations like getting ready for church or making dinner. Act them out in a "grouchy" manner, with kids being crabby and uncooperative. Repeat the scenes with positive behaviors. Which make home more enjoyable? Discuss ways kids can cope when feeling cranky and grouchy. Of course, parents are never accused of being grouchy!
- While it's fun pretending to be grouchy, remind your children how the Bible stresses having a positive attitude. Proverbs 15:13 says, "A happy heart makes the face cheerful." Philippians 4:8 says, "Whatever is true, whatever is noble, whatever is right, whatever is pure, whatever is lovely, whatever is admirable—if anything is excellent and praiseworthy—think about such things."

Celebrate with Crafts

Collect empty film canisters to make a mini "grouch in a can." Stuff a fuzzy green pom-pom halfway into the canister. Glue 2 wiggle eyes to the pom-pom. Glue the top of the canister to the pom-pom. It will look as if your grouch is peeking out from the trash can.

Celebrate with Food

Serve a "sour" meal to go along with grouchy attitudes. How about a menu of:

sweet and sour chicken
sauerkraut
kimchee (if you're brave enough)
sour cream
lemon cake and lemonade

Dictionary Day

Today is Noah Webster's birthday! Sing "Happy Birthday" to Mr. Webster while holding a dictionary. Spend today increasing your word skills.

Celebrate with Fun

- Play Scrabble with a few changes. Players select 14 letters at a time. This makes the game go faster. With older players, play Scrabble using a theme. All the words must have to do with sports or school or history.
- Bring out the dictionary and find a seldom-used word like *jardiniere* or *piste*. Ask family members to guess the meaning. Use the same words and ask people to make up their own definitions.
- Watch a game show such as *Wheel of Fortune*. Pretend you are all contestants and try to win the game by shouting out the answers.
- Come up with a "Word of the Day" every day this week. Write the word in several obvious places. Encourage people to use the word in everyday conversation. It's fun to hear a 5-year-old say, "I find solace in sleeping with my teddy bear."
- Create your own new words never found in a dictionary. Is there a word for the mess left on your son's plate when he smashes the peas and potatoes together?
- Write chalk messages on the sidewalk for people walking by to read. You could write a big "Welcome Home, Mom!" on the driveway so she sees it as she drives over it.
- Collect several dictionaries and compare a word's definition in each one.

Celebrate with Crafts

Purchase some smooth hair clips at a dollar store. Dab a little glue on the clips with a toothpick. Select letters from alphabet pasta to spell out a person's name or "Happy Birthday" on a clip. Let dry. Give as gifts to girls you know.

Celebrate with Food

Make alphabet soup from alphabet pasta, chicken broth, and a few vegetables. When everyone is served, use your spoon to scoop out letters for your name. Have contests to see who can find the right letters for their spelling words. Go ahead and celebrate by playing with your food!

More ideas: www.education-world.com/a_lesson/lesson027.shtml

Watch a Squirrel Day

These bushy-tailed creatures are found in most parts of the country. Celebrate Watch a Squirrel Day by learning more about squirrels and the nuts they eat.

Celebrate with Fun

- How many nuts can your family name? (filbert, peanut, macadamia, almond, walnut . . .)
- Squirrels don't care, but some nuts actually float in water. Purchase several types of nuts to use in "floating" experiments.
- Squirrels hide their nuts in leaves and trees. Hide peanuts in their shells throughout the house. Have everyone put mittens over their hands to look like "squirrel hands." Try to find the peanuts and pick them up with your stubby paws.
- Get your little squirrels involved in learning math. Cut out paper peanuts. Write a number on each peanut from 1 through 24. (Higher numbers if children are older.) Lay the peanuts in a pile on the floor. Have children line up an equal distance from the paper peanuts. Call out a math problem such as 4 + 7. "Squirrels" crawl over to the peanuts and try to find the correct answer.
- Place a number of walnuts, Brazil nuts, or peanuts in a jar. Have family members guess the number. The winner gets to use a nutcracker to shell the nuts for the rest of the family!
- Tree climbing is becoming a lost art. If squirrels can climb trees, why not your children? Find a tree with sturdy branches and let children take turns climbing it. When was the last time you climbed a tree?

Celebrate with Crafts

Take a close look at a peanut. Does the shape remind you of a snowman? It should! Paint peanuts white. While paint is drying, cut out small black top hats from paper or craft foam. Glue hats on top of peanuts. Use markers to make eyes, mouth, and a carrot nose. Make enough for an entire village of snowmen.

Celebrate with Food

Here's a crunchy treat for humans, not squirrels. Microwave ½ cup peanut butter with ½ cup honey for 30 seconds or until smooth. Pour into a medium-sized bowl. Stir in ½ cup raisins, ⅓ cup rice cereal, ½ cup crushed vanilla wafers, and ½ cup granola. Mix well. Drop by tablespoons on waxed paper. Roll into balls. Refrigerate 2 hours before eating.

Caution: Make sure no one with peanut allergies eats these!

More ideas: www.squirrelsrus.com

Boost Your Brain Day

Researchers tell us we only use a fraction of our brain capacity. While we can't guarantee you'll become a genius overnight, these activities will get your brain working overtime.

Celebrate with Fun

- Select items similar in shape or texture to place in a box. Family members reach in and try to identify the objects by feel alone. Can they tell a nectarine from a peach? How about a grapefruit from a softball?

- Set out assorted crossword puzzles and word searches. Everyone starts working on the puzzles. Set a 3-minute egg timer. After 3 minutes, switch puzzles and work 3 more minutes. Keep rotating until most of the puzzles are completed.

- Find the lost and found section in the classifieds. Read about poor little Pootzi who is lost. Make up creative stories about how and why the animals were lost. What would your family do with the $10,000 reward offered for finding Pootzi?

- Test your family's power of recollection. Take turns asking, "Sondra, name 10 things you'd find in a dentist's office," or "Jason, tell us 10 things you see in a post office." Other locations could be a candy store, classroom, bathroom, fire station, or beauty shop.

- Have everyone select a library book on a subject they know little or nothing about. Dad can select a book on flower arranging while 12-year-old Cameron comes home with a book about making sushi. Read your books and report back to the family. Dad might even give a demonstration on how to arrange those carnations in a vase.

Celebrate with Crafts

Use your noodle making some noodle sculptures! Place different-shaped pasta on the table. (Purchase a few unusual varieties ahead of time.) Spread glue on the pasta pieces with toothpicks. Glue the pasta shapes together to create free-form sculptures or tiny creatures.

Celebrate with Food

Since eating fish supposedly increases brain power, make some tuna fish sandwiches and see if your IQ rises.

Here's a recipe you *don't* want to eat. Make a "brain." Mix together 1½ cups instant mashed potato flakes, 2½ cups hot water, and 2 cups clean sand. Pour into a gallon-sized resealable bag. The potato-sand mixture is the weight (3 lbs.) and consistency of a human brain!

Order a brain Jell-O mold from www.mcphee.com/bigindex/current/10375.html

Pretzel Day

Most everyone knows what a pretzel looks like. Try to explain the shape verbally and see how complicated it gets! Tradition says a monk rolled leftover bread dough into a coil, shaping it to look like arms folded in prayer.

Celebrate with Fun

- Any contortionists in your family? Demonstrate your ability to twist yourself into a pretzel by doing back bends and other feats of flexibility. Adults, be careful—no need to stretch and damage your muscles!

- Form a line holding hands. The first person starts twisting the line into a pretzel shape. Still holding hands, follow the leader as she crawls under people's legs and climbs over their connected hands. When the group is thoroughly twisted, reverse the process and try to form the straight line again.

- Look at a box or bag of pretzels. How many do you think are inside? Have family members guess, then count to see whose guess is closest.

- Have everyone put a plastic spoon in their mouth. Slip a large pretzel over the handle of 1 person's spoon. Without using hands, they try to slip the pretzel over the spoon handle of the next person. Keep going until the pretzel has been passed to everyone.

- Tie a 10-foot piece of yarn to a large, crunchy pretzel. Stand in a line. The first person takes the pretzel, puts it down the front of his shirt, and passes it to the next person. That person repeats the process until all of you are "woven" into 1 line. Stay that way or cut the yarn.

Celebrate with Crafts

Give everyone a piece of lightweight cardboard and different-sized pretzels and pretzel sticks to make a picture. Glue the pretzels on the cardboard. One pretzel might be the head of an alien with tiny pretzel sticks poking out as alien hair. Use markers to embellish the pictures.

Celebrate with Food

Make some yummy pretzels. Mix 1 Tbs. yeast, ½ cup very warm water, and 1 tsp. honey. Let sit for 5 minutes. Mix 1½ cups flour and ½ tsp. salt. Add yeast mixture to flour. Stir and then knead on a floured surface for 5–8 minutes. Let rise in a warm place for 2–3 hours. Punch dough down, then shape into pretzels. Let rise 30 minutes. Bake on a greased cookie sheet at 350 degrees for 10 minutes.

Halloween

Halloween is a day for dressing up and enjoying candy. In many communities a concern for children's safety has led to carnivals and "harvest festival" activities replacing the traditional trick-or-treating.

Celebrate with Fun

- Get your children's costumes ready in advance. Let children have a say in choosing and designing their costumes. (There's nothing wrong with telling children no scary or evil costumes are allowed.)
- If you feel uncomfortable having children celebrate Halloween, suggest your church plan a harvest carnival. Children can dress as Bible characters while bobbing for apples or making paper scarecrows. Other harvest-related activities could be:

Have a pumpkin seed–spitting contest. Judge attempts on accuracy as well as the ability to spit the seed into a can.

Use permanent markers to number minipumpkins on the bottom. Float pumpkins in a tub so children can scoop them out. Children win a prize according to the number on the bottom of their selection.

Hand children 2–3 ears of corn. Have a race to see who can shuck their corn the fastest. Afterward, boil, douse in butter, and enjoy.

Have scarecrow relay races. Kids run to a designated point to put on scarecrow clothes—a flannel shirt, overalls, and a straw hat. Tag the next person in line to repeat the process.

Celebrate with Crafts

Pumpkin carving can be messy as well as dangerous. Instead of using sharp knives, hand children paintbrushes. Painting pumpkins is easy and gives children plenty of opportunities to be creative. Their pumpkins can be transformed into clowns, smiling scarecrows, or even rock stars.

Celebrate with Food

Pumpkin bread is a tasty way to enjoy a harvest festival. Stir 2 boxes bran muffin mix (6½ oz. each) in a bowl with 1 cup water and 1 cup pumpkin. Mix well. Pour into a greased and floured bread pan. Bake at 400 degrees 15–17 minutes.

Purchase a small pumpkin for each family member. Cut off the tops and use an ice-cream scoop to clean out the insides. At dinner, ladle homemade soup into everyone's pumpkin bowls.

NOVEMBER

International Drum Month
National Aviation Month
International Creative Child and Adult Month
Good Nutrition Month

Weeks to Celebrate

Thanksgiving Week • National Bible Week
Thanksgiving Week • National Game and Puzzle Week

Days to Celebrate

3rd Thursday   Great American Smokeout
4th Thursday   Thanksgiving

 1 National Family Literacy Day
 3 National Sandwich Day
 5 National Doughnut Day
11 Veterans Day
14 National Teddy Bear Day
15 Sadie Hawkins Day (or closest Saturday)
15 America Recycles Day
15 National Clean Out Your Refrigerator Day
16 *The Sound of Music* Day
17 Homemade Bread Day
29 Historical Figure Day

International Drum Month

Whether tapping on an empty oatmeal box or on a professional drum covered with genuine cow skin, most people enjoy beating a drum.

Celebrate with Fun

- Give everyone a pot, box, or can to use as a drum. Select a leader to walk through the house and beat out a certain rhythm. Everyone follows in a line and tries to imitate the beat.

- Sit around a table holding a pencil in each hand. A leader taps out a certain rhythm such as "fast-fast-fast-pause-fast-pause." Everyone tries to repeat the exact rhythm.

- See if anyone in your community plays the steel drums. These pans originated from Trinidad after World War II, when people used empty oil barrels as drums. The distinctive sound of steel drums will have your children banging on your kitchen pans.

- Discuss the famous quote about "marching to the beat of a different drummer." What does that mean? Ask children about a time they took a stand that was different from their friends. Should a person march to their own drummer if it means going against God's will?

- Have you ever seen the people from Stomp perform? They use every item imaginable to beat out a rhythm—garbage can lids, broom handles, and pan lids all become instruments. Put on your own Stomp performance. Send the family to find unusual items to bang together. Invite Grandma over to hit a wooden spoon on the toaster!

Celebrate with Crafts

Give everyone empty cans of various sizes to make dual-purpose drums. (Check for sharp edges.) Use pencils to beat rhythms on the cans. Fill cans with water and freeze. Hit the frozen cans with pencils again. Is the sound different? Have an adult put a can full of ice in a vise grip. Hammer a large nail or screwdriver repeatedly into the can to create a "holey" design. When ice melts, put votive candles inside for a special lantern.

Celebrate with Food

Pretzel sticks are edible drumsticks. Beat your "drumsticks" on the table, a metal bowl, or your head to get different sounds. Then eat them!

Bake a round 2-layer cake. Frost top and sides with your favorite frosting. Use another color frosting to decorate the cake like a drum the Little Drummer Boy would carry.

National Aviation Month

The Wright Brothers got their start in aviation by building a 2-wing kite. When that proved successful, they went on to build a 17-foot glider at Kitty Hawk, North Carolina. What would the Wright Brothers think if they saw a 747?

Celebrate with Fun

- Have a family paper airplane contest. After everyone makes their incredible flying machines, see who can hit certain targets. Whose plane flies the farthest? Which airplane plummets back to the ground the fastest?

- Visit an air and space museum this month. Call ahead to find out about behind-the-scenes tours or special classes. Most museums offer free guided tours on weekends. These tours give you a greater understanding of the exhibits than you would get on your own.

- Rent the movie *Those Amazing Men and Their Flying Machines*. Watch the movie while wearing jackets and swim goggles so you look (somewhat) like aviators flying single-engine planes without windshields.

- People have always been fascinated with the idea of flying like a bird. Instead of jumping off the roof with a pair of homemade wings, try to get a stuffed animal to fly. See how you can make a parachute or other "contraption" to help your teddy bear land safely after you throw him in the air.

- Take a walk and try to spot airplanes in the sky. Look out the window at night to find planes with their lights on.

Celebrate with Crafts

Make gliders from Styrofoam meat trays. (For extra precaution against germs, rinse trays in a mild bleach solution.) Experiment with different designs. Begin by cutting out the body of the glider, then cut slits ¾ of the way back to slide the wings through. Keep experimenting until your glider flies at least a few feet.

Celebrate with Food

Pretend you are eating on an airplane tonight. Set out rows of chairs side by side as if they are on an airplane. To get the real airplane effect, make sure seats are close together so everyone is crowded! Select a "flight attendant" to walk down the airplane aisles and serve food and drinks. Put the TV on so it seems like you are watching an in-flight movie.

International Creative Child and Adult Month

Creativity. Do you have it? Do your children? While many definitions of creativity exist, most people agree on one thing: Creative people are "innovative" thinkers. They look at ordinary situations in new ways.

Celebrate with Fun

- Set the tone for a creative day. Assign 1 family member to plan a creative breakfast. Maybe you'll eat cereal listening to disco music.
- Have children share a disposable camera and record their day in pictures. After photos are developed, discuss why they took each photo.
- Have a family "Creativity Brainstorming" session. Discuss a problem like why there is so much arguing over the TV. Write down everyone's solution ideas. Remember the number 1 rule of brainstorming: No idea is discarded in the beginning of the process. The more wild and creative ideas you write down, the closer you come to finding a solution.
- Take a different route driving children to school or ballet lessons. Go down a side street and notice a new house being built. Drive behind your grocery stores and notice the delivery trucks. Creativity is looking for new experiences even in mundane places like an alley or side street.
- Foster your family's creative thinking by asking them to come up with untraditional uses for ordinary items. Hold up a roll of masking tape. What unusual way can masking tape be used? Allow time for the wild ideas to develop. Repeat with other items such as coat hangers, toy cars, or coffee mugs. You may just come up with a new idea to patent!

Celebrate with Crafts

This isn't quite a craft, but it shows children how to use "ordinary" objects in "extraordinary" ways. Crush 2 Ex-Lax or other laxative tablets. (Make sure children don't eat tablets.) Have an interesting discussion to explain what laxatives are for and how they work. Add 1 tsp. rubbing alcohol to the crushed tablets. Stir well. Rub mixture on your hands. The alcohol will dry quickly. (Don't rub your eyes with alcohol on your hands!) Slightly wet your hands and wash with soap. Watch out—you'll have foaming lava coming from your hands!

Celebrate with Food

Pack your children's lunch in a totally creative way. Serve rolled-up flour tortillas instead of an ordinary peanut butter and jelly sandwich. Decorate the lunch bags with inspirational sayings.

More ideas: International Association for Creative Children and Adults 513-631-1777

Good Nutrition Month

Sure, it's great fun to eat junk food. Those orange cheese puffs that leave goo all over your fingers can't be beat. Use this month to steer your family toward slightly better eating habits.

Celebrate with Fun

- Parents often say their children won't eat healthy foods. Maybe that's because most kids seldom feel real hunger pains. Get kids playing outside or riding bikes. It's amazing what they will eat when hungry!

- Show your children just how much sugar and fat junk food contains. This eye-opening experiment will have them reaching for an apple instead of a candy bar. Read the label to see how many grams of sugar a bottle of soda contains; 4 grams sugar equals about 1 tsp. If your soda contains 44 grams of sugar, measure out 11 tsp. sugar. That's a lot! Do the same with fat content. Ten grams fat equal 1 Tbs. margarine. Measure out the amount of fat in 1 serving of chips. Disgusting!

Celebrate with Food

Avoid going cold turkey and banning all junk food from the house. Instead, begin with a few substitutions. Set out granola bars instead of doughnuts. Switch to pretzels rather than bowls of chips. Purchase low-fat pudding snacks.

Cookie cutters are a great tool for creating interest in healthy foods. Serve cranberry jelly slices cut into heart shapes. Whole-wheat sandwiches look appetizing when cut into star shapes.

Purchase wooden skewers at any dollar store. Cut up chunks of fresh fruit and cheeses to poke onto the skewers. Have younger children use chopsticks, which have blunt ends.

Somehow all vegetables taste better dipped in ranch dressing. Purchase the low-fat dressing so your kids can enjoy a healthy treat.

Desserts don't have to be full of sugar. Set out supplies to make your own "spiders." Spread peanut butter between 2 crackers. Poke in 8 small pretzel sticks to form your spider's legs. Use a dab of peanut butter to "glue" on 2 raisins for beady little eyes.

Celebrate with Crafts

Create a pleasant mealtime atmosphere with interesting centerpieces. Assign each family member 3–4 days to be responsible for having a centerpiece on the table. It can be as creative as a Lego model dinosaur or as traditional as pretty candles surrounded by flowers.

295

National Bible Week

The Bible is God's blueprint to us for living a Christian life. Spend Thanksgiving week reading and appreciating this special book.

Celebrate with Fun

- Dress up as Bible characters. Old bathrobes and sheets work fine for Moses, Jonah, or David costumes. Your toddler can bring out his fuzzy pajamas and be a sheep on the Ark.

- Ask church members to bring in unusual Bibles they own. Help your family set up a display at church showing the wide variety of Bibles. Compare a colorful toddler's Bible with an antique Bible that's been in a family for generations. Perhaps you'll find a Bible in another language. Set the display where people can easily see and discuss the Bibles.

- Gather all the Bibles in your house. Select a Psalm or a few verses and have everyone read them aloud in different Bible versions. Which is easiest to understand? Which conveys a new understanding of the message?

- Let your children organize daily family Bible reading this week. Ask them to select the verses and then lead a discussion. When guests arrive for Thanksgiving, include them in the child-led Bible study.

- Collect all the loose change in your house. Use the money to buy a new Bible for someone in the community who doesn't have one.

- The Gideons are known for distributing Bibles in hotel rooms, prisons, and sometimes schools. Check the drawers next time you're in a hotel. You're sure to find a Bible donated by the Gideons. Write a letter thanking them for their hard work in making Bibles available.

- Ask the pastor to preach on the importance of Bible reading.

Celebrate with Crafts

Make a set of Bible verse leaves for the Thanksgiving table. Cut out 10–12 paper loaves. Everyone writes their favorite Bible verses on a few leaves. Decorate with fall drawings like pumpkins. Scatter the paper leaves on the table so guests can read them while eating turkey.

Celebrate with Food

Use an Oreo cookie to teach a biblical concept. Carefully twist apart an Oreo cookie. Show children how 1 side is a dark cookie. This is the world before God created light. The other side of the cookie with the filling represents the light God created. Eat the cookies afterward.

More ideas: www.nationalbible.org

National Game and Puzzle Week

The weather is cold and everyone is tired of TV. Celebrate today by playing games and bringing out the puzzles.

Celebrate with Fun

- Take the family to a store to purchase a new game or puzzle. Some libraries offer a game-lending program. See if you can check out some new games using your library card.

- Invite friends over for a game night. Ask them to bring their favorite board game. You may discover a new family favorite.

- Make your own puzzles. Select a picture from a magazine and glue it on a piece of paper. After the picture dries, cut it into several puzzle "shapes." Take turns putting the puzzles together. Store pieces of each puzzle in separate envelopes.

- Here's an unusual game: Dampen a paper towel and place it over an empty glass. Use a rubber band to hold the paper towel in place. Take turns gently placing a penny on the taut paper towel. Add more and more pennies. The person whose penny rips the paper towel is the "loser" and has to replace the paper towel.

- Use the garage floor to make a giant maze. Draw a design on the floor with chalk, creating a maze with dead ends, twists, and turns. Time each other to see who completes the maze in the shortest amount of time.

- Play a rousing game of shoe grab. Take off your shoes and put them in a pile in the middle of a room. Have everyone stand an equal distance from the shoes. On "Go!" race to grab your shoes, put them on, and return to your original place.

Celebrate with Crafts

Create a new family board game that will give Monopoly some competition. Bring out a large piece of cardboard along with an assortment of scrap paper, glue, and scissors. Design your own game board and come up with the rules for play.

Celebrate with Food

Make a set of edible dominos. Use graham crackers as dominos. With frosting, make "dots" on each half. Play a game of dominos before eating your game pieces.

Great American Smokeout

Parents are often overconfident in assuming their children will never smoke. Statistics show 1 million children under age 18 begin smoking each year. Of people who smoke, 89 percent started before they were 18. Use today to warn children about the dangers of smoking.

Celebrate with Fun

- The average smoker spends $700 a year on cigarettes. Ask your children what they could buy for $700.

- Try this experiment to show children the effects of smoke on their lungs. Put a cotton ball in a 12-oz. empty plastic water bottle. Seal the top shut with clay. "Borrow" a cigarette from a smoker. Use a pencil to poke a hole in the clay bottle top. Stick the filter end of the cigarette through the hole. Light the end of the cigarette sticking outside the bottle. Gently squeeze the bottle, causing it to "smoke" the cigarette. Repeat 8—10 times. Remove the cotton ball and look at its dingy color. Explain how smoke damages hearts and lungs.

- Sometimes shock therapy works best. Find pictures of a "healthy" lung and the lung of a smoker. Children can graphically see the difference smoking makes.

- Do you know a smoker who is trying to quit? Ask him or her to talk to your children about the difficult experience of giving up smoking.

Celebrate with Crafts

Give children paper and old magazines to make a smoker's collage. Cut out pictures and captions from cigarette ads. Glue them on the paper. Discuss how advertisers try to get people to buy their cigarettes.

Celebrate with Food

Set out 8–10 candles on the kitchen table. Serve everyone a simple snack such as crackers and cheese. In the middle of eating, blow out all the candles at once. (Careful—you don't want to spray wax everywhere.) Smoke will fill the room and possibly set off your smoke detector. Try eating with the smoke wafting around you. Have you lost your appetite? Now you know why restaurants have nonsmoking sections!

More ideas: www.cancer.org

Thanksgiving

Did you know Ben Franklin wanted to make the turkey our national bird? That's an unsettling thought since turkeys have been known to drown while looking up at the sky when it rains!

Celebrate with Fun

- Begin the day by waking children up not in the usual way, but by squawking and strutting into their bedrooms like a turkey. Too crazy for you? Wake them up by gently tickling them with a "turkey" feather.

- Many books suggest volunteering to serve dinner at a mission on Thanksgiving Day. Often this is impractical with out-of-town guests or toddlers in the family. Instead, before Thanksgiving ask a shelter what you can do to help at home. One family ended up taking 50 lbs. of potatoes and peeling them at home!

- When baking for Thanksgiving, have children set aside a few cookies or muffins to deliver to neighbors as a simple Thanksgiving treat.

- Play a rousing game of "Pin the Feather on the Turkey." Have the artist in your family draw a large turkey body. Cut out paper feathers and ask each player to put her name on one. Rules are just like "Pin the Tail on the Donkey." Tape the paper turkey on the wall. Attach a tape "doughnut" to the back of each feather. Blindfolded participants try to tape their feather on the correct part of the turkey.

- As you set the table, place 2 kernels of dried corn next to each plate. After the meal, pass around a small basket labeled "Our Basket of Blessings." Everyone drops their kernels in the basket and says 2 things they're thankful for.

Celebrate with Crafts

Select a small tree branch. Place it in a flowerpot filled with dirt. Ahead of time, cut out construction paper leaves. Punch a hole in each leaf and add a yarn "loop." Throughout the day, as family and friends arrive, encourage people to jot down what they are thankful for on the paper leaves and hang them on the tree. After the hearty meal, bring in the tree and read the notes.

Celebrate with Food

Why stick with tradition? Serve spaghetti and meatballs for a change. Not really! Do set a goal of serving 1 new food. Maybe you'll serve fresh cranberries instead of canned or add mushrooms to your stuffing. You might just create a new family tradition.

National Family Literacy Day

This national program encourages parents, schools, and children to participate in literacy activities. Have fun spending time reading together.

Celebrate with Fun

- Plan a "Read-In" after dinner. Pile all the pillows and soft blankets in the living room so people are cozy. Turn off TVs and phones so the atmosphere is conducive to reading. Have 10 minutes of silent reading followed by 10 minutes of someone reading out loud.
- Visit a used bookstore to beef up your book collection. Give each child a set dollar amount to spend as they like on books and magazines.
- Pretend none of you knows how to read. Ask children how they would tell shampoo from conditioner. How could they tell if pudding is instant? Many traditional Campbell's soup cans simply list the type of soup without a photograph. Discuss how difficult it is to get through a day without reading skills.
- If a family member has difficulty reading, consider an eye exam. Vision problems are often overlooked when children struggle with reading.
- Begin writing notes to your children to improve reading skills. Stick notes in their coats and lunch boxes and on their toothbrushes in the morning.

Celebrate with Crafts

Teachers use "Big Books" to interest children in books. Make your own Big Book: Cut boxes to make 6–8 cardboard pieces 24" x 48". Cover pieces with plain paper to make blank pages. Number pages consecutively. On page 1, write the title for an all-original family story. Print your story a few lines per page, then pass out pages for family members to illustrate. Have an adult punch holes through the thick cardboard pages with a screwdriver. Put them in order and stick chenille stems through the holes to tie the pages together. Twist the stems shut in loose "circles" so pages turn easily. Donate your Big Book to a kindergarten teacher after your family reads it.

Celebrate with Food

Mix up lollipop cookies to munch while reading a good book. Spread peanut butter on the flat side of a vanilla wafer. Place a clean wooden craft stick on top of peanut butter. Add another vanilla wafer to form your sandwich. Microwave 1 cup chocolate chips 60 seconds. Stir and microwave 20 seconds longer if needed to get smooth chocolate. Hold cookie by the stick and dip into chocolate. Let cool before eating.

More ideas: www.famlit.org

National Sandwich Day

What would a brown-bag lunch be without a sandwich? This handheld meal can be a dainty open-faced sandwich or a hearty 6-inch submarine sandwich.

Celebrate with Fun

- Enter the Ziploc National Sandwich Contest by contacting Dow Brands Food Care Division, Box 68511, Indianapolis, IN 46268, 317-873-7000.

- Have children help you make a list of possible sandwich foods. Keep the list handy so you never run out of creative ideas. The list could include:

Breads	Fillings
Bagels	Peanut butter and bananas
Croissants	Cream cheese and cucumbers
Rolls	Sprouts and tomatoes
Pita Bread	Leftover spaghetti!

- Draw a picture of your own "Dagwood Sandwich." Dagwood is known for making huge sandwiches stacked so high they almost topple over. What creative fillings would you use to make your sky-high sandwich?

- Play "Human Sandwich." The "bread" adults try to catch the "filling" children between them and "squish!" Great hugging time!

Celebrate with Crafts

Mustard adds great flavor to sandwiches. Use a mustard squeeze bottle to play a joke. Tie a knot in a 12-inch piece of yellow floss or yarn. Put the knotted end in the bottle. Thread the opposite end up through the nozzle so it extends 1 inch from the top. Announce, "I can't get this mustard to come out. I keep squeezing and squeezing . . ." Point bottle at a child and squeeze. The air will force the yellow string to come shooting out like a stream of mustard. Great fun!

Plan an old-fashioned box social. Pass out small gift bags or decorate lunch bags. Everyone makes a special sandwich complete with a name such as "Allan's Awesome Avocado Surprise." After sandwiches are inside the decorated bags, hold an auction. Have family members "bid" on the sandwiches. (Give younger children money to participate.)

Celebrate with Food

Eat a sandwich today in honor of National Sandwich Day. How about making a "dessert sandwich"? See what foods you can put together to create a sweet sandwich. Try spreading jam between 2 pieces of pound cake. Put a layer of frosting between 2 plain wafer cookies. Scoop slightly softened ice cream between 2 chocolate-chip cookies.

More ideas: www.ziploc.com

National Doughnut Day

Some people actually argue over the taste of Krispy Kreme doughnuts compared to Dunkin' Donuts. Instead of arguing, have fun celebrating with doughnuts today.

Celebrate with Fun

- Set out a "doughnut smorgasbord" for breakfast. Display powdered, jelly, and chocolate doughnuts. Cut each doughnut into fourths so children can sample each type. Pack kids an extra-healthy lunch so you don't feel too guilty about serving doughnuts for breakfast.

- Instead of tossing your stale doughnuts, use them for an outside game. One child holds the spoon end of a wooden spoon, leaving the handle to catch the doughnut. Another child gently throws a doughnut as the other person tried to catch it with the wooden spoon.

- Doughnuts have a hole in the center. What else has holes? List as many "holey" things as possible. How many foods have holes in the middle?

- In the olden days, kids played with a hoop by trying to keep it moving with a stick. Use a long-handled wooden spoon to get a hula hoop upright and moving. Run alongside the hoop for as long as possible.

- Call a local bakery to arrange a behind-the-scenes tour of doughnut making. You may get some free samples!

- Play "doughnut toss" using a hula hoop to represent a doughnut. Ask a child to hold the hoop horizontal to the floor. Another child tosses an inflated beach ball into the skinny doughnut hole.

Celebrate with Crafts

Make low-calorie giant doughnuts. Trace a dinner plate–sized circle on paper. Cut out the "doughnut" and cut a small doughnut hole in the center. Use craft supplies to decorate the doughnut. Glitter becomes sprinkles. Buttons and sequins make great doughnut toppings.

Staple 2 paper plates together. Cut out a 3-inch circle from the middle to form a paper doughnut. You've just made a doughnut Frisbee. Try tossing your paper doughnut back and forth.

Celebrate with Food

Here's the world's easiest doughnut recipe: Heat 1 cup oil in a frying pan. (Adults only!) Separate a package of refrigerator biscuits. Use a thimble or cap from a pill bottle to cut a hole in the middle of each biscuit. Gently drop the "doughnuts" into the hot oil. Fry 1–2 minutes. Drain doughnuts on a paper towel, then roll in a mixture of cinnamon sugar.

Veterans Day

Veterans Day began on November 11, 1918, when a truce was signed ending World War I. Today we celebrate this day as a way of honoring the men and women who served in our armed forces.

Celebrate with Fun

- Check the paper for listings of local Veterans Day programs. Attend with your family. Your children will see veterans from World War II who need wheelchairs to get around, along with Vietnam vets who look like the person next door. Many ceremonies take place in cemeteries. Take along some American flags to put on any unadorned graves.

- Fly your American flag all day, and wear red, white, and blue in honor of our veterans. If Grandpa or other relatives served in the military, call and thank them for what they did.

- Do you know people who have served in the armed forces? Invite them over for dinner. Have them share their experiences in boot camp where they had to take 2-minute showers. Where did they serve? What was it like adjusting to "normal" life when they left the service? Thank them for their part in preserving our freedom.

- Check if there is a local Veterans Administration hospital in your area. Arrange to visit and bring along some games or cards. Many of the residents receive very few visitors, so they'll enjoy chatting with your family. If the visit is a positive experience, visit regularly.

Celebrate with Crafts

Poppies are the traditional Veterans Day flowers. They grew wild in the battlefields of Europe and became a symbol of the bloodshed that took place. Make your own poppies by cutting pieces of red tissue paper into circles the size of a saucer. Place 3–4 circles on top of each other. Poke a hole in the center to insert a green chenille flower stem. "Scrunch" up the flowers individually, layer by layer, to form a bright red poppy.

Celebrate with Food

Check with local Army-Navy surplus stores to see if they carry dehydrated foods. Purchase a bag of macaroni and cheese or beef stroganoff. Explain to children that soldiers in WW I and WW II often didn't have access to fresh food. They used C-rations or dehydrated foods. Serve dinner using the dehydrated food from the Army-Navy store. End the meal by serving dehydrated ice cream. It actually tastes good!

303

National Teddy Bear Day

Did you know a president gave us the name "Teddy" bear? Teddy Roosevelt went bear hunting—with no success. An aide brought a cub for the president to shoot at close range. He refused, and people called the cub "Teddy's bear."

Celebrate with Fun

- Organize a stuffed animal hunt. Gather together all the stuffed animals in your house. As everyone waits in 1 room, select a person to hide the stuffed animals. (You might make a rule that a portion of each animal must be showing. No fair hiding a teddy bear at the bottom of the clothes hamper!) On "Go!" everyone looks through the house for the stuffed animals. After they've all been found, let another person hide them again.

- Take a group photograph of your family surrounded by all your teddy bears and stuffed animals.

- Calling all superstars for a Teddy Bear Talent Show! Let each family member select a teddy bear or stuffed animal and take a few minutes to practice a special talent for the Teddy Bear Talent Show. You'll be amazed at the feats of these amazing plush pals. Teddy bears can sing, do incredible gymnastic routines, and even be tossed on the ceiling and survive the landing.

- Have a clothes-washing party. Collect all the clothes from your stuffed teddy bears. Set out a tub of soapy warm water. Let kids wash, rinse, and dry the miniclothes.

Celebrate with Crafts

Use plain brown paper bags to cut out teddy bear shapes. Decorate with scrap pieces of ribbon, fabric, or leftover construction paper. Tape the bears' paws together to make a long teddy bear chain.

Celebrate with Food

For the easiest treat, serve teddy bear graham crackers. If you want to get more creative, set out bowls of colored frosting. Using toothpicks, spread the frosting on the teddy bear graham crackers to create colorful clothes and fur styles. Then eat, of course.

More ideas: www.teddybearandfriends.com/history.html

Sadie Hawkins Day

Many high schools celebrate Sadie Hawkins Day with dances that the girls ask the boys to attend. Sadie lived in the town of Dogpatch, where life moved at a slow pace. Slow down today with a more relaxed schedule.

Celebrate with Fun

- Bring out the overalls and gingham shirts. Sadie Hawkins is usually depicted with freckles. Use an eyeliner pencil to give all family members a healthy smattering of freckles. Don't forget to go barefoot all day!

- Play some country music. If possible, listen to a live radio performance from The Grand Ole Opry in Nashville. This weekly radio show is syndicated to hundreds of local radio stations.

- Find a comic strip about Lil' Abner and Daisy Mae. Girls can dress like Daisy with pigtails and square dance–type dresses. Be sure to find a frilly petticoat from the dress-up box to wear under the dress.

- Plan a hog-calling contest. A few children pretend to be hogs wallowing in the mud. Contestants try their best official hog-calling voices to see if the pigs respond.

- Set out a dishpan of "clean mud": Mix 2 cups warm water with ¼ cup liquid soap. Give children a roll of inexpensive toilet paper to add to the water. The tissue forms into "globs" that can be sculpted and squished like clean mud pies.

- Add some Sadie Hawkins atmosphere to the living room by hanging up a clothesline with socks and underwear attached. Get hold of spring-clasp clothespins. Many children have never seen clothes hanging on a line. They enjoy pinching the clothespins and hanging up clothes.

Celebrate with Crafts

Shuck some corn to make cornhusk dolls. Soak cornhusks in warm water for an hour. (Many grocery stores sell dried cornhusks.) Bunch 4–5 husks together. With string tie a "head" about 1 inch from the folded end. Draw a face on the head, then fold out 2 husks from each side as arms. Use fabric scraps to make your doll some clothes.

Celebrate with Food

Along with serving some Mountain Dew today, pack individual lunches or dinners in bandanna bags. After wrapping sandwiches, chips, and fruit, place on a bandanna. Bring up the 4 corners of the cloth and tie shut. Take a walk out to the "back porch" and eat hillbilly style, preferably sitting on rocking chairs.

America Recycles Day

Today is the day to Recycle—Reduce—Repair—Reuse! Get your family in the habit of thinking about saving our earth's resources.

Celebrate with Fun

- Take a trip to a recycling center. Ask management to give you a behind-the-scenes tour. Ask how much garbage is delivered every day.
- Begin collecting aluminum cans to take to the recycling center. Tell your family the money can go toward a special family activity. Get Grandma and Grandpa involved by asking them to collect cans also. Walk around the neighborhood and carry bags to store any cans you find.
- Get a book on how to make an easy compost bin. Call your local Master Gardener's program for more details. Composting reduces waste and teaches children how organic items break down into compost.
- When children ask you to drive them to a friend's house, do some errands on the way. Try to combine trips to save on pollution and gasoline.
- When packing school lunches, use washable sandwich and snack containers. Avoid individual juice packs when a thermos works just as well.
- Encourage children to take shorter showers. Remember the Girl Scout rule to always turn the water off when brushing your teeth.

Celebrate with Crafts

Recycled items can be great for craft-related activities. Use empty egg cartons to mix small amounts of paint in each "cup." Decorate cans to hold crayons and markers. Store beads in metal breath-mint containers.

Hate to toss out your favorite shirt that's too small? Reuse it to make a pillow. Turn clean shirt inside out. Sew both sleeves shut along with the neck. Turn shirt right side out. Stuff entire shirt with fiberfill batting until it is firm. Sew bottom edge of shirt shut and rest your head on your new pillow!

More ideas: www.americarecyclesday.org

Celebrate with Food

Recycle your leftovers! Have some leftover ham? Use it for omelets or frittatas. Freeze extra coffee in an ice cube tray. If coffee is too hot, add a coffee ice cube. Leftover chili? Put chili inside a taco. Add lettuce, tomatoes, and cheese. Extra pie dough? Roll it very thin, dot with butter, then sprinkle with cinnamon sugar. Roll up dough. Bake at 350 degrees 8–10 minutes.

National Clean Out Your Refrigerator Day

Are you brave enough to go to the back corners of your refrigerator and check the mold growing on containers of leftovers? Today's the day!

Celebrate with Fun

- If you are like most families, there are bits and pieces of leftover foods in your refrigerator. Plan a "smorgasbord buffet" for dinner. Have children set out paper plates as serving dishes and creatively label each leftover by writing on the paper plates with permanent markers. That bit of mashed potato can be formed into a mound topped with a pat of butter. Call it "White Volcano." Let people pick and choose their interesting meals. Afterward, simply toss the paper plates.

- After the leftovers are gone, go back to your refrigerator and check out those condiment bottles of barbecue sauce and little-used gourmet mustards. Have kids help you rinse and recycle the bottles. Make a note not to buy the ones your family doesn't use, like cranberry vinegar salad dressing.

- Offer to pay a family member to wipe down the racks and drawers in your refrigerator. (Saves you the work!)

- Make an educational game out of cleaning your refrigerator. When all the items are out of the refrigerator, ask kids to line up the foods in alphabetical order.

Celebrate with Crafts

Is the outside of your refrigerator a hodgepodge of school newsletters, old photographs, and chipped magnets? Have a family conference and decide how to unclutter the outside of the refrigerator. After you have a clean "canvas," add some family artwork. Let each person decorate an inexpensive magnetic frame with sequins, paint, and stickers. Add favorite photographs to proudly display.

Celebrate with Food

Use your freezer to make a nutritious snack as you celebrate your clean refrigerator. In the morning, let children mix a concoction of juice, yogurt, and fruit in the blender. Pour mixture into ice cube tray and add a wooden craft stick. Eat your minipopsicles while decorating the magnetic frames.

The Sound of Music Day

In 1959 this Rogers and Hammerstein musical opened on Broadway. Later, the movie reached millions around the world. Who hasn't felt the joy Maria conveys as she twirls on the open meadow and sings, "The hills are alive with the sound of music"?

Celebrate with Fun

- You may not be able to see *The Sound of Music* performed on Broadway, but you can participate in a homespun version. Assign groups of 2–3 people different scenes to practice. Get ready for an amazing display of talent as Dad and Grandma perform "I Am 16, Going on 17." Your 2 sons might do a talented rendition of the nuns singing, "How Do You Solve a Problem Like Maria?"

- In many places, movie theaters show the sing-along version of *The Sound of Music*. Captions are provided so the audience can heartily sing along. Invite friends over for your own modified sing-along. Most people know the songs anyway, so just show the movie and sing. One catch: Guests come dressed as a person—or object—from the movie. You might find yourself standing next to people dressed as "brown paper packages tied up with string" or "girls in white dresses with blue satin sashes."

- Remember the "Lonely Goatherd" puppet show with the expensive puppet stage and complicated marionettes? No need to get so involved. Simple puppets or socks over your hands work fine to put on a puppet show.

- Every parent wants to hear their children sing, "So long, farewell, auf Wiedersehen, goodnight." Let your children stay up an extra half hour if they can come up with a cute and clever "goodnight song."

Celebrate with Crafts

Maria used curtains to make matching outfits for all 7 children. Instead of cutting up your drapes, pass out plain white handkerchiefs to everyone. Use puff paint to draw designs and decorate. Wear your matching bandannas together.

Celebrate with Food

After singing "These Are a Few of My Favorite Things," eat the food mentioned in the song. The second verse includes "schnitzel with noodles." (Make pork chops if you don't know how to make schnitzel.) Serve "crisp apple strudel" for dessert, of course.

Homemade Bread Day

Yes, it's easy to buy a loaf of ordinary white bread. Today, however, make bread that fills your house with the comforting smell of homemade bread.

Celebrate with Fun

- Show children how yeast works. Pour 1 tsp. yeast in ½ cup very warm water. Sprinkle in a pinch of sugar for yeast food. Stir gently. Have an enlightening discussion with your children about the ways yeast comes "alive" by releasing gas. Observe how the yeast changes consistency while producing a distinct odor.
- Add some math to the bread-making process. Select an easy recipe with your children. Let them figure out how to double the recipe so you can bake an extra loaf for a friend.
- Get a library book that describes the types of bread people eat around the world. Find recipes and try baking cornbread, tortillas, matzos, bagels, or pitas.
- You'll need something to do while waiting for your yeast bread to rise. Ahead of time, ask a Sunday school teacher if you can borrow some of her flannel-board stories. Use the felt pictures to share Bible stories.
- Tell your children how God provided manna from heaven for Moses and his people. They always had plenty of manna, but soon began complaining about the lack of variety in food. See if your family can "survive" without complaining by just eating bread for a whole day. (Don't worry, no one will suffer nutritional deficiencies by eating bread for 1 day.) This is one way to make a Bible story come alive!

Celebrate with Crafts

Here's a colorful, edible craft. Mix up bread dough and divide into 3–4 piles. Add a few drops of food coloring to each pile of dough. Knead color into dough thoroughly. Using the different colors of dough, make teddy bears or caterpillars. Small pieces of dyed dough can be eyes, fur, or other embellishments. Bake as recommended.

Celebrate with Food

Borrow a friend's bread machine. (Or dig yours out from the back of the pantry.) Make bread with the machine doing most of the work. You'll still get that great homemade bread smell!

Historical Figure Day

Many children today look at SpongeBob SquarePants and Barbie as role models. Expose your children to the wide range of historical figures who have influenced our country's development.

Celebrate with Fun

- Dress up as a historical figure. This may take some research. Look up famous people like Marie Curie, Cleopatra, John the Baptist, Louisa May Alcott, and Albert Schweitzer. How did they live their lives? What values did they hold? Who was an influence on their lives? After you know something about your historical character, dress up like them and in character, present a brief introduction about "yourself" to your family.

- Wheaties cereal frequently features pictures and stories about sports heroes on its boxes. Pretend Wheaties selected your historical character to be on a box. Write up a description to include on the Wheaties box for all the world to read.

- Select a Bible character to "interview." One person pretends to be the reporter, while the other person is Jonah or Noah trying to answer questions and staying in character.

- Pretend you are keeping a journal of your life as a historical figure. Jot down a few notes about how you spend your days. What problems are you overcoming? Share your journals with the rest of your family.

- Pretend your historical character suddenly appeared in today's time period. Dress up as your selected person. You've miraculously appeared in your living room. Ask other family members about modern conveniences like electric lights and TVs.

Celebrate with Crafts

What kind of crafts would your historical character like to do? Would Abraham Lincoln like to whittle on a piece of wood? Did Laura Ingalls Wilder enjoy needlepoint? Did Helen Keller have any hobbies or enjoy crafts? Read some biographies to see.

Celebrate with Food

Think about the food your historical person ate every day. Could they go to a store to buy any food they wanted? How did they provide their food? Discuss what it would be like to be a missionary in a foreign country and suddenly have to eat unusual and unfamiliar foods.

DECEMBER

Give a Child the Gift of Camp Month
National Stress-Free Family Holidays Month
Museum Goer's Month
Read a New Book Month

Seasons to Celebrate

Advent • Four Sundays before Christmas
Hanukkah • 8 Days between November 25 and December 26
Kwanzaa • December 26–January 1

Days to Celebrate

 4 Ribbons and Wrap Day
 8 Anniversary of Beach Boys' 1st Single—"Surfin USA"
12 Beginning of Boys Town
20 Exercise Day
21 First Day of Winter/Winter Solstice
22 Flashlight Day
24 Christmas Eve Day
25 Christmas
26 Boxing Day
31 New Year's Eve

Give a Child the Gift of Camp Month

This holiday season, give your children a coupon for summer camp. They'll have fun and develop self-confidence. After all, would you organize rock-climbing expeditions or make a life-sized papier-mâché dinosaur at home?

Celebrate with Fun

- Get kids excited about camp, especially if they've never attended, by planning a few camp activities at home. Select "camp names" for everyone like Laughing Squirrel, Silver Moon, or Shiny Braces to use this month. Don't forget to write "Falling Rock" on your son's lunch bag.

- Mail call is a camp highlight. Write a letter to each children to distribute at "mail call" during dinner. Follow the camp tradition of having to perform a silly task to get the letter. Have children squawk like a chicken or sing "Rudolf the Red-Nosed Reindeer" before getting their mail.

- Like camps, offer a crazy "Clean Cabin" (or "Clean Room" at home) award daily this month. Motivate children to try to earn the coveted "Pink Plastic Flamingo" award for an immaculate room.

- One popular camp activity is having children "Dress the Counselor" in outlandish costumes. Shed your inhibitions—let your children dress you up in a tutu, frizzy wig, and oversized glasses. Take a picture.

- Register your child for camp soon. Camps fill by early spring. Check if camps have an American Camping Association accreditation (see www.acacamps.org) to ensure high safety and staff training standards. Your local church or denomination might offer camping programs also.

Celebrate with Crafts

Camp wouldn't be camp without craft projects. Make family camp T-shirts. Put newspaper inside a T-shirt so paint doesn't soak through. Buy inexpensive rubber fabric stamps and, using a paintbrush, dab fabric paint on your stamp. Firmly press the stamp onto the T-shirt. Add stamp designs until you have just the look you want. Let paint dry and wear your shirt to the family camp sing-along in the living room.

Celebrate with Food

Serve a kid-friendly meal of spaghetti or grilled cheese sandwiches. Pretend you are at camp where a designated "runner" goes to the kitchen to get the food. She brings it to the table, where people help themselves. After the meal, the runner scrapes the plates and carries everything back to the kitchen. Rotate runners every day.

National Stress-Free Family Holidays Month

Y ou survived Thanksgiving. As your family gets ready for Christmas and other holidays, set a goal to simplify things and enjoy stress-free holidays.

Celebrate with Fun

- Plan holiday activities earlier in the month. Invite friends for a cookie swap the first week in December instead of closer to Christmas. When you all entertain later in the month, it's easy to serve a variety of cookies!

- Collect gift-wrapping supplies ahead of time. In a 1-level house, put the tape, scissors, bows, paper, and tags in a small wagon. Whoever is wrapping just rolls the wagon to their area. Or put the supplies in a storage container that can be easily carried from place to place.

- Simplify gift giving—select a general item to give everyone possible on your list. Find a suitable book and add personalized bookmarks. Think how much stress you avoid by shopping in one store.

- Will you need new clothes for holiday concerts or parties? Shop early in the morning or during dinnertime when stores are least crowded. Trade child care with a friend so you can shop in relative peace.

- This time of year, TV commercials entice children with the latest toys and gadgets. You hear pleas of "I've got to have that toy, Mom!" Ask each child to make a wish list, but here's the catch: only 5 items allowed on the list at one time. This means they have to delete something else when they suddenly decide they need the "Jump and Skip Robot." The list helps them narrow choices and figure out what they really want. You can then decide which items to purchase.

Celebrate with Crafts

Enjoy December with 31 simple family activities. As a group, decorate a coffee can or plastic container with stickers. Glue on magazine pictures of fun holiday activities. Spread glue or decoupage over the can to give a glossy finish. Distribute paper strips and have everyone write low-cost, low-preparation ideas like "Walk the neighborhood to look at lights" or "Wear Santa hats at dinner." Place activity strips in the can. Select 1 paper daily and carry out the idea.

Celebrate with Food

Keep it simple! Instead of elaborate holiday meals, serve cold cuts and soup. Enjoying a meal is more important than feeling stressed over the baked Alaska.

Museum Goer's Month

Most communities have at least one museum. Use this month to explore the museums available to you and your family.

Celebrate with Fun

- Hands-on children's museums let children touch and feel without being told to keep their hands to themselves. Let your children spend as much time as possible at the closest children's museum. Allow children to explore their favorite exhibits over and over.

- When visiting a "serious" museum, extra effort is needed to keep kids interested. Stop at the gift shop first to select 3–4 postcards depicting items in the museum. Follow children as they try to find the actual exhibit. This involves reading signs or asking staff for directions.

- Play "Museum Statues." As you view a painting, have children stand in front of it and use their bodies as a statue of the painting. Do the same with actual museum statues. Take pictures of your children standing in front of the statues and mimicking the poses.

- Check if a museum offers parent/child classes. These low-cost programs often give children a behind-the-scenes look at museum exhibits or teach skills in painting and clay work.

- Turn a room in your house into a museum. Use boards to add a few extra shelves for displays. Let children set up "exhibits" of stuffed animals or windup toys. Encourage children to make information cards for each display. Guests at their museum will learn, "This display of 24 Beanie Babies was collected by Amber Clark from 1998 to 2001. She bought many of the stuffed animals with her allowance." Invite friends and relatives to visit the grand opening of your museum.

Celebrate with Crafts

Let your children make an entrance sign for their museum. They can outline the name in glue and sprinkle on glitter to create a sparkly eye-catching sign. Include hours of operation and admission price.

Celebrate with Food

Stop by the cafeteria at the museum you're visiting. They often have tasty food. Check the menu for creative titles like "Picasso's Plum Pie" or "Michelangelo's Magnificent Meatball Sandwich."

For some unusual museums, check out: www.bananamuseum.com; www.foodmuseum.com; www.unusualmuseums.org

Read a New Book Month

We all know the importance of reading, but with hectic holiday schedules, it's sometimes difficult to slow down to read. Celebrate this month by encouraging your family to read a new book.

Celebrate with Fun

- Assign each family member to select a library book for another family member. That means 8-year-old Jenny chooses a book for 3-year-old Kevin. Kevin, on the other hand, picks a book for Mom. Read the books, and after a few days share together what the books are about and thank each other for selecting the books.
- Buy a new Christmas book the entire family can read aloud. Spend time discussing the true meaning of Christmas.
- If older children feel it's too babyish to have books read aloud, start a joint reading program. Read the same book as your children, then discuss the plot together. You might be surprised at the insight your young teen shows when he brings up aspects of the book you never considered.
- Give your children a high-quality "coffee-table" book each Christmas. They cost more, but show your children you value their interest in books. Years from now they'll have a collection of books reflecting their interests as they grew up.
- Get Dad involved in reading. It's important for kids to see a male role model reading. Invite Grandpa over to cuddle and read to the grandkids.
- Challenge children to read a book slightly above their reading ability, one that's also available to rent on video after your child completes the book. Discuss the differences between the book and video.

Celebrate with Crafts

Have everyone in the family write their own book. It doesn't have to be elaborate, just a "new" book to use during Read a New Book Month. Use ordinary typing paper to write the book by hand or on the computer. Add illustrations. Take the books to a quick copy printer where for about $1 each you can have them spiral bound, creating a very professional image.

Celebrate with Food

Find a new recipe book with simple recipes children can make. Select a few and vote on which gourmet treat you'll make. As a family, try the new recipe. Write a "review" as if you were food critics at a restaurant.

315

Advent

Since *advent* is a Latin word for "coming" or "arrival," it makes sense that the 4 Sundays of Advent are set aside to prepare for the arrival of Jesus.

Celebrate with Fun

- Make or buy an Advent wreath with 4 candles. Traditionally 3 are purple and 1 is pink. Light a candle each Sunday, beginning with the purple ones. The wreath, which has no beginning or end, symbolizes God's everlasting, continuous love for us.

- On the first Sunday of Advent, set out a can labeled "loose change" in an obvious place. People drop in their change and look under couch cushions for even more. Donate the money to a favorite charity.

- This Advent season acknowledge the good things God has given us. Get the book *Material World* by Peter Menzel (Sierra Club Books). This amazing picture book shows material possessions of people around the world. Each double-sided page shows a family standing in front of their home and all their belongings. You can imagine the difference between the items a family owns in Uganda compared to a family in the U.S.

- On each Sunday of Advent, plan a secret "mission" to bring joy to someone. Purchase 4 inexpensive Christmas stockings. Decorate them with puff paint or colorful buttons. Fill each with fun items ranging from candy to new pens to colorful socks. On each Advent Sunday, secretly deliver the stocking to someone's door. Let the person guess who gave them the unexpected treat.

Celebrate with Crafts

Decorate 4 cardboard tubes to represent the Advent candles. Cover 3 rolls with purple paper and 1 with pink. Crumple yellow and red tissue paper to stick in the tops like candle flames. Label each candle: number 1—promise, number 2—love, number 3—light, number 4—hope. Each week as you light the real candle, take turns holding the cardboard candle to discuss what it represents.

Celebrate with Food

One Advent Sunday make a surprise cake. The surprise is a batch of sweet cherries in each bite. Mix up your favorite vanilla cake. Pour into a greased 13 x 9 cake pan. Gently press 45–50 pitted cherries into the batter. (Fresh, canned, or frozen all work well.) Bake according to directions. The cherries give extra moisture and a surprise in each bite.

Hanukkah

Hanukkah is also known as the Festival of Lights. Jewish people celebrate for 8 days, lighting 1 candle in the menorah each day. Hanukkah begins on the 25th day of the month of Kislev.

Celebrate with Fun

- Decorate with traditional Hanukkah colors—royal blue, white, and silver.
- Set a special table for children. Put name tags and small gifts at each place.
- Start a tradition of videotaping family members during Hanukkah. Share memories from the past year, sing songs, and tell jokes. Review the video each year before adding to it.
- Purchase some chocolate coins to have a "gelt" hunt (*gelt* is Yiddish for money). Hide coins throughout the house. Give children a time limit in which to find the chocolate.
- Use your musical talents to sing this song to the tune of "Farmer in the Dell": Oh light the candles bright, And dance around the light, Heigh-ho the Derry-oh, It's Hanukkah tonight. Little treats to eat, And family to greet, Heigh-ho the Derry-oh, It's Hanukkah tonight.

Celebrate with Crafts

Make a Star of David. Glue 3 wooden craft sticks in a triangle. Make 2 sets. Cover all the wood with glue, then sprinkle with glitter. Let dry. Glue 1 triangle on top of the other to form the Star of David.

Try making silver and blue candle holders. Wash several baby-food jars after removing the labels. Use a dark blue permanent marker to draw the Star of David on the glass. Fill the jar with clear marbles for a silver effect. Press a blue candle in the marbles until it stands straight.

Celebrate with Food

Potato "latkes" are a traditional Hanukkah treat. Grate 4 large potatoes. Drain excess water. Mix in 1 small grated onion, 1 egg, 2 tsp. matzo meal, and a pinch of salt. Heat ½ cup oil in frying pan. When hot, carefully drop in large spoonfuls of potatoes. Fry on both sides until golden brown.

Make an edible menorah with pita bread. Give children 1 piece of pita bread. Fill with your favorite "sticky" filling like cream cheese or peanut butter and jelly. Stick 9 small pretzels in the filling to look like candles. Make sure the center shammash stands higher than the other "candles."

Kwanzaa

This African-American family celebration was created in 1966 by Dr. Maulana Karenga. The 7-day festival focuses on self-reliance and the unity of the black family. *Kwanzaa* means "first fruit" in Swahili.

Celebrate with Fun

- Kwanzaa colors are black, red, and green. Find ways to decorate at least 1 room with these predominate colors. Black, red, and green streamers along with an African print tablecloth help carry out the color scheme. Ask a local travel agent for posters of Africa to use as decorations.
- At Kwanzaa, *vibunzi*, or ears of corn, are displayed. Set out 1 ear of corn to represent each child in the family.
- Each day of Kwanzaa stresses a principle African Americans should live by. Discuss these traits with your children: Day 1—Unity; Day 2—Self-determination; Day 3—Collective work and responsibility; Day 4—Cooperative economics; Day 5—Purpose; Day 6—Creativity; Day 7—Faith.
- Many children's books are now being written about Kwanzaa. Purchase a colorful book to read together as a family.

More ideas: www.officialkwanzaawebsite.org

Celebrate with Crafts

Make 7 "candles" representing the 7 principles of Kwanzaa. Cover 7 paper towel tubes with construction paper. The black center candle represents the richness of African-American skin color. The 3 red candles on 1 side depict the struggles of life. The 3 green on the other represent the hope of the future. Crumple yellow and orange tissue paper. Tape the paper to the top of the candles as "flames."

It's traditional to give a *zawadi*, or handmade gift, during Kwanzaa. Cut a piece of yarn 28–30 inches long. String 3 red beads, then 3 black beads, followed by 3 green beads. Repeat the pattern until the yarn is almost full. Tie knot in end to make a colorful necklace.

Celebrate with Food

Baked plantains are a popular Kwanzaa dish. Wash the plantain with the peeling intact. Cut in half lengthwise. Place in a shallow baking pan, cut side up. Sprinkle with a mixture of ¾ tsp. cinnamon, ½ cup brown sugar, and ¼ cup melted butter. Cover and bake 35 minutes at 350 degrees. Serve warm for a smooth dessert.

Ribbons and Wrap Day

Colorfully wrapped packages are part of the holidays. Your shopping may not be done, but today prepare a variety of ribbons and wrapping paper.

Celebrate with Fun

- Set aside a corner of the house as the "Wrapping Center Station" where all your wrapping supplies are located. Anyone wanting to wrap a present has paper, scissors, tape, bows, and gift labels readily at hand.

- For variety, wrap packages in something besides regular paper. Try colorful comics from the Sunday paper, a road map, or even cotton bandannas.

Celebrate with Food

Instead of using the oven to bake yourself a snack, bake some ribbons. Don't worry—the ribbons are for wrapping packages, not eating. Cut a variety of cotton fabric ribbons into 18-inch lengths. Wet fabric and squeeze out excess water. Wrap each ribbon around a wooden spoon handle or pencil. Tape the ends to keep from unraveling. Place wrapped spoons on a cookie sheet. Have an adult put cookie sheet in oven preheated to 225 degrees. Bake 25 minutes. Carefully remove and let cool. Unravel the ribbon to reveal perfectly curled ribbon for decorating packages. The curled ribbon also looks great in a little girl's hair.

Celebrate with Crafts

Since you have marshmallows around for hot chocolate, use them to make snowman wrapping paper. Press a large marshmallow flat side down in white paint and then on plain blue paper. Repeat 3 times to form a snowman. Make marshmallow-print snowmen all over the paper. Let dry. Draw or paint on snowmen's faces, hats, and arms.

Adorn a child's present not with ribbon but with hand-painted shoelaces. Tape each end of white shoelaces to a flat surface. Use a fine-tipped permanent marker to draw designs on the laces. Use as "ribbons."

Use bright-colored electrical tape to make plaid wrapping paper. Cut tape to fit paper. Place parallel strips across paper lengthwise, then place another color strips across the width of your tartan-plaid paper.

Sparkles and glitter make solid-colored packages special. Make squiggly glue designs on 3 sides of a package. Sprinkle glitter on and tap box gently to remove extra. Let dry and repeat on remaining side.

For an easy way to wrap presents, ask your favorite Chinese restaurant for extra white take-out containers. Decorate with stickers or permanent markers. Stick your gift inside and top with a bow!

Anniversary of Beach Boys' 1st Single—"Surfin USA"

DECEMBER 8

Even though it's winter, throw a wild beach party in honor of the Beach Boys. Put on your bikini, and don't forget the sunscreen!

Celebrate with Fun

- First and foremost, play Beach Boys music all day long. Wake your children by yelling "Surf's up!" as you wave a beach towel over their heads. Hang a bright yellow beach ball from the ceiling. This way you are guaranteed a sunny day.

- Give kids a pretend microphone so they can lip-sync to various songs. Be sure they play "air guitar" to go along with their vocal skills.

- Take pictures of your family standing by a surfboard. What? You don't have a surfboard? Cover your ironing board with a white plastic tablecloth. Tape the ends under and use permanent markers to draw "groovy" designs. Stand next to the board so you look like a real surfin' dude.

- Collect small action figures and tiny dolls. Set them on blue paper so it looks like they are in the water. They need surfboards too! Cut striped Juicy Fruit gum into surfboard shapes. Stand figures on "surfboards" for a tabletop diorama.

- Your kids will be shocked at the simple plot, but rent an Annette Funicello movie. Remember how she and Frankie Avalon cheerfully entertained themselves tossing a beach ball back and forth?

Celebrate with Crafts

People often take a metal detector to the beach and look for treasures. Make your own beach treasures with old costume jewelry. Anything shiny works. Wrap the "jewels" in aluminum foil. (Foil-wrapped dimes also make great treasures.) Mix 1 cup plaster of paris till thick as pudding. Let set 2–3 minutes. Drop foil treasures in plaster, coating all sides. Remove the treasures. Let dry overnight. If desired, paint with tempera paint. Hide treasure "rocks" around the yard so your beach bums can find them. Use a hammer to tap each rock open.

Celebrate with Food

The Beach Boys would love this surfing cake, and kids will love eating the blue "wave" frosting: Bake a 1-layer cake. Mix a batch of frosting. Before adding blue food coloring, set aside ¼ cup frosting. Spread blue frosting on cake. Using a knife tip, dab a few "blobs" white frosting on top of the blue so your waves have whitecaps. Stick some gummy sharks in the waves to scare any nearby surfers.

Beginning of Boys Town

Father Flanagan started Boys Town in 1917 with 6 boys living in a small house. In 1999 over 33,000 boys and girls were served throughout the United States.

Celebrate with Fun

- Rent the award-winning movie *Boys Town* and watch it with your family. Spencer Tracy won an Oscar for his role as Father Flanagan. He donated the Oscar to Boys Town where it's still on display in the main lobby.

- Help your children understand that some children live in unpleasant situations. Don't go into morbid detail, but according to their age and maturity, tell them about homelessness or child abuse. Focus on how your family can help. Can you donate books or clothes to a women's and children's shelter? How about sponsoring a child from a third world country? Childcare International lets you sponsor a child in India, Africa, or Haiti for $30 a month to provide the child food, education, and Christian discipleship. Select a child from their website at www.childcare-intl.org

- Try a "Trust Walk" to help family members gain a sense of security. Pair off. Blindfold a partner. (Preschoolers might be more comfortable simply closing their eyes.) The blindfolded person walks through the house or yard, holding on to their sighted partner, whose job it is to make sure they don't get hurt or bump into anything. Try laying eggs on the ground. The seeing partner guides the blindfolded person in and out of the egg maze. (Obviously, you'll want to try this outdoors!)

Celebrate with Crafts

Make a "Look What We've Got" chain. Cut paper into 2″ x 6″ strips. Write down positive statements that reflect your family on each piece of paper. Examples could be: We can worship where we choose. Our cars work (most of the time). Our refrigerator keeps food cold. Mom and Dad have jobs. Our school is heated and clean. After you've collected phrases of thankfulness, make a paper-link chain like you make in kindergarten. Hang the chain in a prominent location so everyone can see it and reflect on the good things you have.

Celebrate with Food

Encourage a spirit of sharing. Set out 1 cupcake, 1 apple, or 1 cookie for dessert. Cut the treat into several pieces and share.

More ideas: www.girlsandboystown.org

Exercise Day

Sure you are busy with holiday preparations, but you're also busy munching on candy and other treats. Try to get in a few extra minutes of exercise today.

Celebrate with Fun

- Remember your old PE teacher in high school? You had to do Army-style jumping jacks and sit-ups as he or she shouted at you. No need to start shouting, but lead your family in an exercise session. Lift those knees!

- Doing some last-minute shopping? Park the car at the far end of the parking lot. (That shouldn't be hard since the parking lot is surely crowded with shoppers.) If children normally take the bus to school, walk with them to the next closest stop from their usual one.

- Take the dog (or the neighbor's dog) on an extra-long walk. The exercise will clear your head as you think about all the holiday preparations you still have on your to-do list.

- Local gyms and swimming pools often offer special discounts this time of year. Grab everyone's swimsuit and hit the pool!

- Need to make one last trip to the mall? Find out when stores open, then arrive an hour ahead to do some mall walking. Get in some "power walking" before the crowds of holiday shoppers arrive.

- Check out exercise videos from the library. You'll find exercise styles ranging from *Mommy and Me Like to Move* to high-energy, fast-paced videos. When children ask to watch cartoons, tell them, "Sure, watch cartoons — right after you do 20 minutes of the exercise video."

Celebrate with Crafts

Lift your spirits as you exercise with your own water-filled weights. Find 2 quart-sized plastic milk containers. Wash well to remove any milk. Use markers to write exercise slogans such as "Move On!", "No Pain, No Gain!", and "Work Those Abs!" Fill bottles halfway with water. Carry them on your next walk for an extra workout.

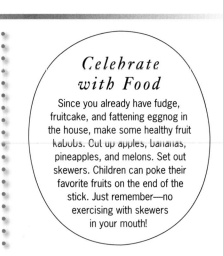

Celebrate with Food

Since you already have fudge, fruitcake, and fattening eggnog in the house, make some healthy fruit kabobs. Cut up apples, bananas, pineapples, and melons. Set out skewers. Children can poke their favorite fruits on the end of the stick. Just remember—no exercising with skewers in your mouth!

First Day of Winter/
Winter Solstice

Even if you live in sunny Hawaii, the first day of winter conjures up images of snowmen and hot chocolate. Celebrate the longest day of the year by creating indoor and outdoor "snowpeople."

Celebrate with Fun

- If you live in snow country, children will want to make a snowman. After rolling the snowballs, they come in yelling, "Mom, Dad, we need charcoal eyes, a long scarf, a hat, and a carrot!" Plan ahead. Put together a "Snowman Kit" box holding worn scarves, stones you collected from the beach last summer, floppy hats, and other accessories. (But don't store the carrot for several months!) When kids want to accessorize their snowman, they'll have everything handy.

- Change the snowman's gender! Make a snowgirl who looks terrific wearing a hula skirt from the dress-up box. Add a wig or fancy flowery hat.

- No snow in your area? Have an indoor snowball fight anyway to celebrate the first day of winter. Cut the legs of old pantyhose into 6-inch sections. Tie 1 end, fill with Styrofoam packing peanuts, tie the other, and start a snowball fight with snowballs so lightweight no one gets hurt.

- It's fun to squish and sculpt soapy snowpeople. Mix 2 cups Ivory Snow detergent flakes and ½ cup water with a hand mixer to create a light fluffy substance. After a while the soap takes on a doughy consistency. Use the soap as white clay to make indoor snowpeople. Use buttons and minicarrots to add facial features.

Celebrate with Crafts

You can never have too many snowmen. These are so easy, children can make several. Give each child 3 paper plates. Punch holes in the top and bottom of 1 plate. The other 2 plates just need 1 hole each. Use paper fasteners to hook these plates together vertically and make a flexible snowperson. Glue on construction paper hats, fancy clothes, and the traditional carrot nose.

Celebrate with Food

It's a cold winter day perfect for hot, steamy snowman soup! Pour cocoa mix for several cups hot cocoa in a mixing bowl. Add hot water and let children stir. Now add the extra ingredients: Stir in 2–3 chocolate kisses until melted. Toss in some mini-marshmallows. Yum! Now have children stir "soup" with a candy cane to add a hint of mint. Ladle into mugs and enjoy!

Flashlight Day

Children love playing with flashlights. Celebrate the day after the Winter Solstice by trying these flashlight-related activities.

Celebrate with Fun

- Get a box with a tight-fitting lid. Cut 2 holes the size of quarters on 1 side. Put an object in the box. Have children shine a flashlight through 1 hole while peeking through the other to guess the object. Repeat with different mystery items.

- Tape colored cellophane over the end of a flashlight. Observe how objects look with different-colored lights. What happens when you put a piece of blue cellophane over a red piece?

- This may not be the most fun activity, but it's practical. Collect all the flashlights scattered throughout the house. Look in the garage and backs of drawers. How many work? List the batteries you need and go buy them so you'll have flashlights that actually give off light!

- Go outside or remove fragile items from the living room. Have children stand in a circle as you shine a beam of light to a spot on the ground. Children try to "catch" the light beam. Try shining the light on a tree, the wall, or the side of the couch. If things get too chaotic with children crashing into each other, let them take turns trying to catch the light.

- Show children the importance of light. Plant 6 identical lima bean seeds in 2 clear plastic cups, 3 seeds per cup. Pour dirt in cups, but place seeds next to the sides for easy viewing. Water well. Place 1 cup in a sunny location while the other sits in a dark closet. After a week, compare the differences in growth between the seeds in the 2 cups.

Celebrate with Crafts

Make a constellation on your bedroom wall. Stretch a paper clip to use as a "poker." Poke small designs shaped like people or animals in the bottom of a paper cup. Place the cup over the end of the flashlight and shine on the ceiling in a darkened room. Come up with names for your new constellations.

Celebrate with Food

Have children help you make finger Jell-O. (The recipe for this concentrated Jell-O is on the packages.) When firm, cut with cookie cutters to make designs. Before eating, hold pieces up to a window or the light. Shine flashlights on the Jell-O to see through your translucent snack.

Christmas Eve Day

I s it almost time to open the presents?" Your children may ask you that hundreds of times today. Whether you open presents on Christmas Eve or the next morning, here are ways to pass the time.

Celebrate with Fun

- Some families traditionally set up the nativity scene in early December. They leave Baby Jesus out of the nativity set until Christmas Eve. You can also have the wise men in another room and slowly move them closer to the manger each day as Christmas approaches. On Christmas Eve, Jesus appears in the manger with the wise men next to him.

- Settle your children for sleep by spending time looking at your special Christmas ornaments. Share your memories about when and where you got each one. Which ornament is your favorite? Which is the oldest?

- Purchase and wrap new pajamas for everyone. On Christmas Eve, when children clamor to open a present, let them unwrap the pajamas. As an added bonus, everyone will look great for Christmas morning photos.

- If setting out cookies for Santa, don't forget the reindeer. Leave some carrots for Rudolph and his buddies.

- Make a stocking for your pets. Glue together 2 large felt stocking pieces. Decorate with buttons and lace. Add catnip toys or a rawhide bone.

- Make a list of the presents you got last year. Can you remember what you received and from whom?

- Children are keyed up today and need a form of physical release, so get some exercise. Take a brisk walk or go to a playground if weather permits.

Celebrate with Crafts

Have some candy canes around your house? Turn them into reindeer. Glue a small red pom-pom on the end of the candy cane's "hook." Add 2 wiggle eyes where the candy cane begins to bend forward. Twist a brown chenille stem above the eyes to form antlers.

Celebrate with Food

Make Christmas star sandwiches instead of sweet cookies. Set out 2 bowls of softened cream cheese. Add 2 different colors of food coloring. Mix well. Use a star-shaped cookie cutter to cut frozen bread slices into star shapes. Spread colored cream cheese on bread stars for a semihealthy snack. (Frozen bread is easier to use when spreading cream cheese. Don't worry, the bread defrosts quickly.)

Christmas

Your children will be overwhelmed with all the toys they receive today, but take time to reflect on the true meaning of Christmas—the birth of Christ.

Celebrate with Fun

- Do your early risers head downstairs at 5 A.M.? The night before Christmas, instruct children to stay in bed until they hear you play Christmas music. Leave a new coloring book and crayons at the foot of your children's beds to keep them occupied until they hear the music.

- Instead of having a mad dash ripping open presents all at once, take turns. Slowly pass out gifts. Watch each person unwrap and acknowledge a gift. Start a new tradition. As you unwrap a gift, stick the bow on your head. You'll have great photos of bow-bedecked family members!

- Take time to look at your Christmas cards. Pray for the senders. Recycle the cards later by cutting them apart to make postcards. Send a "Happy New Year" postcard to the person who sent you the Christmas card.

- As family and friends visit today, write children's names on plastic cups. They can use the same cup throughout the day whenever they are thirsty, and you can do fewer dishes when the celebrating ends!

- If your church offers a Christmas Day service, invite someone who normally doesn't attend church. People are more inclined to go to church on Christmas and Easter.

- Give children a disposable camera to document Christmas Day. Develop the pictures and you'll have insight into how your children view Christmas.

Celebrate with Crafts

Writing thank-you cards is an important courtesy for children to learn. Casually set out card-making supplies like unusual papers and stamps and inkpads for children to use in the afternoon when they get tired of their toys. Gifts are fresh in children's minds, so they can write "Thank you, Grandma, for the toe socks. I'm wearing them right now." Mail cards as soon as possible.

Celebrate with Food

Break with tradition—make homemade ice cream today. A hand-cranked machine occupies children while they wait for the main meal. Mix 3 eggs, 2 cups sugar, 2 quarts milk, 2 pints whipping cream, 3 Tbs. vanilla, and a dash of salt in the tub of the ice-cream maker. Have children add rock salt and crushed ice to the outer container while turning the ice-cream crank.

Boxing Day

Follow the tradition of Great Britain, Canada, and Australia by celebrating Boxing Day. Give small gifts of appreciation to mail carriers, sanitation workers, and restaurant servers. Many years ago, pastors used this day to give bread, cheese, and beer to the members of their church.

Celebrate with Fun

- Today, honor people we often take for granted. Have children make "generic" thank-you cards. Carry them with you to pass out to people you meet. If cards are already decorated, you simply need to add a handwritten personal note. Give one to a store clerk who's dealing with the rush of after-Christmas returns. Hand a thank-you card to the student working at the fast-food drive-up window.

- The day after Christmas you surely have extra ribbon and bows around. Collect the leftover wrapping supplies to keep on hand for giving unexpected thank-you gifts throughout the year.

- Purchase gift certificates from fast-food restaurants or coffee shops. Keep them on hand to pass out with a "Thank you" to people you meet.

- Do something nice for your newspaper carrier. Does she deliver papers by walking door-to-door? Then give her a pair of cute and comfortable socks. If the carrier delivers your paper with a car, how about a gift certificate for a car wash?

- Make small bookmarks that say, "Every good and perfect gift comes from the Father above" (James 1:17). Pass them out to people you meet today.

Celebrate with Crafts

Decorate your mailbox today in honor of your mail carrier. Wrap crepe paper around the pole (if there is one). Fly some balloons around the box. Make a "cover" over it with slogans like "Mr. Johnson is the best!" or "The mail always comes through!" or "Thanks for delivering our mail—even the bills!" Add streamers so everyone driving by will notice. Place a small thank-you gift inside the mailbox too.

Celebrate with Food

Serve a traditional English Boxing Day meal by making Fox in the Hole Casserole. In a dish, layer 1 cup sliced onions with 2–3 cups of sausages. Bake 30–40 minutes at 350 degrees. Remove from oven. Mix together ½ cup flour, ½ tsp. salt, and 1 cup milk. Pour over onion and sausage mixture. Bake an additional 30–40 minutes. Enjoy your English meal! Be sure to speak with a very proper English accent while eating.

327

New Year's Eve

How can the year be coming to an end already? You still haven't accomplished your New Year's resolutions from January 1. Forget about trying to lose those ten pounds and enjoy this last day of the year.

Celebrate with Fun

- Invite families with young children for a New Year's party at 7 P.M. Have guests bring an "Instant Carnival Booth." Give families 10 minutes to assemble their Beanbag Toss or Knock-the-Can game somewhere in the house. Spend the next hour taking turns playing the various games of skill. Set your watches to 10 P.M. When "midnight" arrives, everyone yells "Happy New Year!" and heads home—although it's really 10 P.M.

- While waiting to make noise at midnight, get out your checkbook and date all your checks with the new year. This saves you from writing a check tomorrow and having the clerk tell you, "Sorry—that was last year."

- Compose new words for "Auld Lang Syne." (What does that mean, anyway?) Keep the tune; just update the words so people understand them.

- Have family members draw billboards showing them fulfilling dreams for the coming year. Perhaps they'll draw themselves winning the school geography bee or riding a new bike. Post the billboards in your hall to see throughout the year. Don't forget to add captions!

Celebrate with Crafts

Remember hanging felt pennants from your walls? Get ready for tomorrow's football games by making team pennants. Cut felt pieces the colors of your favorite teams in long pennant shapes. Use smaller pieces of felt to make letters and logos. (Hint: When working with felt, glue 2 pieces together without readjusting the fabric.) Display the pennants tomorrow.

The New Year calls for a new home for your backyard birds. Buy a plain wooden birdhouse and work together to make it look more "rustic." Glue small twigs on it with hot glue or carpenter's glue that stands up under the elements. Paint designs around the door to add charm to your log cabin birdhouse.

Celebrate with Food

Since you're wearing a goofy pointed hat for New Year's, make an edible hat. Set an empty pointed ice-cream cone on a plate. Using frosting and sprinkles, decorate the cone to match the hat you are wearing. Take a picture of you "eating your hat" while wearing a hat.

Still need more wacky and unusual holidays to celebrate? Check *Chase's Calendar of Events* and the following websites:

www.chases.com
www.hicards.com
www.holidays.net
www.web-holidays.com
www.activityconnection.com
www.mydailyplan-It.com
www.teachervision.com
www.bookmarketing.com
www.educationworld.com
www.annieshomepage.com
www.holidayinsights.com
www.childfun.com (click on "Holidays")
www.holidaysmart.com
www.123greetings.com
www.theteachersguide.com
www.holidayorigins.com

Parenting expert **Silvana Clark** is the author of several books, including *Stuffed Animals on the Ceiling Fan*. She has appeared on national television, is frequently quoted in women's and parenting magazines, and is an accomplished speaker presenting addresses to parent and professional groups several times a month. She lives in Bellingham, Washington. Check out her website: silvanaclark.com.